Story Starters and Science Notebooking

Story Starters and Science Notebooking

Developing Student Thinking Through Literacy and Inquiry

Sandy Buczynski and Kristin Fontichiaro

A Teacher Ideas Press Book

Libraries Unlimited
An Imprint of ABC-CLIO, LLC

A B C CLIO

Santa Barbara, California • Denver, Colorado • Oxford, England

Library of Congress Cataloging-in-Publication Data

Buczynski, Sandy.
    Story starters and science notebooking : developing student thinking through literacy and inquiry / Sandy Buczynski and Kristin Fontichiaro.
        p. cm.
    Includes bibliographical references and index.
ISBN 978-1-59158-686-9 (hard copy : alk. paper) 1. Science—Study and teaching (Elementary) 2. Language arts—Correlation with content subjects. 3. Inquiry-based learning. 4. School notebooks. I. Fontichiaro, Kristin. II. Title.
    LB1585.B74   2009
    372.3′5–dc22   2009005965

13 12 11 10 09   1 2 3 4 5

This book is also available on the World Wide Web as an eBook.

Visit www.abc-clio.com for details.

ABC-CLIO, LLC
130 Cremona Drive, P.O. Box 1911
Santa Barbara, California 93116-1911

This book is printed on acid-free paper ∞

Manufactured in the United States of America

Contents

Acknowledgments

We are grateful to our families, students, and colleagues for their ongoing support.

Many *mahalos* to Sherri Garcia, Fred Silverman, and Evelyn Lacanienta of Seabury Hall in Maui, Hawai'i, and to Sue Kohfeldt, Marcia Mardis, Mary Beth Pardington, Julie de Klerk, and Vicki Pascaretti for their valuable suggestions and input. A big thanks also goes to elementary methods professors Dr. Donna Barnes and Dr. Bobbi Hansen and the graduate students in the Pedagogical Processes for Science Educators class at the University of San Diego for their support with "thinking through" inquiry. Thank you to Jennifer Martella, Rob Glass, Barbara Jones Clark, Deborah West, and the staff of Beverly School for their conversations and collegiality. We also appreciate Troy Lee's help in condensing science content knowledge and the useful insights offered by Dominque Fougeré. And finally, we sincerely thank Tony Buczynski for supporting our writing retreats and non-stop conversations about science. Our long-distance collaboration was enhanced by the free telephony services of Skype and the collaborative authoring tools provided by Google Docs.

This book stemmed directly from our work with the professional development program of the American Professional Partnership for Lithuanian Education (A.P.P.L.E.), where we met as lecturers. Our deep thanks to our A.P.P.L.E. colleagues, especially Jim Brousseau, Phil Gorrasi, Sue Kohfeldt, Birute Druckute, and Giedre Stankuniene, who know how to find everything from *ledai* (ice cream) to chicken wire in a Lithuanian town! Blanche Woolls, our colleague there and in the United States, was instrumental in bringing our vision to the attention of our editor Sharon Coatney, whose thoughtful edits helped us give shape to this book.

PART I

Inquiry, Story Starters, and Science Notebooking

1

Introduction to Inquiry and Story Starters

Once upon a time,
there were two educators who lived on opposite sides of the country. One was a science education professor who believed in the power of science inquiry to develop critical thinking skills in problem solving. A former secondary science educator in Hawai'i, she often centered students' inquiry work in environmental science by engaging them in their natural world. The other was a school librarian who envisioned students with strong cognitive skills, inquiring minds, and a quest to pursue personal and aesthetic interests. A former English teacher, she knew how student writing could deepen thinking, and her work as a children's book author informed her about the enduring power of story.

In a city by the sea in a faraway country,
they met as professional development lecturers for the American Professional Partnership for Lithuanian Education in 2005. They guided Lithuanian teachers toward more constructivist and active student learning. Sandy's work focused on transitioning elementary science from lecture to experiential inquiry, and Kristin's worked on using drama to explore story and academic content. Over shared meals, they talked and exchanged ideas, but it was not until they reunited in Lithuania in 2007 that the idea of this book was born. How could the power of stories be harnessed to provide a context for student learning?

Introduction

This is a book about the power of story and inquiry to promote student thinking in science among students in grades 3–6. Original stories (like the sample above) set up a problem scenario that needs an evidence-based solution. Students use guided inquiry to explore a variety of possible resolutions to the problem in the story: documenting their prediction, process, observations, and conclusions in a science notebook. As students investigate the stories' science concepts, they tap into prior knowledge, practice several genres of writing, reflect on their learning, and apply the scientific method. As students begin to consider science as way of thinking more than as a body of knowledge, they start to connect inquiry with the development of scientific knowledge. This sets students on the path toward science literacy.

Foundational Ideas Behind this Book: What we Know About how Students Learn

Though the stories in this book are original, the instructional approach used is grounded in classroom practice and educational research. Donovan and Bransford's (2005) *How Students Learn: Science in the Classroom* (2005, cited in Darling-Hammond, 2008) identified three key components to successful student learning: activation of prior knowledge, organization of information to promote conceptual understanding, and metacognition. This book incorporates these learning components into the structure of each inquiry experience to ensure science concepts are explored in a way that moves each learner toward science literacy.

Activation of Prior Knowledge

Learning proceeds primarily from *prior knowledge* or *schema*. This prior knowledge includes former observations, past experience with a topic, or previous interactions with a subject via print or multimedia resources. Linking new information to this prior knowledge gives students a context and scaffold for new learning. The confidence built by touching on the familiar helps activate students' interest and curiosity. More importantly, it gives students a foundation upon which to add new information.

For each lesson in this book, students are encouraged to activate prior knowledge through open discussions and note-making in a science notebook. Sometimes a learner's prior knowledge can confound an educator's best efforts, especially if a student's prior knowledge is at odds with presented material. Beginning with consideration of previous experiences and understandings gives the instructor an opportunity to redirect misconceptions throughout the inquiry process and to practice formative assessment during inquiry instead of waiting until an end-of-unit test.

Promoting Conceptual Understanding

Mere inquiry does not automatically lead to conceptual learning. Conceptual learning stems from inductive reasoning, which moves from specific observations to broader generalizations about a concept. Students are expected to draw connections between data collected from a topical inquiry to the bigger-picture ideas of science. For example, the concept of attraction and repulsion is basic to science content areas of magnetism, static electricity, hydrophobic/hydrophyllic reactions, molecular bonding, and many more. Similarly, the concept of a cycle is extrapolated from a study of specific cycles, from water cycles to lunar cycles to life cycles.

To facilitate inductive thinking, students design data organizational systems that help them collect, sort, and interpret collected data. Because students take an active role in designing this data-collection system (with guidance from the instructor), they have a greater awareness of *why* they are collecting data and insights into what data might be telling them. Patterns emerge from organized data that help learners draw a valid conclusion that either supports or falsifies a prediction. These patterns may also be a critical element of the scientific concept that students will encounter again in future investigations. Organized data also helps students see connections between ideas and helps them build from specific data to general concepts and, in the process, develop authentic scientific work habits.

Managing One's Own Learning and Reflecting on It

To grow as a learner, a student must be given opportunities to engage in metacognition, or "thinking about his or her thinking." To do this, inquiry-based learning provides a variety of perspectives and behavioral strategies that help learners "own" and understand the work they are doing. Broken down into small steps for elementary learners, these strategies help move students to deeper levels of thinking that can transfer into future learning situations.

In addition, throughout this book, students are encouraged to reflect on both the process and the product of inquiry. Opportunities are presented for learners to be self-reliant, strategic, flexible, and productive as they figure out how to solve a particular problem as presented by the story. Students embark on a journey from prediction to experimental design through to execution. Finally, they reflect on the outcome of the experiment and its relationship to the original prediction. Students consider "what" happened, "so what" does it mean, and "now what" do we do next. By asking students to take what they have learned during inquiry and relate it back to the story, these lessons give elementary students regular practice in the skills that support metacognition.

What is Inquiry?

Inquiry is a student-centered learning strategy that implies a *need* or *want* to know. The focus is not on finding *the right answer* but rather on the process of seeking answers. It brings together the best practices identified above promoting students' curiosity and guiding explorations that lead to new understandings. John Dewey (1916) described how true learning begins with the curiosity of learners. This curiosity is the foundation of inquiry. Curiosity involves personal interest about how things work and why things are the way that they are. To inquire is to seek answers. This is really the motivational foundation for science learning (Rosebery & Warren, 2008). Inquiry-oriented curriculum harnesses students' natural curiosity, urges them to verbalize that curiosity as a question, and supports them in their quest to seek answers. Guided science inquiry empowers students to gain conceptual understanding through student-created investigations. Rather than following a prescribed series of steps and arriving at *the* correct answer, students identify a problem and then develop, carry out, and reflect on their own experiments to arrive at *an* answer.

The story starters in this book offer up problems designed to motivate learners to raise measurable questions to address these dilemmas. Too often, in school, students are bombarded with simplistic questions that can be answered "yes or no," "true or false," or "pick the best answer"—questions that rarely excite the learner. Scientific inquiry questions are open-ended and require thought, hands-on work, or further research in a search for answers. These questions are satisfying to pursue and often lead to new questions.

To solve problems, students examine relationships such as identifying possible causes and effects or uncovering the connection between independent and dependent variables. The problem-solving process also guides students in developing criteria to help them evaluate the effectiveness of their solution. For example, does the solution solve the problem without creating other, more serious problems? Sometimes students must go through many iterations of the process in order to find an acceptable resolution. Finally, the results of the solution are communicated clearly and effectively, using a variety of tools and strategies.

What does Inquiry Look Like in a Classroom?

Students must learn how to make observations, how to weigh one data set against another, and how to determine for themselves what is important in order to construct their own conceptualizations (Martin, 2006). Inquiry-based classrooms allow time for students to be perplexed, work through their confusion, and arrive at authentic conceptual understanding. Analyzing experimental findings and constructing meaning takes more class time than confirming a prescribed answer to an established experimental procedure.

Science inquiry instruction that uses the science notebooking method (outlined in Chapter 2) encourages development of a thinking skill set. Ultimately, students learn to investigate like scientists, meeting the goals of the National Science Standards (NRC, 1996).

Inquiry-based learning classrooms can be noisy, but it is the noise of engagement and interaction. Student work in an inquiry classroom is student-driven and that means students must take responsibility for their planned course of action and the accuracy of their results. In return, students' observations and formulation of explanations are deeply valued when outcomes are conveyed in an appropriate manner.

Inquiry and the Scientific Method

The scientific method is the procedure that is most commonly used with inquiry-based learning in science. The scientific method has a structured order used to investigate a topic:

1. Define the problem (sometimes called "Ask a question")
2. Conduct background research (in the library or from previous investigations)
3. Develop a hypothesis (a prediction based on knowledge and research)
4. Test the hypothesis by doing an experiment (collect data)
5. Analyze data
6. Draw a valid conclusion
7. Share the results
8. Conduct further inquiry

Although these steps of the scientific method are sequential, not all steps of the scientific method must be a part of every classroom investigation. It is also important to note that the scientific method is not the only procedure that can be used for inquiry. Inquiry-based learning can be accomplished through library research, demonstration, survey, or hands-on laboratories using models or simulations. Multiple forms of inquiry-based learning will be explored in this book.

Distinguishing Between Inquiry Investigations, Hands-On Learning, and Fun

When educators think about engaging students in science, they sometimes think that students will not be interested unless the activity is "fun." We have all observed scientific experiences in which students enjoy the interaction but are unable to explain what has been learned. For example, it's fun to watch a science fair volcano erupt—but too often few students understand the science behind the phenomenon. Other "fun" science activities might include playing games, using technology, going outside, or simply being engaged in activities that are enjoyable and amusing. Fun activities and inquiry-based learning do not have to be mutually exclusive. For fun activities to qualify as inquiry, however, requires more cognitive engagement from the student: questioning, seeking, exploring, and summarizing.

Hands-on or experiential learning emphasizes that students interact with actual materials and manipulatives—from props in a play to counting blocks in math. This type of learning emphasizes the role of kinesthetic interaction in mental engagement. In hands-on learning, students might mix cornstarch and water to create an "ooze" that behaves both as a solid and as a liquid. The students themselves are mixing the ingredients and watching how the ingredients interact. This activity is hands-on as students touch the ooze and may even be perceived as fun as students feel the ooze drip through their fingers. But if they are unable to articulate why this change in states of matter happens or why it is relevant to the science they already know, then the hands-on learning falls short.

In truth, shallow experiments with little more than a "Wow!" factor are less interesting to children in the long run than wrestling with an inquiry question and taking ownership of their own learning. Inquiry can be fun *and* hands-on *and* thought-provoking. Most fun or hands-on experiments can be converted into an inquiry–based learning format. Doing so requires that activities be restructured and made more open-ended, allowing room for students to explore questions and reach possible solutions. The role of the teacher shifts to one who guides—but does not *direct*—the children's inquiries.

Why Science Notebooking?

This book uses science notebooking as a methodology to track student thinking as they proceed through the scientific method in inquiry investigations. This is compatible with how "real" scientists work. Practicing scientists keep digital or handwritten notebooks to track their hypotheses, procedures, outcomes, thinking, and conclusions. Likewise, working in a science notebook gives students a chance to practice thinking and writing concisely and clearly. This systematic documentation also allows teachers to gain a new window into the inner thinking of their students and provides a basis for more effective formative assessment. Science notebooking fits perfectly with inquiry-based instruction because the notebooking process provides a consistent structure in which students are empowered to select and construct inquiries that answer personally meaningful questions (Campbell & Fulton, 2003; Klentschy, 2008; Klentschy, 2005).

Organization of this Book

This book is divided into three major sections. Chapters 1 through 3 provide an overview of the inquiry process and the methodology of science notebooking. Chapters 4 through 10 outline laboratory-based story starter inquiry lessons for science concepts such as transfer of heat energy, attraction and repulsion, and plant growth. Each inquiry lesson follows a consistent format including basic information about the scientific concept to help teachers gather materials and prepare for instruction. Timelines for lessons are intentionally not included because each inquiry can stand-alone, be integrated into existing curricula, used as a whole, or separate parts on consecutive days. Additional time is needed for project presentations and extension activities. The lesson in chapter 11 demonstrates how guided inquiry can be adapted for library research. Chapter 12 offers a technique to help students write their own story starter for future science inquiries.

Each science concept in this book is framed by the National Science Education Standards for science content published in 1996 by the National Research Council for grades K–4 and 5–8. From these content standards, achievable outcome objectives have been divided into two levels: "emerging scientists" and "practiced scientists." Each chapter is also divided into three lesson components: the story starter, the inquiry investigation, and the project/assessment piece.

The Story Starter

In language arts, a writing prompt given to students to jump start narrative writing is called a *story starter*. Story starter sentences build literacy skills by setting a context for writing. In this book, the story starters represent a variety of genres including a fractured fairy tale, reader's theater, poetry, and an e-mail exchange. In each story, a problem arises. Students use an inquiry process to investigate possible solutions to the story's problem, recording their thinking and experimentation in science notebooks. At the conclusion of their investigation, students respond with the results of their research and ideas for resolution of the problem. In presenting solutions, students are speaking from another perspective (writing in the voice of another character), generating presentation formats for the results of their experiment (podcasts or PowerPoint presentations), or writing using various genres (e-mail, an advice column, or a persuasive argument). By asking students to take what they have learned during inquiry and *transfer* it back into the story, students practice the application of their new knowledge.

The Inquiry Investigation

After reading the story starter, students examine the story for relevant information, tap into any prior knowledge they have about the science concept, and record vocabulary power words so that references to science concepts can be made using academic language. Following procedural instructions constructed before the experiment, students measure, observe, and collect data that will serve as evidence for drawing a conclusion that solves the problem. Finally, students reflect on their data by making claims based on the evidence gathered.

Project and Assessment

Rubrics are provided for each investigation's summation project and integrate at least two of the writing traits from Culham's *6+1 Traits of Writing* (2003), which outlines six traits of successful writing and includes presentation as the "+1."

The first trait is *ideas*. In this book, the ideas are the student's scientific understanding. The projects ask students to put what they have learned during inquiry back into the context of the story. In each project, students apply their conclusions about scientific concepts, based on data drawn from experimentation.

The next is *organization:* the arrangement of ideas into an order that is pleasing to the reader. Some story starter projects require students to communicate their experimental results in writing. Projects guide students to organize ideas sequentially, from least to most important, or in another order that promotes flow. Students are encouraged to use transition words and phrases to assist the reader's experience in moving from idea to idea.

The third trait is *voice.* In several projects, students write as themselves. Students with strong voice have writing that can be described as "writing the way they speak." There is an authority and sense of ownership behind the work. In other projects, students are asked to write in the voice of a story character, adopting the vocabulary, tone, and style of that persona.

Culham's fourth trait is *word choice*. This is particularly important when students write in the science content area. Developing a scientific vocabulary helps students precisely describe their activities and thoughts during a science laboratory experience. For each project, student writing incorporates the academic language of science (vocabulary) that is found within each lesson.

Sentence fluency is the fifth and often most challenging trait. When young writers write with choppy, predictable patterns, such as, "I went shopping. I got cookies. I ate a lot," sentence fluency is lacking. Mature writers write with a variety of sentence styles and lengths. Each of these science lessons provides introductory phrases or clauses to help students create varied sentence beginnings and to help create bridges between sentences.

Conventions are the final trait. These are the nuts and bolts of good writing: grammar, spelling, and punctuation. When used well, these elements create an elegant frame around writing that that communicates a sense of competence and professionalism. Each project rubric includes criteria for writing conventions to advance students' writing quality.

Culham's "+1" is *presentation,* or the sharing of ideas with an audience. Podcasts, monologues, slideshow presentations, and sharing a science fair board all develop the oral presentation strengths of students. Written presentations include a brochure, lab report, letter, memo, and e-mail. Being able to communicate scientific results is an authentic norm to measure.

Multitasking

We know that educators are under intense pressure to cover a great deal of curriculum in a compressed period of time, and we find that this story starter lesson approach encompasses several curriculum areas simultaneously:

- **Reading comprehension skills** improve as students analyze the story for clues to use in their investigation.
- **Science skills** improve as students strengthen their abilities to create, test, and evaluate a hypothesis. (In this book, we refer to a hypothesis as a prediction to correlate more meaningfully with language arts.)
- **Note-taking skills** develop as students learn to use their notebooks to track their ideas and thinking. Moreillon (2007) uses the term "note-making" rather than "note-taking." Note-taking hints that information is "taken" or copied from a source, whereas note-making incorporates cognitive decision-making as students choose what to write and what words to use to summarize their thoughts.
- **Writing skills** improve both through the practice of regular note-making and through the end products that demonstrate student understanding (Klentschy, 2008).
- **Vocabulary skills** grow as students use authentic science vocabulary in context.
- **Collaborative work skills** continue to develop as students work together using authentic science tools to solve a problem.
- **Independent work skills** flourish as students gain confidence in their ability to craft their own explorations. Students recognize that teachers are available to support them when they struggle but learn to take responsibility for their learning.

This book's imaginative approach makes it possible for students to question and examine knowledge that they might otherwise ignore while developing literacy skills that are transferable to other content areas.

Integration of Technology

The technology options in this book facilitate more meaningful student learning. Technology integration in the inquiry process supports four key components of learning: active engagement, development of cooperative skills, application of content knowledge, and connection to real-world resources. Technology is also well suited to the project-based learning assessment tasks where students refine their grasp of content knowledge through application of claims, evidence, and perspective to the story starter problem. The technology projects are consistent with the refreshed National Educational Technology Standards for Students (NETS*S) of the International Society for Technology in Education (ISTE, 2007).

Final Thoughts

Drawing on story starters to provide context for inquiry and using science notebooking to document this thinking process develops children's literacy skills by providing opportunities for learners to read, write, and problem solve in one setting. The story poses a question that puts students in the driver's seat. When students have success answering this question with *an* answer rather than *the* answer, then they begin to build confidence that they can answer the next question by using the same set of thinking and writing skills. This combined methodology creates a learning environment where students want to do more and learn more about scientific concepts.

2

What Is Science Notebooking?

Introduction

Science notebooking is a processing tool used by students to document the questions, predictions, procedures, conclusions, and reflections from their inquiry investigation. It is modeled on the real-world journals of practicing scientists. As an authentic instrument, the science notebook serves as an organizational tool, a memory aid, and a chronicle of activities written before, during, and after the experiment. Featuring narrative writing, annotated drawing, data set organization, diagramming, graphing, and table construction, a science notebook follows an organized structure based on scientific inquiry, recording product (results), process (procedures), and metacognition (reflective thinking).

Science notebooks and journals are terms that are often used interchangeably in the field. Although these techniques do share some common characteristics (e.g., both can include question prompts and are creative in nature), these forms of writing differ in format. *Science notebooks* are a more structured type of writing that accompanies the scientific method and uses science process skills as a basis for writing. *Journals*, on the other hand, emphasize a more free-form type of writing that often expresses feelings and is found in literature reflection, fiction, and poetry.

Science notebooks are more than a log of data. Logbooks are a record of "what happened when." Although data are part of a student's science notebook, the science notebook goes further, tracking a learner's cognitive process over time. Harvey and Goudvis (2007) point out that just as animals leave tracks in the snow showing where they have been, student notes leave a trail of their thinking. Science notebooking captures those "tracks" by asking students to record their thinking as an experiment unfolds. These attributes make science notebooks more than mere diaries, portfolios, or scrapbooks. Diaries chronicle personal events and lack a standard structure. Portfolios and scrapbooks collect and sequence artifacts of student's work, including reflection or journaling, but do not repeatedly assist students in refining process skills as a science notebook does.

Science notebooks are an approach to working with inquiry-based learning, not a curriculum. Science notebooks are an instructional approach that function harmoniously with existing science curriculum and with science kits. These notebooks are an alternative to pre-packaged procedures and worksheets and also replace teacher-directed procedures and data collection instruments with student-driven questioning and original student-generated procedures.

Process, Not Product

As a process tool, a science notebook is not intended to be a polished piece of writing. Just as is the case with practicing scientists, the primary audience for a science notebook is the notebook's author—the student. As such, it may look to the adult eye like a rough draft, complete with trials-and-error, grammar mistakes, or quick notations in lieu of complete sentences. However, teachers are encouraged to keep their editing instincts at bay. Real-world scientists do not submit their notebooks for external validation; rather, they process ideas in their notebooks and publish their results as articles, which are then open to public evaluation. Similarly, in this book, students demonstrate understanding of scientific concepts by creating a final project using results from experimental data.

Penmanship can be an issue for scientists of all ages, and it is certainly a factor when viewing science notebooks. Science notebook entries should be legible, but student thinking can be hampered if the approach is too focused on "use your best handwriting" instead of problem-solving thinking. Peers can exchange notebooks to confirm legible handwriting and check for comprehension, but the focus of the science notebook needs to remain on thinking, analyzing, and organizing scientific work for use in communicating final results.

Student-Generated Content

Science notebooks should be populated with student-generated content. Although at times it may be useful for a teacher to provide a sheet of graph paper or a working definition of a vocabulary word, these should be exceptions in the appearance of a science notebook. Science notebooks move beyond copying from the board or stapling in pre-prepared handouts. The science notebook approach addresses good work habits. The overarching life skill is to learn to take responsibility for selecting and organizing data in a way that makes sense, which leads to successful information-management skills in later years of schooling.

More than Text

Science notebooks incorporate many visuals such as sketches, graphs, charts, and tables. This makes them particularly suitable for differentiated instruction. Many students with special needs or students for whom English is not their first language can be on par with their peers when they can use graphics and illustrations to demonstrate their thinking or explain a process. Ralph Fletcher, in his book *Boy Writers* (2006), points out that, especially for boys, illustration is a key method for communicating information.

In *Science Notebooks* (2003), Campbell and Fulton suggest that students try to draw objects as they really look in nature rather than creating a cartoonish "symbol" of the object made of sticks and circles. For example, many children draw a flower as a stick with a circle on top of it, surrounded by a series of short vertical lines representing grass. This type of drawing is a *symbol,* a non-realistic stand-in for the real object.

Instead, encourage students to observe an object before drawing it and to make every effort to draw it as accurately as possible. For example, a real blade of grass is not a straight line but a tapered band with a small ridge going down the midpoint of the blade. To help students draw more realistically, use colored pencils instead of pens, so that lines can be erased if inaccurate or smudged to create shadows. Also, freshly sharpened colored pencils better represent nature's gentle colors than most markers, and their thin lines are more conducive to drawing realistic, color-blended shapes.

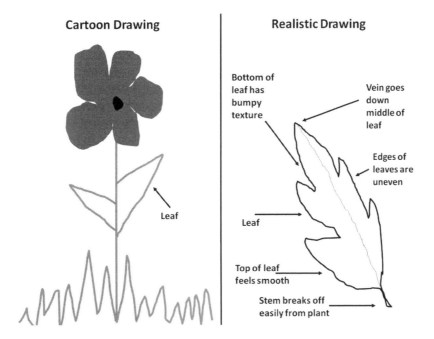

Figure 2.1.

Notice how the more detailed the drawing becomes, the more students are able to identify and discuss the elements present within that drawing. The "cartoon" leaf, on the other hand, lacks features or details, and students are unable to elaborate further.

Why Use Science Notebooking With Inquiry Investigations?

Gilbert and Kotelman (2005) outline five good reasons to use science notebooks with inquiry-based learning. First, notebooks are cognitive tools to help students think. Second, they are formative assessment tools that guide instruction by giving teachers a window into current student understanding. Third, notebooks improve student literacy skills by giving genuine purpose for writing, encouraging details, and giving regular practice integrated into content area learning. Fourth, they support differentiation. And finally, science notebooks support collaborative work among teachers. Each of these reasons is elaborated below.

Science Notebooks as Cognitive Tools

Science notebooks require students to document data and then to think through that data by writing about it. The notebooking process scaffolds cognition so students achieve conceptual understanding instead of simply going through the motions of a procedure.

Most of the work done by students in school is for an adult audience. Over the years, students learn that to be successful, their work must be pleasing to their parents or guardians, teachers, and administrators. A science notebook changes this paradigm. Students are empowered to work in science notebooks because they are writing for *themselves.* This infuses their inquiry projects with a greater level of intrinsic motivation and encourages them to give greater detail and attention to their work and to take pride in their thinking. This motivation sustains students during the intellectual rigors of science notebooking, including data sense-making and metacognition.

Science Notebook Assessment

Assessment drives today's educational climate. Assessment takes into account the process, outcomes, instruction, and activities that lead to final products. Summative assessment generally occurs at the culmination of study on a topic, and students who are unsuccessful on these tests have little opportunity to improve their knowledge. Likewise, it is too late for teachers to modify their instruction if a concept was misunderstood (Black & William, 1998). As a result of relying solely on summative assessment, conceptual misconceptions perseverate and negatively impact future learning. Additionally, some students learn the required content but not in a way that can be assessed on paper, or poorly written assessments can lead to confused student answers. Students "cramming" for summative tests retain the information for only a short time and do not gain enduring understanding Therefore, in this book, performance tasks are utilized as summative assessments for grading, placement, or accountability.

Performance Tasks: Summative Assessment Performance tasks measure students' conceptual understanding and content knowledge of a specific topic by asking them to draw on what they have learned through investigation to explain the concept to another (such as a character in the story starter), to make an informed decision, or to apply their understanding by speaking from another perspective.

These tasks range in format from writing a letter, e-mail, or newspaper column; performing a podcast; making an oral presentation with a PowerPoint slide; to designing a "science fair" type of poster display. Each project is designed so that the application of scientific knowledge and the ability to communicate findings are the focus. Each project also draws from the 6 + 1 traits of Culham (2003) (reviewed in Chapter 1). Each post-notebooking project includes an evaluation rubric that provides a means of measuring the level of student understanding. Each rubric is designed such that a student can use its constructive comments to revise their project and resubmit for advancement to the next level of understanding. While students work in the science notebook, however, *formative assessment* is more effective.

Notebook Entries: Formative Assessment Formative assessment is formal or informal assessment that occurs continuously during the learning process. When teachers conference with students during an experiment, collect "exit slips" to gather feedback at the end of class, or ask students to contribute knowledge to a discussion, they can provide feedback immediately. New knowledge can be either confirmed (if accurate) or corrected (if inaccurate) before a misconception can escalate. Science notebooks provide frequent and timely opportunities for formative assessment by teachers. Teacher comments in a science notebook provide crucial guidance or indicate specific actions that can be taken to close the gap between a student's current level of understanding and the targeted level understanding (NRC, 2001). Science notebooks are both learning tools for students and a source of information about that learning for teachers (Ruiz-Primo, Li, & Shavelson, 2001).

For example, if an elementary teacher collects science notebooks on a regular basis, he or she can track how students' understanding is developing over time. If misunderstandings are discovered during a review of science notebooks, then these can be addressed via individual conferences, mini-lessons, peer coaching, or tutoring. If the notebooks reveal an exceptional mastery of a concept, the student could be fast-tracked into more complex inquiries or extension activities, be referred to the school library media center for more in-depth research, or be placed in another group.

Providing feedback to students in science notebooks is not solely a cognitive exchange. It is also intertwined with issues of affect, motivation, self-esteem, and self-efficacy (NRC, 2001). Studies (Cameron & Pierce, 1994; Kluger & deNisi, 1996) show that students show better learning gains when they receive focused feedback rather than grades. "Grades, and even undue praise, can reinforce expectations of failure and lead to reluctance to invest effort" (NRC, 2001, p. 40). Therefore, when reviewing notebooks, providing comments instead of grades is recommended.

Just as teachers wish to be evaluated based on their classroom performance rather than on the state of their lesson plan book, students need the mental freedom that comes from knowing that their notebooking process will not be graded. It may be useful to compare the ongoing feedback of science notebooking to the kind of feedback received in a writer's workshop. In a writer's workshop, the teacher provides feedback to the student throughout the writing process so that he or she can become a better writer, but only the final piece is graded. Likewise, investigations in the notebook receive critical, constructive feedback only.

Tips for Providing Feedback   Feedback on notebook entries can be verbal or written. Feedback is not limited to areas for improvement; it can—and should—also motivate students by reassuring them where they might be doing particularly well. To enhance the inquiry process, here are prompts that can be used for formative feedback:

- **Inquire** into the student's current knowledge and experience.
- **Challenge the student** in critical-thinking processes (e.g., "Did you make any assumptions when drawing claims from evidence? How certain are you of your conclusion? Would you consider your evidence strong or weak?").
- Allow students to **self-assess** their performance and **diagnose** any areas in need of improvement (e.g., teamwork, accuracy in data collection, or procedural design).
- Provide **constructive feedback** on areas in need of improvement (e.g., "Do you feel you have enough data to support that claim? You might consider measuring …" or "The graph of data was clear and accurate. What does it mean?").
- **Observe** how the student's thinking has changed. Point this out to the learner to reinforce his or her scientific thinking.

Additional formative assessment questions are found in each of the science notebooking stages described in Chapter 3.

Keep feedback simple, constructive, and specific. Rather than giving many suggestions for improvement, work with the child to set a single goal for the next science notebook entry. For example, a student might focus on realistic drawing, designing a meaningful data chart, or using text to better explain a procedure. Science notebooking provides practice in student self-assessment as well. One key hallmark of successful adults is their ability to self-monitor and self-evaluate their work. Developing self-assessment skills must be deliberately incorporated into student learning. How do students make judgments about their own work? How accurate are they? How might these judgments be improved? One strategy for developing self-evaluation skills was created by the National Research Council (2001), which uses a system of red, yellow, and green colored dots. Students draw or apply adhesive dots in their notebook to indicate their level of confidence with their efforts, as measured by specific criteria. Green dots represent confidence, yellow symbolizes lack of sureness, and red indicates a student's impression she did not understand the assignment. This simple method can, at a glance, guide instructional decisions such as which students have accurate self-perceptions and which need additional support in evaluating their own work.

Science Notebooks as Literacy Tools

Ask any author how he or she developed a talent for writing, and the answer is almost always, "Practice, practice, practice." Science notebooks provide that practice and are conducive to a variety of writing genres, including:

- **Procedural writing** (e.g., listing the steps of a project: "Step One. Fill the bowl halfway with water."). Practicing scientists know that their experiments may be replicated by others. Therefore, students develop the skill, over time, to describe their investigations in enough detail to allow another student scientist to repeat the process and achieve similar results.

- **Narrative writing** (e.g., "When we added dye to the water, the water turned pink."). This "tell what happened" style of writing is often found on state assessment tests. In science notebooks, students become accustomed to telling a story of what transpired during experimentation.

- **Descriptive writing** (e.g., "By the third day in the sun, the green grapes were starting to turn brown with small wrinkles."). Being able to make detailed observations is an important scientific skill. In science notebooks, these observations are recorded and communicated through descriptive writing.

- **Note-making** (e.g., "The apple got all shrively."). Note-making requires that students process and make sense of new information and observations before rephrasing them in their own words.

- **Defining** (e.g., an entry in the glossary at the back of the science notebook). This type of writing uses familiar vocabulary to construct a description of more academic or scientific terminology.

- **Summarization** (e.g., "We tried the experiment three times. Every time, we got the same result. Opposites attract."). When summarizing, students give a quick synopsis of the overall experiment. Summarizing the main points of an inquiry process prepares students for identifying the main idea or message on standardized tests.

- **Persuasive writing** (e.g., "Because there was salt left on the tray after we put the saline solution in the sun, we believe that the saline solution was a mixture, not a compound.") (Gilbert & Kotelman, 2005). Persuasive writing takes a stand and encourages others to adopt the same point of view. Understanding persuasive messages is another skill found on many state assessments.

- **Types of print** (e.g., captions, labels, table of contents, page numbers, and a glossary). These are elements and text features students use repeatedly in their science notebooks. Students' ability to use these features to help navigate textbooks and research materials is crucial for success in later grades.

Science Notebooks for Differentiation

Differentiation is the process of modifying or adjusting instructional design to best fit the learning needs of an individual student. This is often a very difficult and time-consuming task for teachers. Because science notebooks are written in the student's own voice and students have guided independence in deciding how best to represent data and information, notebooks naturally provide differentiation options. Because students can use graphics, drawings, tables, charts, and graphs to communicate what they are discovering, there is greater flexibility for students of different learning abilities and for students for whom English is not the primary language. Differentiation is also enhanced during the inquiry investigations, which frequently group students of varying academic strengths together. Students learn that there are a variety of viewpoints, not only their own, and students who struggle to find meaning are often supported by their peers.

Science Notebooks for Teacher Collaboration

When teachers work in collaboration with one another, student achievement can improve. One of the best-known models for teacher collaboration is that of Professional Learning Communities, or PLCs (DuFour, 2004). In a high-functioning PLC, teachers who teach the same curriculum gather to plan instruction, design and evaluate formative assessments, and minimize gaps in student understanding. Examining student work is key to these collaborative meetings. Bound in a single volume, a science notebook shows teachers a student's thinking at the present time as well as his or her progress over time. In a meeting of the special-education team, a science notebook helps educators understand the level of thinking, effort, or comprehension of a student.

What Style of Notebook is Best for Young Students?

Paper Notebooks

Composition books, stock-bound (9-3/4″ by 7-1/2″) with a marbled cover, are best for use as science notebooks. These books are generally smaller than a spiral notebook or 3-ring binder, making them easier to store and to use on lab tables or classroom desks. The pages are securely stitched into the binding and withstand heavy use. The permanence of the pages helps provide a sequenced record of the student's work. Lined pages facilitate the construction of graphs and tables. The composition book can lay open in a flat, two-page spread, which gives additional room for oversized data-collection organizers.

Spiral notebooks or steno pads are not good choices for science notebooks because pages can come loose, disturbing the page order that delineates progress over time. Three-ring binders are also not recommended, as they are too bulky for lab bench or desktop writing and pages are too easily removed or misplaced.

Digital Notebooks

For science notebooking to be effective, the student must have it at hand for all stages of the inquiry process, and each student should have his or her own notebook. This makes technology-based notebooks impractical in many schools. However, computers facilitate the processing of data. For example, primary students may draw and make textual notations using a drawing and writing software like KidPix. Older students may use Microsoft Power-Point or Excel to create graphs and charts. Students with special needs may dictate their observations via a digital voice recorder to create a podcast. Digital formats have the advantage of uniform readability, spell check, auto graphing of data tables, and easy archiving. Some districts even encourage online submission of science notebooks as a means of publishing student work (North Cascades and Olympic Science Partnership, n.d.).

Elements of a Science Notebook

Organization is an important life skill that facilitates learning. Teachers can help students format their notebooks so that they can easily find their place in them. By dividing a notebook into sections and using tools such as tabs and a ruler, students will be well organized throughout the notebooking process.

Table of Contents

Leave the first few pages of the notebook blank, as this is where the table of contents will be recorded. After an experiment is completed, the title of that investigation is written into the table of contents along with the starting page number for that research.

Investigations

Investigations comprise the major content of the book. Number and date each page to preserve chronology. When starting a new day's work, start a new page and put the subject on the top line. Students should always endeavor to fill at least one complete page during each day of the investigation and spend additional time working in the notebook after the investigation.

If the teacher feels that a teacher- or commercially-created worksheet is essential to the success of the notebook, these sheets may be shrunk to a half of a sheet of copy paper (e.g., 8-1/2″ × 5-1/2″) and pasted or taped into place.

When this or any section of the science notebook is filled, the notebook is archived, and a new notebook is started. Notebooks become part of a student's cumulative learning record, and existing notebooks are continued in subsequent grade levels.

Glossary

Save several pages at the back of the book for the glossary, where science vocabulary words are listed. Some teachers encourage their students to flip their notebook upside-down so that the back cover, upside-down, becomes the front cover of the glossary section. For primary students, it is easiest if a new glossary page is started for each investigation. Older students may create a semi-alphabetized glossary by putting a heading on the top of each page (e.g., "A–C," "D–G," "H–J," "K–M," "N–P," "Q–V," "W–Z") and sorting their glossary entries into the correct sections. For scientific accuracy, glossary entries are generally guided by the teacher but in the student's own words and images. The class may choose to photograph objects and paste the photos into their glossary along with a caption.

Tabs

Students are more productive when they have organized their notebook so information can be accessed quickly. Use sticky notes or adhesive file folder tabs to identify the first page of a new investigation.

Rulers

A ruler for each student is useful during investigations. A laminated paper ruler can be used as a bookmark or taped to the front cover of the book. Metric measurements are used in science. There are several printable rulers available from Vendian.org (http://www.vendian.org/mncharity/dir3/paper_rulers/). When taping a ruler to the notebook, line up the "zero" mark on the ruler with the edge of the notebook.

Final Thoughts

Science notebook methodology has a fundamental role in elementary science instruction with benefits to both teachers and learners. Science notebooks are written with an intended audience of their own author. This provides a safe place for learners to maintain an archival record of their interests, their thinking, and what they have learned. The notebook provides learners with opportunities for differentiated learning through annotating their drawings and constructing their own definitions for science vocabulary. For teachers, notebooks provide indicators that can be used to guide their instruction as well as serving as a window into their students' thinking. Because of the nature of instruction in inquiry-based science, notebooks are the perfect means to capture an individual's input into a group's product as well as opportunities for learners to use academic language and develop positive attitudes toward learning.

3

Working in the Science Notebook

Introduction

If teachers are to truly engage students, then students need to know not only *what* they should be doing but *why*. This chapter spells out both the "what"—the steps of science note-booking—and the "why"—the cognition benefits—behind the science notebooking steps. Most of these steps are derived from Klentschy (2008), whose research has drawn attention to the relationship between science notebooking and improved student achievement in science, reading, and English language acquisition. In this approach, science notebooking is divided into three sections: before the experiment, during the experiment, and after the experiment. A variety of strategies for working through these stages will be found both here and in the sample lessons that follow. A summary of science notebooking can be found on page 22.

Before the Experiment

It may be surprising to discover how much of science notebooking takes place before the hands-on inquiry begins. This is necessary to maximize students' connection to the task when the actual experiment unfolds. Therefore, a great deal of cognitive energy centers on pre-experimental planning. Teachers scaffold the planning stages through class discussions and individual consultations, but the bulk of the cognitive work remains with the student. By actively participating in the design of experiments, students become active learners. The level of intellectual engagement rises and the process of "doing" gives students a true commitment to the science behind the experiment.

Awakening Prior Knowledge

Tapping into *prior knowledge*, or what a student already knows, is the first step in developing reading comprehension in students (Harvey & Goudvis, 2007; Moreillon, 2007). Awakening prior knowledge is equally important in science inquiry. When students articulate what they think and know about key elements of a book (in language arts) or the materials of an investigation (in science), they "wake up" that repository of personal knowledge. For example, a young child may not know the vocabulary word "magnet," but he may be familiar with the objects that stick his school art to his refrigerator. By connecting the new vocabulary to a familiar setting and the associated memories, the student has a greater chance of grasping the concept of magnetic force.

Science Notebooking at a Glance

Before the Experiment

Preparing for Inquiry
- Awaken prior knowledge
- Read and discuss the story starter
- Discuss the science
- Lead Inventory Walk and introduce vocabulary

Student-Written Question
- Investigable
- Avoid yes/no questions

Prediction
- "If I change _____, then I predict _____ will happen because _____."

Identifying Variables
- Independent variable (what is changed)
- Dependent variable (what will be measured)
- Constants (what will be kept the same)

Procedure
- Think through experiment design, materials, and measurement
- Write sequential list or paragraph

Data Organizer
- Chart, table, or text
- Based on procedure and variables

During the Experiment

Conducting the Experiment and Recording Data and Observations
- Follow the procedure
- Record data
- Add drawings and descriptive text

After the Experiment

Claims and Evidence
- Process and calculate the gathered data
- Identify data patterns
- "Because of (evidence), I believe that (claim)."

Conclusion
- Look back at claim and evidence and at the original prediction
- Was the prediction supported?
- "I conclude that (claim) because of (evidence). My prediction was/was not supported."
- Thinks through the possibility of experimental error

Next Steps
- Narrative reflection by students
- Identifies areas for future investigations

Project and Assessment
- Creates a conclusion to the story starter
- Assessed with a rubric

Extensions
- Individual, group, or class activities to continue the exploration of the concept

Figure 3.1.

At the start of each inquiry, students are invited to contribute what they think about and already know about the topic. Students brainstorm their individual ideas in their science notebooks, then pool their information in small group conversations or whole class discussions. In the case of whole group discussions, the teacher acts as a scribe, notating the ideas on a piece of chart paper, on a bulletin board dedicated to science, or on a part of the whiteboard that will not be erased. This recollection of prior knowledge builds a foundation on which new learning can grow and flourish. It provides a real-world context on which new knowledge makes sense. K-W-L charts, in which students outline what they know, what they want to know, and what they learned, use "K" to record prior knowledge.

The Story Starter

The next stage is to share the story starter, which introduces students to a problem that needs resolution. The story starter and ensuing discussion develop a useful scaffold for students to focus prior knowledge. The conversations also inform the teacher about existing vocabulary knowledge, content information, and disposition of the class.

The story starters in this book may be duplicated for classroom use. Students may read independently, in small groups, or round-robin style in the classroom. Alternatively, teachers may read aloud, with students following along. Encourage students to keep a colored pencil in hand while reading to make notes in the margins or circle important information. This is preferable to highlighting, because young scientists tend to over-highlight text without processing the text's meaning. Note-making, instead, requires that students think before they write.

Reviewing the Story

Especially for students with limited prior knowledge, reviewing the story is essential for developing an initial awareness of concepts and motivation to learn more. "What is the problem that needs resolution?" "What events in our lives relate to the content of the story?" and "What do we know from the story that can help us design an inquiry?" are key discussion questions.

Connecting to Science

We wouldn't ask students to navigate a strange city without a map, and we shouldn't let them loose on inquiry without some scientific information to ground the experience. For inquiry to be successful, and not random or hit-or-miss experimentation, students also need some real science knowledge that they can apply in the situation. After reading the story starter, the teacher connects scientific content with events from the story. The inventory walk is an easy first step in making those connections.

The Inventory Walk

An "inventory walk" or discussion about the materials, safety devices, and equipment that will be involved in the post-story investigation, can introduce new vocabulary, review science skills (such as measuring or using senses for observation), and nudge student curiosity (Klentschy, 2008). This concept is similar to a *picture walk* from language arts, which is a pre-reading strategy that stimulates prior knowledge. During a picture walk, a teacher shows a book to the class and, without reading the text, asks questions about the people, places, and interactions depicted in the illustrations. A picture walk is interactive and encourages questioning and discussion. After the "walk," the teacher then shows the book again, this time reading the author's text.

Similarly, an inventory walk in science can lead students through an interactive discussion about the items they will have on hand to design their upcoming investigation. Klentschy (2008) recommends this technique as a way to stimulate curiosity and establish common scientific vocabulary about the items that will be used in the investigation. This is especially valuable for English language learners. Again, the inventory walk both taps into and develops connections to experiences in students' lives that can provide a framework for building scientific interest.

To conduct an inventory walk, the teacher gathers students close so that everyone can see. From an opaque box or storage container, he or she selects one item from the box and holds it up for students to view. (In a large classroom, holding the item under a document camera connected to a data projector will facilitate student viewing.) The teacher asks if someone can name the item, or, if the item is familiar, offer up the specific name used by scientists. It is important to use proper science nomenclature. For example, "beaker" is preferable to the more generic "cup." Once the item is named, the teacher may ask a variety of questions about the object, or students may pose questions that might be answered by other students. Some questions may remain unanswered during the inventory walk, recorded in the science notebook, and revisited during the inquiry.

Following the inventory walk, items may be placed in clear plastic bags and stapled to a science bulletin board, labeled with the proper name. Large objects may be placed on a nearby counter or table. This "exhibit" serves as an ongoing reference and assists students in using real science vocabulary during the experiment.

Vocabulary: Power Words

Many science vocabulary words define processes or scientific phenomena that cannot be represented by an item in the inventory walk. Using a variety of vocabulary acquisition strategies, students are introduced to content vocabulary that names the phenomena they are exploring. As students develop relationships between vocabulary terms, working definitions may be posted to a bulletin board or recorded in the glossary. It can be advantageous to have collective working definitions throughout the inquiry, with the student waiting until the end of the inquiry to craft a personal definition for his or her science notebook glossary.

Student-Generated Questions

Once students have a working understanding of the story's problem and the materials, equipment, and resources available to explore possible solutions, students are ready to design an investigable question. This is a question that comes from their curiosity about the science they were introduced to in the story starter.

A single focus question for each investigation is appropriate for elementary students. Students generate their own questions with the support of their teacher because one's own ideas are always the most interesting to pursue! Some inquiry experiments encourage each student to create his or her own inquiry question; in other cases, a small group may work together, with each student recording the communal question in his or her individual science notebook.

Designing good questions for scientific investigation is one of the most important steps of science inquiry. Throughout this book, several question development-strategies are shared. Questions that focus on *what would happen if _____, comparison,* and *measurement* are often easiest for elementary students to construct inquiry around, as are questions that begin with *how, which,* or *what.* Sample questions in each category include:

What Would Happen If _____

- What would happen to a flower if I added salt to the water in its flower vase?
- What would happen to a potato if we kept it in a dark place for a month?
- What would happen to a nail if I submerge it in 50 ml of cola?

Comparison and Difference

- If I put a cup of hot oatmeal into a glass bowl and another cup of hot oatmeal into a plastic bowl of the same size, which oatmeal will be cooler after ten minutes?
- Which type of milk (fat free, 2%, or whole) do most students prefer?
- Which has a stronger magnetic pull, the large magnet or the smaller one?

Measurement

- How many centimeters will a seedling grow in a week?
- For how long will an object keep its temporary magnetism?
- How much will an ice cube wrapped in newspaper melt in an hour?

Types of Questions to Redirect

Klentschy (2008) cautions against "why" questions for hands-on inquiry. "Why" inquiries are best saved for library research, as shown in Chapter 11. These "why" questions are suitable for library research:

"Why" Questions

- Why do we have solar eclipses?
- Why does rust occur?
- Why does water expand when it freezes?

Questions to Avoid   Chin, Brown, and Bruce (2002) suggest moving student-generated questions away from basic closed questions that have a single, unambiguous answer. These types of *factual questions* would fall on the low level of Bloom's taxonomy (knowledge, comprehension) and are considered **input** questions requiring students to recall information. For example, these questions should be avoided:

- What color is the north pole of a magnet?
- Who discovered Jupiter?

These types of basic questions do not lend themselves to inquiry. Students might also develop *procedural questions* that simply **clarify** how a task is to be carried out but are not open-ended enough to guide inquiry. For example, these should be avoided:

- When should we add this chemical to make the volcano erupt?
- Does _____come before or after _____?

To move these basic questions to higher levels on Bloom's taxonomy (application, analysis, synthesis, evaluation), guide students to develop **"I wonder" questions.** These questions require an application or extension of taught ideas. They may focus on predictions, explanations, and causes instead of facts and procedure, or on resolving discrepancies and gaps in knowledge. These could be *processing* questions (drawing relationships among data) or *output* questions (going beyond data in new ways to hypothesize, speculate, generalize, create, and evaluate.)

"Yes/No" Questions   Questions that can be answered with either "yes" or "no" also do not provide students with the necessary cognitive opportunities to evaluate data, observe patterns, and investigative information, nor do they allow students to delve deeply into exploration. The following types of questions should be redirected:

- Are magnets metal?
- Do rocks contain minerals?
- Is water necessary for plant growth?

Subjective Questions to Avoid   Likewise, questions that can be answered with an opinion, lead to a subjective answer, or are too general to be answered do not make good investigable questions. For example, avoid questions like these:

- Are magnets special?
- Can a rock last forever?
- What color is water?

Practicing with Questions   Giving students practice identifying good inquiry questions builds student expertise and ease with the process. When empowered with a variety of strategies, students can learn to develop more meaningful questions.

Another way to develop questioning skills is for teachers to use the metaphor of "red light, green light" (Levitov, 2005). Even the youngest elementary students know to stop at a red light and that "green means go." Similarly, red light questions are those questions that stop curiosity as soon as they are answered. "Is water necessary for plant growth?" The answer is simply: *Yes*. Red light! Imagine a bicycle squealing to a halt. ERRRRR! Slam on the brakes! We're all done!

A green light question, on the other hand, invites further exploration, just as a green light urges the rider onward. To use this strategy, have the students construct paper traffic lights. Give each student a copy of the reproducible on page 28 that contains two traffic lights. On one traffic light, color the top circle red. On the other traffic light, color the bottom circle green. Cut out the lights and glue them back-to-back on a paint stirrer or staple them to a small wooden craft stick. When the teacher calls out a sample question, students hold up the red side of their traffic light if the question can be answered with "yes" or "no," is too broad for investigation, or does not invite further investigation. Hold up the green side if the question requires more than a "yes/no" answer and can be measured. Teachers may pose questions orally, although using a data projector or document camera to display them in writing will enhance comprehension for non-auditory learners. After modeling the exercise with teacher-written questions, move into guided practice by inviting students to offer their own questions for the class to evaluate using the paper traffic lights. Questions generated by the class can also be placed on the board.

For additional practice in developing measurable questions, post possible questions around the room. Invite students to mark the questions with either a red or a green sticker dot. At science time, examine a few of the questions and discuss why children voted the way they did. As a class, rework red light questions until they become green light questions.

As a kinesthetic alternative, ask students to line up in the hallway with their backs against the wall. A selected student or the teacher calls out student- or teacher-generated questions. Students take one step forward if they believe it is a green light question but stand still if it is a red light question. If it is a red light question, invite students to brainstorm "green" alternatives.

Once students have moved from class practice into writing their own inquiry question in the science notebook, this checklist for the teacher can be helpful:

- Writing a question is the first science notebooking step. Did students begin by dating the entry, writing the page number, and writing the investigation topic at the top of a fresh page in the notebook?
- Have students written a question in their own words?
- Is the question investigable and not simply answered "yes" or "no" or with a single word?
- Is the question clear, concise, and related to the problem being investigated?
- Is the question measurable so that it will generate data needed to answer it?

Creating a Testable Prediction

A *prediction* is a statement of what the learner thinks the relationship is between what action is performed and the consequence of that action. This book uses the word *prediction* instead of the word *hypothesis*. This is done purposefully to more strongly match with the language arts curriculum, where "prediction" is a common nomenclature. A hypothesis is a testable statement, which includes a prediction by proposing a possible explanation to some phenomenon or event. The key word is *testable*—testing how two variables might be related—the one you are changing and the one you are identifying to measure any changes. A prediction is usually based on some previous observation, experience, experiment, library research, or perhaps what happened in the story starter.

Predictions are written in the science notebook before experimentation and are based on the question asked in the previous step and the student's prior knowledge. Predictions are revisited after experimentation as students draw conclusions from data gathered. Teachers can guide students toward strong prediction statements by encouraging them to frame their predictions in this format (adapted from Klentschy, 2008):

If I change _____, *then* I predict _____ will happen because _____.

Note the use of the personal pronoun "I." Students want to be explorers and investigators. Putting them in the driver's seat by framing predictions this way encourages students to respond at their own level of thought. Students are free from the burden of knowing in advance why something behaves as it does and are liberated to put forth possibilities, offer explanations, test ideas, or suggest conjecture upon which to build (Bass, Contant, & Carin, 2009).

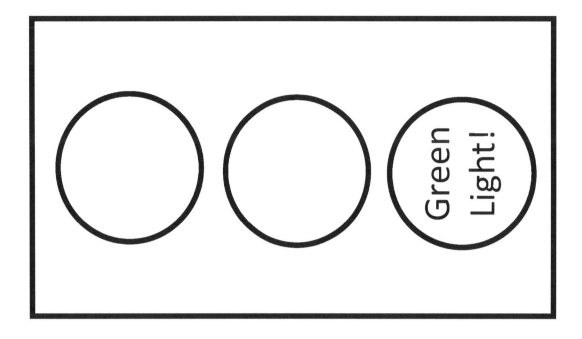

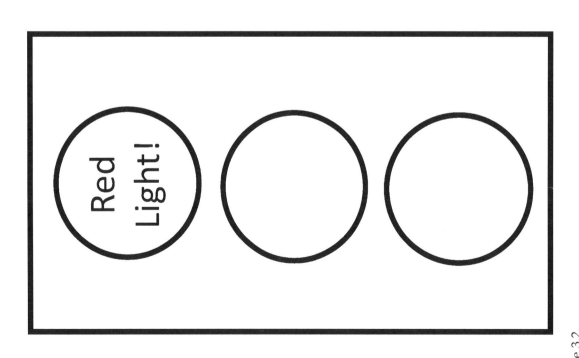

Figure 3.2.
From *Story Starters and Science Notebooking: Developing Student Thinking Through Literacy and Inquiry* by Sandy Buczynski and Kristin Fontichiaro. Santa Barbara, CA: Teacher Ideas Press. Copyright © 2009.

28

The "if/then" pattern correlates with language arts, where students use these same words to determine cause and effect in a story. At a fundamental level, an experiment is a test of the relationship between two variables, similar to the relationship between "cause and effect." Using the word "because" requires learners to provide a rationale for their prediction that is based on prior knowledge or background research. This provides a cognitive anchor for the student's learning and reduces random, disconnected inquiries. This prediction template can be used for students to insert any ideas that might make sense. As they "plug in" various changes, they consider what results might be measured as a result of those changes. Predicting isn't "just guessing." Rather, it is comparative thinking.

Teachers can coach students into creating good prediction statements by asking questions like, "What is something you might like to work with in this experiment?" If students are able to identify a few materials, the teacher can probe further by asking, "What could be done to alter one of these materials?" This helps identify the item that might change, which comes after the "if" clause. What comes after the "then" clause guides students to what types of data to collect, what available data to pay attention to, or possible ways to interpret the data.

To be useful, a prediction must suggest the direction in which the student thinks the outcome will fall. Ultimately, the prediction will be tested through experimentation to determine if it is supported or not supported by the data collected. Therefore, the prediction should suggest what evidence would support it and what evidence would refute or not support it. When formatively assessing the prediction, teachers may ask questions to probe student thinking, such as:

- Is the prediction built on prior knowledge or background research?
- Does the prediction take a stand and forecast an outcome?
- Is the prediction measurable? Does it point to what kind of data to collect?
- What might happen if (aspect of variable) were to be changed?
- How can we use this (change of variable) to explain this (probable outcome)?

Especially well-crafted student predictions can be offered as models to help struggling students make connections between variables and to construct a prediction with a measurable outcome.

Identifying Variables

An *investigation* is the process of testing a prediction. Investigations have variables: things that can be changed, have variation, have differing amounts, or that can be monitored to observe the results of change. These variables are mathematical tools used to maintain control of an investigation in a *quantitative* (measured) way. The dependent variable is what is measured or observed in response to changes of the independent variable. This relationship between the variables enables scientists to attribute experimental results as a function of changes to the independent variable.

When using the prediction template above, it is easy to identify the independent and dependent variables. The *independent* variable comes after the "if" clause, and the *dependent* variable comes after the "then" clause, as shown here:

If (*independent variable*) is done, then (*dependent variable*) will happen.

Independent Variable   The *independent variable* is also known as the *changed* or *manipulated* variable. Because independent variable is the terminology that is used in upper grades, it is easiest to learn this term initially. The independent variable is the component of the investigation that is purposefully changed, altered, or manipulated. This is the only factor that purposefully varies in an experiment.

Dependent Variable   The *dependent variable* is also known as the *responding* or *measured* variable. This is the variable that is being observed or measured in response to changes being made with the independent variable. The dependent variable will have associated units of measure for discrete and continuous data. For example, discrete data are categorical data for measuring the presence or absence of some characteristic as counted in whole numbers, such as number of people, number of phone calls per day, types of coins, gender, etc. Continuous data are usually associated with physical measurements that have values on an uninterrupted scale, such as weight, width, height, temperature, and time. All measurements (discrete and continuous) collected will have an associated label to indicate *units* of measure, such as centimeters, milliliters, minutes, degrees Celsius, grams, number of paper clips, number of people, male or female, etc.

Constants   *Constants* are multiple factors in an experiment that remain stable: deliberately unchanged. To define the constants of an experiment, look back at the independent variable. What aspects of the experiment would need to be held steady so that any results observed can be attributed to the independent variable? Holding all variables constant, except the independent variable, helps make the experiment a "fair test." If a test of the prediction is a "fair" one, then every aspect of the investigation is identical, with the exception of the variable that is deliberately being changed (the independent variable).

In identifying constants, students are seeking any factors that might inadvertently impact the outcome of the experiment. For example, when doing experiments involving the temperature of objects, as in Chapters 5 and 6, a constant is the ambient air temperature. Students repeating that experiment on a different day with a changed ambient temperature might get another result. Imaginative young students may need help reining in their list of constants. Students can omit from their list of constants anything that might *not* influence results. For example, if students are designing a fair test to determine if the boys of the class are taller than the girls, then constants might include taking off shoes, standing up straight, and using the same measuring device for all students. Each of these factors could affect accurate and consistent measurement of the height for each student. However, students would not need to list factors such as hair color, time of day, or room temperature, as these would have no impact on height.

Students may struggle at first with the concept of variables, but it is important to spend time developing their understanding, as variables are scientific concepts that apply to all fair test (controlled) experiments, whether they occur at school or in the scientific field, such as a medical drug trial. For additional practice, students can practice picking out independent, dependent, and constant variables for the following examples:

- **If plants are grown in dark and lighted environments, then the plants in the dark will be the tallest.** (*Independent variable:* amount of light. *Dependent variable*: height of plants measured in centimeters. *Constants:* amount of water, temperature, type of soil and container for plants, and variety of plant.)
- **A student wants to find out which stain remover works best for removing grass smudges from a shirt.** (*Independent variable:* brands of stain remover. *Dependent*

variable: degree of stain reduction measured by a color scale from 1–5. *Constants:* temperature of water, amount of stain remover used, size of stain, type of fabric, and length of time stain soaked.)

Teachers can also spot-check science notebooks to provide feedback on students' ability to identify independent and dependent variables. The following checklist is helpful:

- Did the student correctly label the independent variable by identifying the aspect of the experiment that is being manipulated (changed)?
- Can the dependent variable be measured (centimeters, milliliters, days, hours, grams, number of people, degrees Celsius, etc.) or observed (greener, wrinkled, pale, stinky, sweet, etc.)?
- Are experimental factors that need to be held constant listed and logical?

Student-Written Procedures

A *procedure* is the series of steps that scientists follow in carrying out an experiment. Procedures are important because they provide the information needed to repeat experiments. Each repetition of an experiment is called a *trial*. It is common for scientists to repeat experiments in the exact same way, many times, to make sure the data being gathered are accurate and consistent (or, to use scientific terms, valid and reliable). Reviewing procedures after an unsuccessful experiment or an experiment with unexpected results can help scientists identify experimental error.

Procedures should be brief and to the point and recorded beneath the variables in the science notebook. In writing a procedure, students must consider sequential action steps, materials to be used, amounts and units of measurement, timing (how often and when measurements will be taken), and when data should be gathered. If the investigation will be repeated, that should be noted at the end of the procedure.

A written procedure helps keep students on track and prevents "fooling around" during the inquiry. Writing down steps can slow down young students' impulsive thinking and encourage them to think more methodically through the process. The following checklist for formative assessment is useful:

- Are procedural steps in sequential order?
- Can the investigation be completed safely, with available resources and time?
- Does the procedure match the prediction?
- Are measurements (data) being collected?
- Could someone else follow these directions to repeat the experiment?
- Are directions clear and easy to follow?

To help students think sequentially in designing a procedure, ask one student to hide an object on the playground and then write directions to find it. These written directions are then handed to a partner who must follow them to find the hidden object. This demonstrates how much detail is needed to provide solid procedural instructions.

Data Organizer

Data organizers are charts, tables, or graphs that hold numerical or text data. No single data organizer works for every experiment, and there are often multiple ways to express the same data. Teachers can assist students' thinking about data organizer construction by asking students to consider putting dependent variable data on the vertical plane (axis) and independent variable data on the horizontal. Examples of data organizers are shown throughout the sample lessons in this book. Creating the data organizer *before* beginning the experiment sharpens students' focus and points to the kind of data to collect. Because data organizers are pre-drawn, during experimentation the input of data is immediate. Students can also pre-fill the unit of measurement (degrees, centimeters) on the data organizer to assist with clarity.

To assist with formative assessment, the following questions at this stage are useful:

- Has the student constructed a data organizer that will collect useful data?
- Can the data organizer be completed using the data from the procedure?
- Is the data organizer labeled, including measurement units such as inches or grams?

During the Experiment

Conducting the Experiment and Recording Data and Observations

Because students have invested so much pre-thinking into their experiments, they are now fully equipped to carry out the experiment with little adult intervention. One advantage of prewriting the question, prediction, variables, and procedure is that this thinking and writing can be completed far in advance of the experiment itself if necessary. For teachers with limited time for science, this is a big advantage and maximizes "lab time" for hands-on investigation.

With cooperative group structure for labs, it is useful to assign specific roles and responsibilities for group members. This minimizes "tourist" students who hide behind the work of the rest of the group. Over time, each student should have an opportunity to fill one of the laboratory roles. One possible group configuration is to assign these roles:

- **A runner,** who gathers the necessary materials (in some inquiries, each work group will be using a slightly different set of materials, depending on the experiment they design);
- **The administrative assistant,** who keeps good notes of observations made and data gathered;
- **The manipulator,** who actually administers the experiment and is in charge of operations.

Other possible roles for group members might include a discussion leader, who asks and records the answers to supplementary questions during wait times; custodian, who is in charge of set up, take down, and clean up of materials; or a spokesperson who communicates final results to whole class discussion. Although students design and run the experiment, the teacher is always available for formative assessment, advice, and support. Student-centered design does not imply an absence of teacher input!

During the experiment, it is important that students also write supplementary observations in their science notebooks that cannot be represented by numerical data. This further sharpens observational skills and gives students authentic practice in writing with details. Any anomalies or "mistakes" can also be recorded as a written observation, as this experimental error may help illuminate why the students achieved the results they did.

"Mistakes" are not a crisis; one group's errors may lead to new or different understandings, but all data should be documented with integrity. Falsification or invention of data is a serious offense in the scientific research community. Besides, many scientific "mistakes" end up as creative new inventions or medical miracles!

Students can also draw a sketch of their experiment. Drawings express action. Making illustrations is an appealing communicative approach, especially for males (Fletcher, 2006). Coloring drawings with colored pencils also provides a valuable means of expressing the details of observational data.

Questions to help teachers formatively assess this stage include the following:

- Have data been collected and measured accurately?
- Has the metric system of measurement been used?
- Have labels for units of measure been applied correctly?
- Was the procedure followed exactly or modifications noted if procedure altered?
- Are data recorded truthfully?
- Are team members working safely and effectively together?
- Do drawings appear realistic and support the experimental outcomes?

After the Experiment

After the hands-on investigation is complete, students find data patterns and derive meaning from them, reflect on the experience, and identify future areas for investigation. These post-experimental steps do not need to take place on the same day as the experiment itself.

Making Claims Based on Evidence

In this stage, students look at their collected data, seeking patterns from which to make claims. Claims must be justified by data (*evidence*) from the experiment. Just as in the prediction step, the use of the word "because" provokes students into thinking about the reasons behind their claim. Some younger students, despite the results of their experiment, will cling to false preconceptions and want to use those misconceptions in determining the claim. "Because" requires that students use evidence (their collected data) to back up their assertion. At this stage, students cannot use their prior knowledge to justify a claim.

Classroom discussions in which students with related inquiries pool their data to help students formulate a claim with a larger pool of supporting evidence (Klentschy, 2008). Manipulating data by calculating the mean or median, displaying results in a chart or graph, or performing mathematical calculations are all mechanisms that help students process and interpret data. These calculations are recorded in the science notebook. If a technology tool such as PowerPoint or Excel is used to calculate data, the results can be printed and taped or stapled into the notebook.

When students are ready to make an assertion, this is a useful template based on Klentschy (2008):

Because of (evidence), I claim that _____.

Notice the avoidance of phrases like, "I proved" or "that proves." In science there are no absolutes. Scientists also keep in mind that their data may have been flawed due to unforeseen or yet-undiscovered errors during the inquiry. It is also important to note that claims from one set of experimental data may not be valid under alternative experimental conditions.

Identifying claims and evidence reveals the relationship between the independent and dependent variables, and for that reason, teachers should check in with students and be certain that they have reached their claim in a logical manner that is consistent with the collected data.

Teachers may consider the following while monitoring student progress:

• Does the evidence (data and observations) support the claim (assertion)?
• Does the claim mention the independent variable and is the evidence based on the dependent variable?

By responding strategically to students' claims and evidence, teachers can open up critical discourse and improve students' ability to communicate their results. According to Bass, Contant, and Carin (2009), three strategic responses are:

1. **Accept student responses without judgment.** Because the inquiry process encourages risk taking, students have the "right to be wrong" (p. 194). A teacher's initial positive attitude toward a student's idea that contains mistakes, errors, or alternative conceptions will create an inviting, non-threatening environment that opens up further discussion. To accept a student response, teachers can (a) repeat a student's idea back to him, (b) list it on the board for consideration, or (c) praise the effort of risk taking.
2. **Extend student responses by adding something new.** This strategy is helpful for vague, unorganized, incomplete, or partially correct student responses. Teachers can (a) add a clarifying remark by paraphrasing, simplifying language, or reorganizing the idea, (b) compare or contrast two student responses for modeling purposes, or (c) focus an idea or claim by stating that the student is "on the right track" but might want to consider XYZ.
3. **Probe student thinking by asking penetrating questions.** This differs from a teacher extending a student's response—now it is the student who is clarifying and focusing their response. Teachers' probing questions seek justification of a response, explanation of terms, or expansion of ideas. Probing question stems include:
   • "What do you mean by (vocabulary term)?"
   • "Is that claim an assumption?"
   • "Why do you think that?"
   • "Could you explain this to me?"
   • "How would you restate that?"
   • "Show me the evidence that supports this claim."

Drawing a Conclusion

The conclusion of an investigation returns to the prediction statement to determine if the experimental evidence supported the prediction or did not support it. A conclusion answers the measurable inquiry question and should be concise and to the point. Using data to answer the question is the difference between *drawing* a conclusion and *jumping* to a conclusion. This is especially important with elementary learners, who often rely instinctively on prior knowledge and may need encouragement to trust the data over their internal schema.

A conclusion also examines experimental error, anything that might have gone wrong in the investigation that impacted the outcome, such as: not holding the constants steady, using a different measuring apparatus each day, not timing accurately, losing or mixing up results, or not entering data in the correct spot on the data organizer.

A conclusion addresses what was learned from the experiment, what was particularly effective, or what students might do differently next time. Any other questions that students have about the topic are raised in the conclusion as points for future investigation. Klentschy (2008) suggests:

> **Conclusion:**
>
> **I conclude that (new scientific knowledge) because (evidence). My prediction was/was not supported.**

Mary Beth Pardington, a veteran fourth-grade teacher in Michigan's Birmingham Public Schools, uses the checklist on page 36 to guide her students through the conclusion process. Her checklist asks students to consider their results and also potential errors.

Young learners need to know that an unsupported prediction does not indicate a failed experiment. Real scientists learn by repeating experiments again and again, using results to guide their next iteration.

In examining student notebooks, the teacher might reflect on these questions:

- Did the student note whether his or her prediction was supported or not supported based on the collected data?
- Did the student draw a valid conclusion by connecting claims and evidence?
- Did the student examine the process for possible experimental error?

Next Steps and Reflection

Children's curiosity does not stop when their experiment is finished, and this stage captures and validates that curiosity. As "Next Steps and Reflection," students write a few sentences about what they might like to explore next on this topic as well as reflecting on the overall experience.

Often, their inquiry journey will reveal new questions that students wish to explore. Students could conduct some "next steps" as another classroom inquiry. Identify time during which curious students can generate new questions, predictions, and experimental designs. Students can rotate through a science "center" during silent reading time or reading groups, for example.

Other questions that might be difficult for elementary students to solve in a hands-on way can be researched in the school library. The school library media specialist can identify expert resources that fit the student's area of interest and work with individuals or small groups to find answers.

What to Include in Your Conclusion

» **Compare your PREDICTION with your CLAIMS AND EVIDENCE:**

> **I conclude that (claim) because of (evidence).**
> **My prediction was/was not supported because . . .**

» **Answer the QUESTION or state whether the PROBLEM has been solved.**

» **Explain why you think your RESULTS turned out the way they did. Were these results expected?**

» **Did anything unusual occur to affect your results? Report any oddities or events that occurred that could have affected your RESULTS.**

Figure 3.3.

From *Story Starters and Science Notebooking: Developing Student Thinking Through Literacy and Inquiry* by Sandy Buczynski and Kristin Fontichiaro. Santa Barbara, CA: Teacher Ideas Press. Copyright © 2009.

Project and Assessment

In this book, a final project reunites students with the dilemma that arose in the original story starter. Each chapter has a different kind of project that brings together the story's crisis with the results of the scientific experiment. These projects have an important cognitive role: they require students to take their claims and evidence and apply them back to the original situation, solving a problem. This is higher-order thinking applied to an authentic setting, so don't miss them!

The final project occurs *outside* the science notebook but uses the observations, data, and conclusion as recorded in the notebook as the basic information for creating the project. Although the authors do not recommend that the notebook itself be evaluated, the summative project *is* designed for assessment, and a sample rubric is included in each chapter.

Extensions

In this book, each chapter ends with several related extensions that build additional knowledge about areas related to the unit of study. These can be used for enrichment, differentiated instruction, or undertaken by the entire class. Many of the extensions focus on an authentic, real-world activity.

A Team of Teachers

Because science notebooking individualizes learning, some teachers may feel intimidated at attempting it alone. We encourage classroom teachers to partner with parent volunteers, scientists from the community, preservice university programs, or existing professional staff in the building that can help facilitate this meaningful instructional approach.

For example, school librarians have a vested interest in developing inquiry habits in children, can be collaborative teaching and assessment partners, and act as an extra set of helping hands and watching eyes. In 2007, the American Association of School Librarians released its *Standards for the 21st Century Learner* (AASL, 2007, available for download at http://www.ala.org/aasl/standards). The table on pages 38 and 39 illustrates that inquiry is at the focus of these standards, which map strongly to the inquiry process of learning using science notebooking (Fontichiaro & Buczynski, 2009).

Final Thoughts

Story starters are intended to motivate and inspire students to take responsibility for experimental design and execution. At the same time, teachers need to be prepared to release some of that responsibility to their students and to recognize that students need time to develop their inquiry skills and self-expressions. With enough practice and scaffolding, story starters and science notebooking can provide both learners and their teachers with integral roles for developing very high quality inquiry and literacy skills.

Note: A version of the correlations chart in this chapter originally appeared in the March 2009 issue of School Library Media Activities Monthly.

Notebooking Stage	What Happens	Role of the School Library Media Specialist	AASL Standards Correlation
Planning for Learning	The teacher selects a science concept focus and, optionally, finds a story that introduces students to a content-based problem needing solution. The teacher and SLMS select an inquiry focus (e.g., questioning, predicting, making meaning of data, conclusion, etc.) that will be especially monitored.	Provide age-appropriate introductory content materials and/or stories related to the scientific problem; plan co-teaching, formative assessments strategies, project, and rubric with teacher.	Common Belief 8, Common Belief 9
Story Starter, Connecting to Science, Inventory Walk, Vocabulary	The teacher taps into and strengthens prior knowledge. In this book, teachers present a story that introduces students to a science concept and problem to be solved. Teacher introduces basic science concepts, begins vocabulary development, and reveals materials available for students to use in designing an investigation.	Provide cameras so students can create labeled photo display of inventory items as a visual reference throughout inquiry. Recommend books for additional reading. Co-lead discussions.	1.1.2 , 4.1.5
Questioning	Students generate an open-ended measurable question. Counting, cause and effect, or comparison questions are effective. Avoid "yes/no" questions.	Guide students in designing open-ended questions that will lead to fruitful exploration.	1.1.3
Formulating a Prediction	Based on the measurable question, students determine what they think a logical outcome will be and then make a prediction (via writing or drawing) about the direction of that outcome.	Assist students in creating an "if, then" statement that reflects the student's vision of a possible outcome of the experiment.	1.2.1
Identifying Variables	Students identify the experimental elements (variables) that will change, be measured as a result of that change, and remain constant.	Guide students in their efforts to identify variables using word clues such as "if, then."	Common Belief 7
Designing the Procedure	Students further define their experimental process by visualizing the steps they will take to test their prediction. In a sequential manner, students write or sketch steps to be followed during the experiment.	Help students visualize steps needed to gather data; review procedural thinking for thoroughness and materials needed; monitor for gaps.	4.4.3
Creating the Data Organizer	Reflecting on their variables, students consider the types of data they will need to collect in order to test their prediction. They create an empty graphic organizer (table, chart, graph, etc.) for use during the experiment.	Provide examples of graphic organizers. Help students envision data to collect. Monitor that the organizer relates to the procedure and prediction.	2.1.2

-- *Continues on next page* --

Figure 3.4.

From *Story Starters and Science Notebooking: Developing Student Thinking Through Literacy and Inquiry* by Sandy Buczynski and Kristin Fontichiaro. Santa Barbara, CA: Teacher Ideas Press. Copyright © 2009.

-- Continued from previous page --

Notebooking Stage	What Happens	Role of the School Library Media Specialist	AASL Standards Correlation
Conducting the Experiment; Recording Data and Observations	In groups, students conduct the experiment and record data. In addition, they sketch images of the experiment in progress and record observations.	Circulate throughout groups to monitor progress, discuss progress with students, give oral feedback, and assist students with accurate measuring.	3.2.2, 3.2.3
Claims and Evidence	Students review data, looking for patterns or trends that lead them to make an assertion (claim). Students justify their claim with data (evidence) collected during the experiment. The cognition in this step moves students away from reliance on prior knowledge and into consideration of collected data.	Help students make meaning of data and distinguish between inference and evidence. Assist with using technology to sort data, calculate, or construct graphs to make patterns/ trends visible.	1.1.6, 2.1.4
Conclusion	In their notebooks, students compare their claims and evidence to their original prediction. They determine whether their original prediction was supported and what new scientific knowledge they have gained. Students reflect on possible experimental errors. The notebook will be used in subsequent steps as a reference in creating a work product that demonstrates what has been learned.	Collaboratively guide students through this thinking process. Remind students that unsupported predictions are not failures and provide examples of "failures" that yielded new discoveries.	2.4.2, 2.4.3, 3.4.1
Project	Students use findings to create an authentic work product (brochure, podcast, monologue, etc.) that requires students to apply content knowledge, interpret results of investigation in context of original problem, take a different perspective (speak from another voice), or use technology to communicate findings. Students receive rubrics in advance to guide them in identifying quality work. Students have opportunities to re-submit final project after constructive feedback.	Provide support or co-teach necessary writing or technology skills. Support student work in creating the final product that demonstrates level of conceptual knowledge. Share in evaluating student work and revising the project for resubmission.	2.1.6, 3.1.1, 3.4.2
Next Steps	Like real scientists, students consider what new hands-on or library inquiries they might like to explore next. Future investigations are recorded in the same science notebook, creating a long-term portfolio of student thinking.	Work with groups to pursue new hands-on or library inquiry. Share evidence of learning with administrators. Plan next inquiry with teacher.	2.4.4

From *Story Starters and Science Notebooking: Developing Student Thinking Through Literacy and Inquiry* by Sandy Buczynski and Kristin Fontichiaro. Santa Barbara, CA: Teacher Ideas Press. Copyright © 2009.

Part II

Science Notebooking in Action

4

Observation: Going Bananas

Lesson Overview

Students are introduced to basic science notebook formatting and an investigation that helps develop observation skills. After being presented with a banana-ripening problem in the story starter, students in grades 3 and up investigate variables that might hasten this ripening process. The teacher models the steps of science notebooking so that in future lessons, some scaffolds can be removed and students will be able to take on these steps with guidance but also with a great deal of independence.

National Science Education Standards

Abilities Necessary to Do Science Inquiry

- **Use data to construct a reasonable explanation**. Students learn what constitutes evidence and judge the merits or strengths of the data and information that will be used to make explanations (Grades K–4).
- **Design and conduct a scientific investigation.** Students should develop general abilities, such as systematic observation, making accurate measurements, and identifying and controlling variables (Grades 5–8).

Outcomes

Emerging scientists will be able to:

- Predict a possible outcome of an investigation based on known patterns of data.
- Gather information using all appropriate senses and instruments that extend the senses.
- Group objects according to one or more common properties.

Practicing scientists will be able to:

- Formulate a measurable question about an everyday experience.
- Identify experimental variables.
- Use observations as evidence to formulate principles and generate explanations to answer the initiating question.

Awakening Prior Knowledge

To stimulate students' thinking about the process that a banana goes through as it ripens, invite them to engage in ''science talk'' (Gallas, 1995) around a parallel process: why do leaves change color? For the science talk, students sit in a circle to encourage conversation among themselves, listen respectfully, ask clarifying questions, and build on each other's ideas. These talks reconcile the creative and imaginative exercise of thinking about areas that are completely unknown. The teacher's role is to listen and ask questions if the discourse stalls:

- **What color is a (maple, oak, palm, banana, etc.) leaf?** (Typical answer is green.)
- **Have you ever seen a leaf change color from green to beautiful shades of orange and yellow?** (Perhaps show some leaves or pictures of leaves in various fall colors.)
- **In what season does this usually happen?** (In the autumn.)
- **Is the whole leaf one color or a mixture of colors**? (Mixture.)
- **Do all of the leaves on one tree change to a particular color at exactly the same time?** (No, process is gradual; coloring is in gradient.)
- **How do you think a leaf can change from green to orange or yellow?** (Orange and yellow pigments are always in the leaf, but hidden; because there is more green pigment, the leaf's overall appearance is green. Changing temperatures cause green pigment (*chlorophyll*) in leaves to break down revealing the underlying red, orange, and yellow pigments.)

Science talks can be messy and sometimes chaotic in style and content but reflect the vitality of children's lives and ideas; a ''living'' science language that acknowledges the desire to understand the most complex kinds of questions (Gallas, 1995).

Now show students a green banana and a yellow banana speckled with black. Through careful observation, can the explanation of what happens in leaves be applied to the state of these two bananas? (As a banana ripens, green pigment in the peel is broken down to reveal yellow pigments already there.) How do you select a banana for eating? (Color of peel, firmness, smell, and/or size.) Outwardly, does the color of a banana's peel reveal its stage of ripeness? (Yes.)

One way to introduce this story to students is to duplicate a copy of the letter from page 45 and mail it to yourself at school. On the morning of the experiment, open the envelope, withdraw the letter, and place it where it can be displayed for the class on a document camera. (Alternatively, copy the letter onto a transparency and use an overhead projector.)

Story Starter

Please see the reproducible on page 45.

Preparing for Inquiry

Reviewing the Story

Read the letter from Mildred aloud. Then model how you might respond to it, saying, ''Look at this, a letter from my friend Mildred. I am so excited about seeing her on Saturday. And I am famous for my banana bread. But there's a problem. To make banana bread, I need really ripe bananas. All I have are these green ones. They'll never ripen in time for my visit with Mildred on Saturday. What can I do to ripen these bananas faster?''

FROM THE DESK OF
MILDRED B. KREPPELMEYER

Dear Friend,

I am so glad that you are coming to visit me on Saturday. I am looking forward to seeing you again.

I hope you will bring a loaf of your famous banana bread with you.

See you soon!

Your friend,
Mildred

Figure 4.1.

Now open up the conversation to students. What do they know about ripening a banana that could help solve your problem? Document their ideas on chart paper, on an undecorated section of a bulletin board, or on a portion of the whiteboard that does not need to be erased each evening. Students might tell you that bananas are kept on the counter and not the refrigerator, that they ripen in a day or so, and that they have a pleasant odor when they are ripe. Or students may reveal that bananas turn black when they are ripe and that the insides ooze when they are overripe.

Connecting to Science

Making Observations   When making observations, people have a tendency to see what they expect to see and focus more on differences than similarities (Bass, Contant, & Carin, 2009). As a rule, initial observations tend to be global, potentially missing relevant fine points. Learning to observe for detail, to see what is actually there, and to pay attention to both similarities and differences are important skills to develop through inquiry (Harden & Jelly, 1990).

To begin developing students' observation skills, set up "observation stations" of several bananas at varying stages of ripeness. Each station should have one whole banana and one banana that has been peeled and sliced. Ask students to use their five senses to make detailed observations about each of these stages of a ripening banana. Does the outward appearance of a banana reveal what is happening inside the banana as it ripens?

Feel: Touch both the whole banana and a slice of banana. Describe its texture and consistency. What happens to the texture of a banana as it ripens? (A carbohydrate known as *pectin*, which makes plants' cell walls stiff, is being broken down in the ripening process making the banana feel less firm.)

Taste: Taste a slice of banana. Describe this flavor. What changes in taste occur as a banana ripens? (As a banana ripens, complex starches are being converted to simple sugars, sweetening the taste of the banana.) (SAFETY NOTE: When allowing students to taste in the laboratory, make sure students do not have a banana food allergy, that the banana has been sliced and stored in a sanitary manner, and that students' hands are clean.)

Sight: Look carefully at each banana peel. How does a ripe banana look different from an unripe one? (Visually, the chlorophyll [green pigment] in plant cells is deteriorating causing the peel to morph from green to dark yellow.)

Smell: Sniff the banana slices. Do green bananas have an odor? (No.) Do yellow ones? (Yes, what you smell are *esters*, organic molecules evaporating from the fruit.)

Possible Solutions to Consider for Ripening Fruit   Say to students, "I want to ripen these bananas faster so I can make banana bread for Mildred. However, farmers, agricultural transporters, and grocers also need to know how long it will take for bananas to ripen so they can keep bananas fresh in transit and in grocery stores." Give students an opportunity to rate the bananas from the "observation stations" as to which state of ripeness they would pick to eat. These results can be graphed in a simple bar graph. By using graphs as well as a head count, data are differentiated so that many types of learners can understand the relative popularity of each phase of ripening. Sharing student choices will reveal that ripening increases the desirability of fruit, but only up to a point. Too much ripening results in fruit spoilage.

Next, ask students to brainstorm factors to consider that might influence the speed at which a banana will ripen. They may brainstorm alone in their science notebooks first, and then share their ideas as a class, with the teacher recording their thoughts on chart paper or on a bulletin board. Their brainstorming may include temperature, light exposure, exposure to air, discarding the peel, humidity levels, putting the banana in a closed space, or waiting until later to pick the banana from its plant.

Starting with temperature, ask students, ''Has anyone ever put a banana in the refrigerator?'' If so, then they know that bananas are very sensitive to temperatures. Chilling a banana will cause the peel to have a smoky, dull gray appearance but will slow the ripening process of a banana's flesh. On the other hand, bananas exposed to heat (cooked) will have a peel with a brown to orange appearance, softer flesh, and a shorter shelf life.

Next, discuss their idea of a closed space. Ask students, ''Where in the kitchen do you keep bananas?'' The usual response is on the open counter, although some students may say that their family keeps bananas in a paper bag. This is a popular storage method because paper bags trap and facilitate the recirculation of a ripening gas (*ethylene*).

Ethylene, a plant hormone, plays a regulatory role in many processes of plant development. Fruits and vegetables produce ethylene within their tissues and release it into the surrounding atmosphere, where it initiates more production of ethylene. Ethylene causes the destruction of chlorophyll (green pigment) allowing the red and/or yellow pigments in cells to become unmasked and the fruit or vegetable to ripen.

Paper bags are porous enough to allow certain gases, such as *carbon dioxide*, to pass through. However, ethylene gas can build up even inside a porous paper bag. On the other hand, plastic bags are not porous. What might happen to a banana left in a plastic bag?

Inventory Walk

Return to the ''observation stations'' of bananas in various stages of ripeness. From observations made with their senses, students generate common vocabulary for use in discussing the ripening process of a banana. Descriptive words (nouns such as ''peel'' and flesh'' or adjectives to distinguish various shades of yellow and green) may arise. What classification system could students devise to put bananas into categories? They may develop classification categories such as, ''just right to eat,'' ''too ripe,'' or, ''not ripe enough.'' What characteristics of the bananas are students using as criteria for these categories? This process of defining and classifying is useful to students throughout their scientific careers.

Vocabulary: Power Words

Content vocabulary for this inquiry arises naturally as students generate names for the parts of a banana (peel to describe the outer portion and flesh, the inner) through their observations. Working definitions for fruit terminology emerge.

- **Fruit:** The part of a plant that contains seeds. Yes, bananas have seeds, an evolutionary carryover from the past.
- **Peel:** The outer covering of fruit.
- **Flesh:** The part of the fruit that is eaten.
- **Ripen:** To become mature (i.e., ready to be eaten or used).

Students build on these basic terms by applying descriptive words to detail their observations. Using sensory details is the hallmark of descriptive writing. Use this sentence prompt: "The banana is ripe." Give students three to five minutes to create a "quick-write," or rapidly written description of what the ripest banana might look like, in their science notebooks. Students' writing should create a strong mental image of a ripe banana.

According to Roth (1993), the importance of observational data is not how precisely all details are described. Rather, the importance lies in how the observed phenomenon is used to develop more powerful and complete explanations. For example, in the quickwrite, the initial impression ("The banana is ripe") expands to "The brown splotched, dark yellow banana peel was beginning to dry. Also, the banana's flesh felt spongy and smelled sweet, but a bit rotten. I would not want to eat this banana. It is past its prime!" Recreating an image through deliberate, graphic word choice conveys observational details that are so important to the process of developing scientific concepts.

Students can also use this descriptive vocabulary to discuss other fruits. For example, does an apple have a "peel" and "flesh"? Can you tell the difference between a "ripe" apple and an "unripe" apple? What about with other fruits?

Working in the Science Notebook: Before the Experiment

Student-Generated Questions

For this guided inquiry and "fair test" investigation, the teacher models developing a measurable question. Questions, as discussed in Chapter 3, should come from the students' usual inquisitiveness and should avoid being answerable by "yes" or "no." "Red light" questions, like, "Will a banana float?" are too facile to hold the attention of young scientists, and such questions are disconnected from the problem described in the story starter. This type of question also does not have any context from nature.

However, tweaking the question so that it searches for a relationship between objects ("Which will ripen fastest, a banana in the refrigerator or a banana on the counter?"), a measurable outcome ("How many bananas [out of 10] will turn from green to yellow in the first 24 hours in a paper bag?"), or a problem-oriented question ("How will a banana change if we leave it in the dark 24 hours compared to one left in the light?") provides more interesting, engaging, and relevant answers.

One of the reasons inquiry-based learning is so powerful is that it puts much decision-making in the hands of the student. The sample inquiries provided in this book are merely used to illustrate how science notebooking *could* be used with a particular science concept. **It is not meant to be a prescription that *must* be followed.**

A sample inquiry question from this story starter might be:

Question:

What will make a banana ripen faster?

The teacher turns to a new page in her science notebook (or models on an overhead transparency or chart paper), records her name and date, puts the title "Going Bananas" at the top of the page, and records the question. The students do the same in their science notebooks. They are now ready to move on to predicting an answer based on prior knowledge as gained through the observation stations.

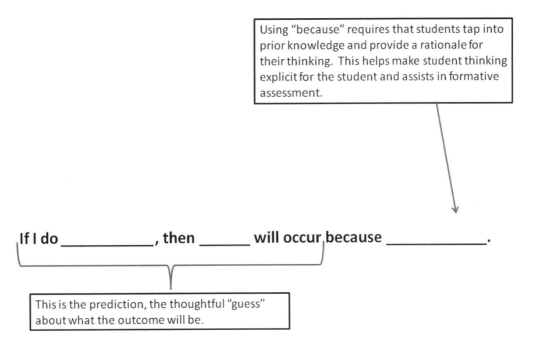

Figure 4.2.

Testable Prediction

A *prediction* is a thoughtful speculation about what might happen as a result of an action during the experiment. The sentence template above can help students craft a prediction and further develop their inquiry in future steps as well. Notice how it includes both a prediction and a rationale that supports inductive thinking (making a generalization from specific observations).

"Because" provokes powerful cognition, pushing students to justify why they believe their prediction is sound. It often reflects a student's prior knowledge, or for older students, a literature review or background research.

It is important to note that students may have flawed prior knowledge. It is not necessary for the teacher to correct misconceptions that might show up in a student's "because" clause. Rather, this misconception is addressed during the conclusion stage of the experiment.

For this sample inquiry, the teacher models some thoughts that guided her prediction statement. For example, she might recall a time when she brought her lunch in a paper bag and forgot to eat her banana. A few days later, when she opened the bag, the banana was really overripe and sweet smelling. She wonders aloud if the paper bag hastened the ripening process.

She might have a similar memory of a time she forgot to unpack one plastic bag of groceries, and by the time she unpacked it, the bunch of bananas inside had gone bad. Or, she might recall the time she left a banana in her beach bag with a wet towel on top of it and the banana was still fresh after several days.

She might also think aloud that she notices that all of her friends keep their bananas on the counter, not in the refrigerator or freezer, and that she has also noticed that bananas are not in a refrigerated section of the grocery store. She puts her bananas in a plastic produce bag at the grocery store but always takes them out of this bag when she gets home.

In thinking through all of the conditions that could be changed that might affect the process of fruit ripening, students consider the options in the following table.

Light	Water	Exposure to Air	Temperature
A dark or a light place	A damp towel or dry towel	A sealed or an unsealed bag	A cooler or warmer place
In light 24 hours or in light 12 hours and dark 12 hours	Misted with water every day or not	A plastic bag or a cloth bag	Frozen or not frozen
		Talking to it (blowing carbon dioxide over the banana) or staying silent	In the sun or in the shade

The table above shows four possible independent variables that could be manipulated in a variety of ways. Students select one independent variable for experimentation. After deciding which environment will be manipulated, the student considers possible answers to this question, "How can you measure the response of a banana to being placed in one of these environments?"

- **Time:** ripens faster or slower (measured in days).
- **Visual Appearance:** ripens into a more desirable fruit or does not look as appetizing (measured on a color scale of 1–5).

When these two elements (what will be changed and what the expected outcome is) are combined, then the teacher has the necessary information to form a prediction, using the template below. The prediction has to take a position and choose an expected result. The Teacher "thinks aloud," then writes the prediction in her science notebook below the question. The students do the same. For example:

Question:

What will make a banana ripen faster?

Prediction:

If I put a banana in a paper bag and one on the counter, *then* I predict the banana in the paper bag will ripen faster *because* in the past, when I left a banana in my lunch bag, it got very ripe, very fast.

Identifying Variables

Variables can be a difficult concept for elementary scientists to understand. Variables represent the various elements present in an experiment. A "fair test" experiment involves (1) intentionally changing one variable, (2) observing the effect of this change on another variable, while (3) keeping all other conditions exactly the same (Bass, Contant, & Carin, 2009).

Independent Variable   Imagine that an experiment is in a state of rest. If nothing is done to change the environment of a green banana, then we assume it will ripen at the

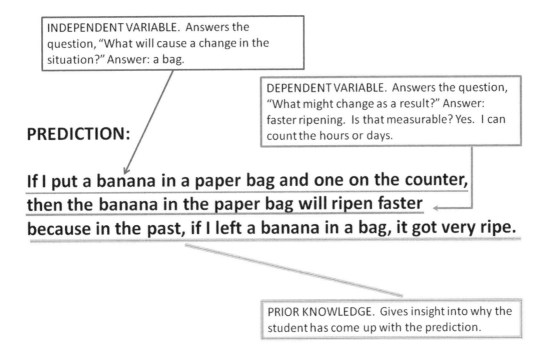

INDEPENDENT VARIABLE. Answers the question, "What will cause a change in the situation?" Answer: a bag.

DEPENDENT VARIABLE. Answers the question, "What might change as a result?" Answer: faster ripening. Is that measurable? Yes. I can count the hours or days.

PREDICTION:

If I put a banana in a paper bag and one on the counter, then the banana in the paper bag will ripen faster because in the past, if I left a banana in a bag, it got very ripe.

PRIOR KNOWLEDGE. Gives insight into why the student has come up with the prediction.

Figure 4.3.

''normal'' rate. The *independent variable* is changing the ripening environment of the banana to see if it will ripen at a ''different'' rate. In the sample template above, the independent variable is the clause that comes after ''if.'' In the sample, putting the banana in a bag is the variable that we are changing, therefore the independent variable. Two environments are being compared: one is the banana in a bag (proposed ''different'' rate of ripening), and simultaneously, the other environment is a banana *not* in a bag (on the counter) (proposed ''normal'' rate of ripening). What is the difference between the two? This difference is what will be measured and thus is the *dependent variable.*

Dependent Variable   The *dependent variable* is what results as a function of changing the independent variable. In the example, what is predicted to change? (The speed or rate of ripening.) How can we measure how long it takes something to ripen? We can measure (count) the number of hours or days. Another consideration is how we will measure ripeness. We could make a ripeness scale and compare each banana to the scale to give it a rating of ripeness:

1 = Green, firm, no smell, hard to peel
2 = More yellow than green
3 = Light yellow with green necks
4 = All yellow
5 = Dark yellow flecked with brown, mushy texture, strong smell

Control   The banana that will be used to show what would have happened if we had done nothing (left the banana on the counter) serves as the *control.* A control serves as a standard for comparison. By comparing the ripening time of the banana in the bag to the ripening time of the control ("normal" rate of ripening), the class will be able to find out if the independent variable had an impact on the speed of ripening.

Constants   Finally, experiments have several *constants*. These are the factors that will remain the same throughout the experiment. For example, during this ripening experiment, the bananas being compared need to be at the same ripeness, size, and type *to begin with*, while temperature and humidity in the room will also stay the same. Keeping all conditions exactly the same, except the independent variable, allows for a more reliable measure of the dependent variable.

Having identified the variables, the teacher writes them in her science notebook. She can list them, create a simple table in which to store the information, or try another organizational technique of her choosing. Students will do the same. For example:

Independent Variable	Dependent Variable	Control	Constants
Putting banana in a paper bag	Days it takes banana to ripen to a "4" on ripening scale	Banana on counter	Air temperature Humidity Size and type of banana

Having had time to think about what she wants to test in the experiment, the teacher is now ready to think about how she wants to conduct the experiment. This series of steps is called the *procedure*.

Procedure

The easiest way to write a procedure is with a numbered list, though writing in paragraphs may be desirable for a language arts connection and will be explained later in this book.

Again, the teacher thinks aloud to model this process for her class. "Let's see—I know I want to test if a bag makes a banana ripen faster. I think I want to use two bags: a paper one like the time I left a banana in my lunch bag, and a plastic one, because of the time I forgot about a bag of groceries and found an overripe banana inside.

"It's OK for me to use two kinds of bags. I can compare the results of each of these bags to each other as well as to the control banana that was not put in any bag. I should try to find two bags that are a similar size and block the light through both, so these factors are constant."

"So that means I'll need to set up three stations: a paper bag with a banana in it, a plastic bag with a banana in it, and a banana with no bag to be the control. It is important that I do each of the stations twice so that I can be sure that what is happening to one banana is not just a freak occurrence but I can get the same results the next time I do it."

She places her science notebook under the document camera (or uses chart paper or an overhead transparency) and thinks aloud as she writes this procedure, soliciting help from the students.

Procedure:

1. **Gather two paper bags and two opaque plastic bags of similar sizes.**
2. **Get six bananas that are an equal shade of green (unripe) and a similar size and type.**
3. **Rate each banana on the ripeness scale (rating of 1, 2, 3, 4, or 5).**
4. **Leave two bananas out on the counter.**
5. **Put one banana in each of the paper bags and fold it closed.**
6. **Put one banana in each of the plastic bags and fold it closed.**
7. **At the beginning of the next school day and again at the end of the school day, rate each banana on the ripeness scale and then return the bananas to their assigned bags or countertop.**
8. **I will know that the banana is ripe when it scores a 4 on the ripeness scale.**
9. **Every time I check on the bananas, I make notes in my data organizer.**

The students also record the procedure in their notebooks. The teacher models how she would check this procedure with *her* teacher for feedback, not for a grade, much as students share their rough drafts during writer's workshop. She is then ready to move on to the next step: designing the data organizer.

Data Organizer

Using organizers and teaching students to design their own charts, tables, Venn diagrams, concept maps, and graphic organizers promotes knowledge organization. Students are thinking deeply about what needs to be measured, what needs to be recorded, and how some data should relate to other data.

To create a data organizer, students look back at their prediction, variables, and procedure. They must ask themselves what will need to be monitored. In this sample inquiry, they will track the ripeness of six bananas in three environments, twice a day. So the data organizer must provide for a place to record time and condition (ripeness scale). They must have room to record this information for each of six bananas. The experiment calls for six bananas, two for each environment, to rule out the possibility that the resulting rate of ripening might be attributed to the uniqueness or genetic makeup of any particular banana. If two bananas are placed in the same environment and they both ripen at the same rate, then the results are more likely attributed to the environment and not the banana.

Because we all think differently (some linearly, some visually, and some in other ways), science notebooking avoids a "one size fits all" approach to data organizers. Throughout this book, a variety of data organizers are offered as examples, but they are far from the only approach. By encouraging students to organize information in a manner that makes sense for them, we are helping them achieve a lifelong skill.

In modeling this process, the teacher decides that she wants to both write and draw her observations, so she opens her science notebook and turns it sideways. This gives her room to draw a large chart as depicted in the following table.

Date/Time	Type of Data	Bananas on Counter (Control)		Bananas in Plastic Bag		Bananas in Paper Bag	
		Banana #1	Banana #2	Banana #3	Banana #4	Banana #5	Banana #6
Monday, 9 A.M.	Rating (1–5)	1	1	1	1	1	1
Baseline data	Observations						
Monday, 3 P.M.	Rating (1–5)						
	Observations						
Tuesday, 9 A.M.	Rating (1–5)						
	Observations						
Tuesday, 3 P.M.	Rating (1–5)						
	Observations						
Wednesday, 9 A.M.	Rating (1–5)						
	Observations						
Wednesday, 3 P.M.	Rating (1–5)						
	Observations						
(continue as needed)							

The "1" notations in the row marked "Monday, 9 A.M.," reflect baseline data for ripeness, which will be discussed in the next step.

Students also record a data organizer and baseline data in their science notebooks.

Working in the Science Notebook: During the Experiment

Conducting the Experiment and Recording Data and Observations

At this point, the teacher invites the class to divide into groups and set up their experiments in the classroom. For this chapter only, as it is primarily a modeling chapter, each group's experiment is similar. (Once students understand fair test experimentation, each group will design its own experiment, as shown in future chapters.)

Baseline Data   Because it is Monday at 9 A.M. when the experiment starts, the teacher records *baseline data* using the banana ripeness rating scale developed as a measure of the dependent variable. Baseline data are the measurements taken at the start of the experiment. The teacher records a "1" to represent the beginning ripeness stage of the bananas, according to the 1–5 rating scale developed earlier by the class. Recording baseline data is a good practice for all experiments. Although not essential to this observation-based example, many experiments call for the students to measure the change from the beginning to the end of an experiment. The lab groups follow the procedure, and at the designated times each day, they record observational data and ripeness ratings. To maximize the effectiveness of the experiment, bananas should be out of their bags for the shortest possible amount of time while being observed.

Remember that the prediction referenced "faster" ripening, and so students will be looking for when each banana achieves a ripeness rating of "4." In the boxes of their chart, they will be writing what they observe.

Asking students to use their senses—especially touch, smell, and sight—can give students guidance in making specific observations. Teachers can help students determine which senses are most useful for a given experiment. For example, tasting has been removed for this observational data because that would require the banana to be peeled, which would alter the results. The sense of hearing also has no value in this experimental setting.

The following chart provides an example of what the baseline data might look like at the start of the experiment.

Date/Time	Type of Data	Bananas on Counter (Control)		Bananas in Plastic Bag		Bananas in Paper Bag	
		Banana #1	Banana #2	Banana #3	Banana #4	Banana #5	Banana #6
Monday, 9 A.M. Baseline Data	Ripeness Rating (1–5)	1	1	1	1	1	1
	Observations	Sight—peel is green Smell—no odor Touch—peel feels hard; banana feels solid		Sight—peel is green Smell—no odor Touch—peel feels hard; banana feels solid		Sight—peel is green Smell—no odor Touch—peel feels hard; banana feels solid	
Monday, 3 P.M.	Ripeness Rating	1	1	2	2	2	2
	Observations	Sight—peel is green Smell—no odor Touch—hard		Slight—peel is yellow Smell—like a banana Touch—hard		Slight—peel is yellow Smell—like a banana Touch—hard	

Students can also draw images in their chart that represent what they are seeing. Colored pencils help students create realistic drawings, not "symbols" for what they are seeing (see Chapter 2).

Working in the Science Notebook: After the Experiment

Claims and Evidence

The experiment can stop at three potential points: (1) on a particular day, when several of the six bananas have achieved a 4 on the ripeness scale; (2) when one of the bananas becomes so overripe that it turns black (if bananas start to ooze, however, stop the experiment so that the ooze does not attract insects); or (3) after one calendar week.

Now students have a chart full of data. What happened? How long did it take for the banana in the plastic bag to become overripe? When did the banana in the paper bag become ripe? What is the sequence in which the bananas ripened? These are all questions that can help children make sense of what has happened during the experiment and answer the story starter question.

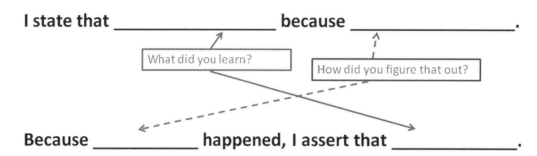

Figure 4.4.

When students examine data, discover patterns, and make a statement based on those patterns, they are creating the experiment's *claim* (Klentschy, 2008). Claims are supported by *evidence,* the supporting data or observations that lend veracity and credence to the claim.

In making a prediction, students used prior knowledge or background research. But in making a claim, students must put prior knowledge aside and look closely at their data—the words, numbers from the ripeness scale, and pictures—and decide what it is that the data are telling them.

Consider this format (Klentschy, 2008) for writing the claims and evidence in the science notebook:

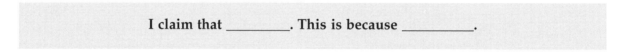

For this sample lesson, students can come together as a whole class, share their found data, and discover trends and patterns. With the teacher's guidance, students come up with a claims and evidence statement for their science notebooks such as these:

Claims and Evidence:

I claim that a closed paper bag helps a banana ripen faster. This is because bananas in a closed paper bag became ripe 2 days before bananas left on the counter.

or

I claim that closing a bag is not what speeds up the ripening of bananas because the bananas in the closed paper bags ripened fast but the bananas in the closed plastic bags ripened slowly.

These claims are merely samples; in practice, teachers and students may generate claims and evidence of their own.

Conclusion

Students have now made a claim, but they have not yet looked back at the prediction. By doing so, they identify misconceptions and gain new scientific understanding.

Consider this conclusion template:

I conclude that (new scientific knowledge) because of (evidence). My prediction was/was not supported because ...

More scaffolding of the conclusion process can be found on page 36.

In this modeling lesson, the teacher might look at the original prediction and the claims and evidence (below) and think aloud. The teacher's sample prediction, which was adopted by the class, was as follows:

Prediction:

If I put a banana in a paper bag and one on the counter, then I predict the banana in the paper bag will ripen faster because in the past, when I left a banana in my lunch bag, it got very ripe, very fast.

One claim and evidence was:

Claims and Evidence:

I claim that a closed paper bag helps a banana ripen faster. This is because bananas in a closed paper bag became ripe 2 days before bananas left on the counter.

The teacher's think-aloud might sound like this, "Let's see. I predicted that a paper bag would make a banana ripen faster. It did ripen faster in a paper bag. I think I will write this for my conclusion:"

Conclusion:

I conclude that if I am in a hurry, I can speed up the ripening of a banana by putting it in a closed paper bag. This is because the banana in a closed paper bag ripened faster than a banana left out on the counter. My prediction was supported. This will help me have ripe bananas ready by Saturday for my visit with Mildred. But if I want bananas to last for a while, I can put them on the counter where the ripening process happens slower.

Notice how the conclusion demonstrates scientific understanding that transcends this particular experimental design. The information learned by the student can be applied to other situations.

Having samples of banana bread, intended for Mildred, for students to taste is an enjoyable way to end this inquiry.

Next Steps and Reflection

In this stage, students reflect on the experience. This metacognition may yield new questions or identify experimental error.

New Questions Some students' curiosity will extend beyond this experiment. They may have additional questions: "Will this work the same way with tomatoes that we also keep out on the counter? What would happen if we combined a tomato with a banana in the same paper bag? How would the data be different if we stored one banana in the refrigerator or freezer? Or wrapped one banana in cling wrap or a damp cloth?" The teacher can model writing a list of her questions in her science notebook.

Consider having a science center or station set up where these experiments can be carried out, and where science notebooks are used outside formal class time.

Experimental Error In addition, the teacher can model the process of reviewing for experimental error. Thinking aloud, she might say, "I wonder if I made many mistakes in doing this experiment. I wonder if there were any extra variables that I didn't think about but that could change the results of the experiment." These, too, should be written in the notebook.

Project and Assessment: Designing a Banana Flyer

Using a word processing or desktop publishing program, students design an informative flyer, tri-fold leaflet, card, bookmark, or brochure that can be distributed at the local library or grocery store. The brochure should tell banana lovers how to take care of bananas that they want to have ripen early, ripen on time, or ripen late, using what they learned doing this inquiry. This would have been just the information the teacher would have liked to have had to prepare her bananas for making bread for Mildred. The flyer should be easy to read, informative, and well organized. It should include the following elements:

1. Scientifically accurate information about the natural ripening process of bananas;
2. Scientifically accurate information about altering (speeding up or slowing down) the ripening process of bananas;
3. The use of descriptive words from the students' observation of the banana-ripening process;
4. Illustrations or other graphic design elements.

Rubric

A sample rubric can be found on page 60.

Extensions

Cross and Long Sections Teachers may also choose to continue the banana inquiry by including a lesson on the difference between a *cross section* and *long section* of a banana. A cross section is the equivalent of cutting something in half the short way. If you cut a cross section slice of a banana, you end up with a round slice. A long section cuts lengthwise along the length of a banana, showing you a stretched, oval-shaped interior (Figure 4.5). Both cross sections and long sections help scientists and researchers learn more about the inner workings of objects.

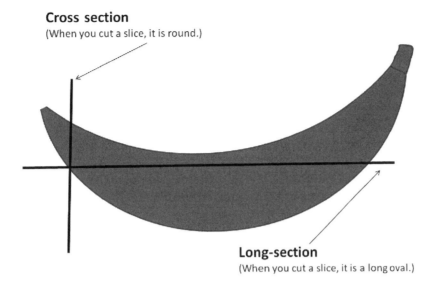

Cross section
(When you cut a slice, it is round.)

Long-section
(When you cut a slice, it is a long oval.)

Figure 4.5.

Cross and long sections can appear in non-fiction material in print and online. Ask your school library media specialist to provide a series of books or Web resources showing how authors and illustrators use these sections to educate the reader.

Library Research

- **What role do hormones play in plant development?** (Plant tissues communicate by means of hormones, produced in one location yet affecting another location; i.e., ethylene, produced and released by rapidly growing plant tissues [meristematic] has multiple effects on plants. For example, in seedlings, ethylene will inhibit stem elongation, increase stem thickening, and increase lateral growth.)
- **What chemical changes occur as a fruit ripens? Why?** (During fruit ripening, stored starch is converted to sugar. The sweetness of fruit attracts animals to disperse seeds contained in fruit.)
- **How could an iodine stain be used to indicate the chemical difference between fruit flesh that is ripe or unripe?** (Iodine is a chemical indicator for the presence of starch, a complex carbohydrate. Iodine binds to starch, turning from yellow to blue-black, but not to sugar, remaining yellow.) SAFETY NOTE: Adult supervision is required to work with iodine solutions, including protective gloves, eyewear, and clothing protection.
- **Cut fruit, such as apple, turns brown when exposed to air. What might prevent this oxidation?** (Lemon juice, vinegar, or vitamin C [citric acid]).

Applying Inquiry Learning to a New Setting   You have heard the saying, "A rotten apple spoils the whole barrel." Does a rotten banana spoil the whole bunch? How would you find out? What solution might you propose to prevent this from happening?

Name _____

Going Bananas Rubric

	Apprentice Grocer (2 points)	Grocery Clerk (3 points)	Master Grocer (4 points)
Information on speeding up ripening	Be clear about what exactly will speed up the ripening of a banana and how you know that it works.	You claim a particular action will speed up ripening, but how can you be sure?	You are able to back up the information provided on speeding up ripening with evidence and data!
Information on ripening at a normal rate	Can you tell us what to expect when leaving a banana on the counter to ripen?	Could a banana go from green to yellow with brown flecks while sitting on the counter overnight? Why or why not?	This is clear, accurate information on the normal pace of banana going through stages of ripening.
Aesthetics	Consider the use of white space as well as text to draw attention in your flyer.	Is it possible to add graphics or text features to enhance the look of your flyer?	Looking at your work is like enjoying a banana split—a pleasure!
Organization	Your ideas will flow better if you cluster similar ideas together and sum up each suggestion for a quick read.	In this format, a reader wants to be able to pick up the main ideas at a glance. The flyer must be organized so this can happen.	Your ideas are organized logically and summarized for quick reading necessary in a flyer.
Conventions	Banana lovers are counting on you for great spelling, grammar, and punctuation! Review the parts of a banana and what happens to those parts in the ripening process.	Bana, bana, bo, fanna, be sure to run spelling check before printing a handout. Use vocabulary to paint a picture of a banana ripening.	This flyer is ready for publishing and distributing at the grocery store or library. Good use of a descriptive vocabulary.

Figure 4.6.

Drama   Students act out a culinary question-and-answer show after researching answers to questions that have been posed. For example:

Q: Do you think microwaving a banana would make it become ripe faster?

A: Ripening is a chemical process that might be accelerated with heat; however, cooking a banana is not the same as ripening one.

Q: What would happen if you put your banana in a paper bag along with an apple? Or a tomato?

A: Because the apple and tomato are both also emitting ethylene (ripening gas), the process should go faster for all the fruit in the bag.

Consumer Science   Students may also have seen infomercials for Debbie Meyer Green Bags™, which claim to preserve produce ten times longer than "normal." These storage bags are coated with a mineral that is supposed to absorb ethylene gas, thus delaying the ripening process. Do these bags really work? How many times can a bag be reused effectively? What is the cost-benefit? How do these bags actually work?

Art   Get started collecting the stickers found on bananas. It's sort of a cult thing.

5

Insulation: A Royal Home

Lesson Overview

Students examine potential insulating materials to think about how heat is transferred. The effectiveness of these various materials is examined by designing an insulation system to prevent an ice cube from melting. Students in grades 3 and up ask, "How do I know a particular insulating material is effective?" To answer this question, they collect quantitative data and use the data as evidence to support a reasonable answer. Students make accurate measurements by using cylinders (to measure volume) or scales (to measure weight) and keep clear and accurate records of their investigation and observations.

National Science Education Standards

- **Transfer of Energy**: Heat moves in predictable ways, flowing from warmer objects to cooler ones, until both reach the same temperature (Grades 5–8).

Outcomes

Emerging scientists will be able to:

- Accurately weigh an object or measure an amount of liquid.
- Explain the purpose of insulation.
- Use evidence-based claims to explain how some materials are better insulators than others.
- Value the process of making a hypothesis, even if the hypothesis is not supported by the data collected.

Practiced scientists will be able to:

- Illustrate that when cold objects are surrounded by an insulating material, the cold object gains heat at a slower rate than an uninsulated cold object.
- Describe how *insulation* can slow down or reduce the transfer of heat.
- Use math to build a supporting argument in problem solving.

Awakening Prior Knowledge

Ask students if they can think of any objects they are familiar with that keep things inside the object one temperature when the atmosphere outside the object is hotter or colder. Sample responses might include a thermos, refrigerator, plastic or Styrofoam cooler, freezer, building or car with air-conditioning, wet suit, or an insulated lunch box. Students brainstorm a list of these insulation ideas in their science notebooks before sharing their ideas with the class.

Then ask students what component is present in all of these examples that keeps the exterior and the interior environments at different temperatures. Note their suggestions on the overhead or whiteboard. Students might brainstorm ideas including a barrier, metal, foam, double windows, the exterior of a home, and more. All of these heat transfer barriers can be grouped together under the word *insulation*, which is defined as any material that can slow down or reduce the transfer of heat.

Next, ask students to process the discussion and record their understanding in their science notebooks. Students may use a variety of recording methods to do so, perhaps drawing a picture that portrays how they think the insulation is slowing or reducing the transfer of heat, constructing a table that lists possible insulating materials and what they are used for, or considering if some insulating materials are more effective than others. Allowing some students to draw instead of write is a simple differentiation strategy.

Story Starter: Designing a Royal Home

Introduce the story of "Designing a Royal Home" (pages 65 and 66) to students. The story may be read aloud or distributed to students for individual or small group reading.

Preparing for Inquiry

Reviewing the Story

Interesting storylines help students delve into concepts better than when using textbooks alone (Butzow & Butzow, 1994). As students read the story starter purposefully for science information, they look for ways to connect it to their personal experiences. It can be useful to begin by reviewing what information in the story starter is relevant to solving the royal couple's problem and what is not.

- **Which facts are the most relevant to solving the problem for the royal couple?** (A home that is cool inside and warm outside; a home that pleases two kinds of pets.)
- **What parts of the story are not important to solving the problem?** (Names of characters, school they went to, the professor's name.)
- **What is the royal couple asking the class to figure out**? (A house that stays cool inside even in a warm climate.)
- **Are there any words in the story that you are not familiar with?** (Use context clues to help determine meaning.)
- **What category (genre) of story would "Designing a Royal Home" fit into best: biography, non-fiction, fairy tale, personal narrative, or science fiction?** (Fairy tale.)

Making Text-to-Self Connections
Harvey and Goudvis (2007) stress the importance of students making connections with the text. By doing so, students deepen their capacity for understanding and are drawn more deeply into the narrative. Invite younger students to identify temperature control information from the story and from their own lives. Bring their prior knowledge and story understanding together by creating a chart that includes information from each.

Designing a Royal Home

ONCE UPON A TIME, long before the days of air-conditioning, there lived a prince and a princess. Prince Piquant was from the Land of the Blazing Sun, where the sun's rays made the sand so hot that you would hop to keep it from burning your feet. Luckily, Prince Piquant often rode on his camel Blister, so his royal feet rarely touched the ground.

Princess Frostiana lived in the Kingdom of Chillington, where even on the warmest days, her ladies-in-waiting wore a wool sweater over their palace gowns. Two golden retrievers, Snowflake and Icicle, were her constant companions.

When Prince Piquant and Princess Frostiana were each twenty years old, their parents sent them to the Royal Academy for Future Kings and Queens on the Island of Temperate to learn the sorts of royal duties they would perform when they inherited the throne. In Professor Whist's class, Royal Decision-making 101, the prince and princess met and fell in love. Their engagement was announced soon afterward.

Soon, both kingdoms were preparing for the royal wedding of the century, which they agreed to hold in the chapel of the Royal Academy. The town criers heralded every detail of the plans, from the custom-made saddle blanket for Blister to the corsages that Snowflake and Icicle would wear as they accompanied Frostiana down the aisle.

Oh, what a wedding it was! It was not until the servants had cleared away the plates from the wedding supper that the prince and princess realized that they had never discussed where they would live.

"I assumed that you would come and live with me, in the desert," said Piquant. "You will love the warmth of the sun on your shoulders."

"Oh, I could never live there," said Frostiana. My dogs would be too hot and panting to try to cool down! They need cool air to be happy."

Figure 5.1.

"But Blister could never survive in the cold air. He needs warmth and the feeling of sand between his toes," replied the Prince. "Couldn't your dogs just live inside my castle in the desert?"

"Your castle is a tent. It's just as hot inside as it is outside. That will not work at all. Plus, my dogs are used to a castle that has floors and windows. A tent has neither," said Frostiana.

"Your dogs need a cool house in which to live, and my camel needs a warm, dry climate. We'd better ask Professor Whist for help."

So they summoned Professor Whist (very politely, because he was their favorite professor). He suggested that they invite the citizens of their kingdoms to help them solve their problem. That very evening, a royal proclamation was issued:

Dear Citizens of the Land of the Blazing Sun
and the Kingdom of Chillington,

We need your help. We want to build a royal home
we can both enjoy. Can you help us design a home
that will keep the Princess and her dogs cool while
still letting the Prince and his camel enjoy the hot
sun outdoors? A royal reward will be given to the
citizen who can solve this dilemma for us.

With gratitude in advance,
Prince Piquant and
Princess Frostiana

Figure 5.2.

What I Know from the Story	What I Know from My Own Life
The camel needs a warm outdoors.	When I got my new lunchbox, the label said it was "insulated." Mom says it helps me keep my soup warm until lunchtime.
The dogs need a cool indoors.	We put stuff in a cooler that we want to stay cold during a picnic.
The prince and princess want a palace where all of the animals can be happy.	The temperature inside my house can be made warmer (furnace) or cooler (air-conditioning).

Older students needing more challenge might make a four-column table or T-chart, as shown here, to include inferences or questions about controlling temperatures. An *inference* is an idea that is not stated explicitly in the text but that is extrapolated based on ideas in the text. Note that creating inferences is an important standardized test skill that can be developed via this chart:

What I Know from the Story	Inference/Question	What I Know from My Own Life	Inference/Question
The camel needs a warm outdoors.	We can't change the temperature of the air outside, so that is a constant. And camels can only live outdoors, so building a special house for them isn't a choice.	When I got my new lunch box, the label said it was "insulated." Mom says it helps me keep my soup warm until lunchtime.	Insulation keeps things warm.
The dogs need a cool indoors.	We can control inside temperatures. The dogs would do fine living indoors if we could control the inside temperature.	We put stuff in a cooler that we want to stay cold during a picnic.	Coolers keep the cold in. (Note: students later discover that insulators really keep the *heat* from moving, not the cold, but this is a common misconception).
The prince and princess want a palace where all of the animals can be happy.	They want to live together, and so we need a solution that works for both of them.	The temperature inside my house can be made warmer (furnace) or cooler (air-conditioning).	The windows at my house have two pieces of glass with air in between. How does this help keep the inside of our house warm in winter and cool in summer?

No matter what a student's background is, he or she brings important and useful ways of knowing and talking about scientific concepts. While these real-world experiences and prior learning may be sources of misconceptions, a pedagogy (including frequent formative assessment) that identifies and addresses these initial impressions in a content area will ultimately improve conceptual understanding.

Connecting to Science

How Heat Energy Transfers

Although it is not immediately evident, heat is actually caused by molecular vibrations. The measure of heat energy is temperature. The higher the temperature reading, the greater the number and frequency of molecular vibrations. Cold is the *absence* of heat, not the *opposite* of heat. Cooler objects *cannot* transfer cold to warmer objects. This is a common misconception.

Heat energy can be transferred in three ways: *conduction, convection,* or *radiation.* Conduction transfers heat energy between materials that are in direct contact with each other. Examples of conduction include a pan acquiring heat energy from contact with a hot stove burner or a metal spoon becoming warm in a cup of hot cocoa.

Convection is the transfer of heat via the movement of gases or liquids. The application of heat to a gas causes the molecules to move faster and the gas to expand, generally resulting in a net upward movement (e.g., hot air rises). The gas cools (loses heat energy) as it expands, causing it to condense and sink. This creates what is known as a convection current as observed in the movement of ocean currents and atmospheric air streams.

Radiation is the transfer of heat energy without any direct contact between materials, such as when sunlight transfers heat energy through space to Earth.

How Does Insulation Work?

Students have inferred from the story starter that insulation is what is needed for the palace. Before they can grapple with the function of insulation and the insulating properties of various materials, they first need an understanding of heat transfer.

Begin with the question, "Why do ice cubes melt when left out on the counter?" By couching the answer in terms of heat transfer, the concept of insulation begins to come into focus. When a warmer item is put with a cooler one, the warm one loses heat energy and the cool one gains it, until they are both at the same temperature. In the case of the ice cube on the counter, the air is the warmer object, and the ice cube is the cooler object. Warmer air surrounding the ice cube transfers heat energy to the ice cube. The solid cube warms and eventually begins to melt, changing into liquid form. Ultimately, the "cube" is completely transformed to liquid as it reaches room temperature. If a barrier were placed between the ice cube and air, how would that change the movement of heat energy?

Insulators

A good insulator reduces the transfer of heat energy. Remember that a common means of heat transfer is conduction, where heat is transferred from an object of higher temperature to another of lower temperature through direct contact. This heat transfer happens when the more energetic molecules from the warmer object bump into those of the cooler object imparting some of their energy. Air is a great insulator. Air molecules are far apart, so they are less likely to bump into one another, making it more difficult to transfer heat energy. That is why wet suits are designed to trap a layer of air between the suit and your body and why most insulation materials contain many tiny air spaces, such as foams used for thermal insulation.

Insulation materials range from batting to loosely filled fiberglass and are rated for their resistance to heat flow (R-value). Insulation materials include snow, straw bale, mud/adobe, cardboard, Thinsulate ™ clothing insulation, cellulose, fiberglass, polystyrene, urethane foam, and vermiculite loose fill. Of course, the best insulator of all is a vacuum (not a vacuum cleaner!), because a vacuum is empty space. Absence of molecules means no heat can be transferred by conduction.

Inventory Walk   As discussed in Chapter 3, an inventory walk is an opportunity for students to view available materials, develop science-specific vocabulary, and build curiosity about the inquiry to come. The following items can be used in this chapter's inventory walk:

- Scale or balance (the lesson can be adapted using a cylinder or measuring cup if no scale is available)
- Timer or a wall clock with a minute hand
- Ice cubes of similar size
- Small, sandwich-sized zip top plastic baggies to contain the ice cubes
- Small plastic tubs with lids (5″×5″) to serve as the "framework" of the castle
- Possible insulating materials, from which students select one to try:

  - Full sheets of newspaper
  - 8-1/2″ × 11″ pieces of corrugated cardboard
  - 8-1/2″ × 11″ pieces of bubble wrap
  - 8-1/2″ × 11″ pieces of aluminum foil
  - 8-1/2″ × 11″ pieces of cloth
  - Foam peanuts
  - Extra zip top baggies
  - Sandbox sand
  - Large container of table salt
  - Feathers
  - Lard
  - Water
  - Mud

- Possible conduction materials, from which students select one to try:

  - Aluminum foil
  - Water

Vocabulary: Power Words

Terms to Know   Simply copying words and definitions is not enough for a student to make connections that link meaning to vocabulary. Some familiarity with vocabulary will occur before the experiment, but deeper associations with the meaning of the words will manifest as students test and refine their definitions of vocabulary during the inquiry. Relevant vocabulary for this chapter includes:

- **Insulation:** A material that slows the passage of heat energy.
- **Conduction**: Transfer of heat energy between materials that are in direct contact with each other.
- **Thermal:** A word used to refer to heat (as in thermal springs, thermal air current, thermos, and thermal underwear).
- **Heat energy:** A form of energy transferred by a difference in temperatures.

Working Definitions

To place vocabulary in the context of the story, say to the class,

"In order to think about a royal home that meets both the prince and princess's needs, we need to explore the idea of *insulation* and how things can be kept cool. Insulators help slow the transfer of heat from a warmer object to a cooler object. That's what the royals are asking for, right? A castle wall that blocks the transfer of as much of the outside heat energy as possible. Which kind of materials do you think the Royal Architects need to use to create a home that stays cool inside and warm outside? For our investigation, we'll use an ice cube to represent the inside of the castle. Our question for this part of the inquiry is, 'How well can you keep an ice cube frozen?'

"Strategies we discover in this part of the inquiry for keeping the ice cube frozen can be used later to give our advice to the royal couple. However, not all materials are good insulators."

"Explain Yourself" Game   To actively engage students in the use of vocabulary, play the "Explain Yourself" game. In pairs, students ask each other,

- **Would you rather be an insulator or conductor material? Why?** Explain yourself.
- **Would you prefer to be heat energy or a cold object? Why?** Explain yourself.
- **To keep a drink cold, would you choose a thermal insulator or a thermal conductor? Why?** Explain yourself.
- **If it is cold outside, would you rather wear thermal underwear or regular? Why?** Explain yourself.
- **If you were heat energy, which direction would you flow, hot to cold or cold to hot? Why?** Explain yourself.

These questions help students think beyond definition and into application.

Working in the Science Notebook: Before the Experiment

Student-Generated Questions

The most efficient way to encourage critical thinking is to invite students to ask questions (Tompkins & Blanchfield, 2005). Teachers can help their students develop questioning skills when they ask students to think about three factors when developing a question: topic, purpose, and type of outcome the question will generate. In the context of the story starter, the topic is insulation, the purpose is to block heat transfer, and the outcome is achieving a cool interior while the exterior stays warm. Although the topic and purpose of inquiry questions for this context would not change, the type of outcomes would. Outcomes include counting or measuring, a comparison between materials or conditions, and action steps derived from "What would happen if _____."

Counting and Measuring Questions   Counting and measuring questions often lead to a single numeric answer. Students frame measurement questions as: "How many ___, How long ___, How often ___, How hot___, How much___, or How strong___." Students also consider what instruments might be used to measure outcomes, such as a clock, thermometer, ruler, cylinder, or scale. For example:

- How many layers of cardboard are required to keep an ice cube from losing 50% of its weight in one hour?
- How long will it take for an ice cube wrapped in bubble wrap to completely melt?

Comparison Questions   Comparison questions encourage sharper observations. Students look at similarities and differences in their results. Experimental outcomes can differ in many aspects: shape, color, size, texture, structure, amount, temperature, function, density, effectiveness, etc. Comparison questions urge students to define relationships between variables, to classify variables into categories, and to bring order to variety.

Sentence prompts for comparison questions help students organize their inquiry to collect measurable data. Question starters are helpful, such as "How are _____ and _____ different? Which _____ is the most effective? How much (longer, heavier, hotter, etc.) is _____ than _____." Sample comparison questions include:

- How much longer will it take for an ice cube container wrapped in newspaper to melt than an unwrapped ice cube?
- Which material will be more effective in keeping an ice cube from melting, cardboard or aluminum foil?
- Is water or sand a better insulation material for an ice cube?
- How much more effective are foam peanuts than feathers for keeping an ice cube from melting?
- How are sand and aluminum foil different in their insulating capabilities?

Questions That Pose Problems   "Can you find a way to _____?" is a more complex question because it challenges finding a solution to the problem. Students might be overwhelmed and think, "No, I cannot find a way to _____." One motivational tool that can be implemented is the "I-can." This is an ordinary, empty, cleaned soup can that has had the label removed and replaced with a sheet of construction paper. On that paper are glued pictures of "eyes" that have been cut out of magazines. This "I-can" is placed on the desk of students who might be feeling a bit unsuccessful. The I-can brings a smile and confidence boost. Problem-posing questions might look like:

- How can we make an ice cube last the longest period of time using the materials given?
- Can we find a way to keep the inside of the container (castle) cool when it is placed in a hot environment?
- Is it possible to rank all of the inventory materials in the order of their insulating properties?

"What Would Happen If" Questions   These types of questions lend themselves to investigation because students are exploring characteristics of materials with unfamiliar properties. "What would happen if" questions could also be phrased, "How does _____ affect the _____?" or "What does ____ do to ___?" This question approach also lends itself to prediction formulation, the next step in the inquiry process. For example:

- What would happen to the ice cube if the ice cube container was packed in sand?
- How does wrapping the ice cube container with bubble wrap affect the melting rate of the ice cube?

Tompkins and Blanchfield (2005) suggest a gallery walk of student-generated questions as a strategy to engage peer review. Students write their questions on a strip of handwriting paper to be posted anonymously around the room. Students walk around and engage in the question rather than with the author of the question. Students provide helpful hints to the question's author by writing on sticky notes that are then attached to the posted question. Question authors retrieve their question and make revisions as needed. Because this chapter models how an entire class can work together to answer the same question, students form groups and come to a consensus on a question to be forwarded from the group to the entire class and one question is agreed upon.

By closely reading the letter in "Designing a Royal Home" and dialoguing to form a consensus, a question that identifies the underlying problem may emerge, such as the following question, which will serve as the sample question for our model inquiry:

Question:

What insulating material would be most effective for the castle?

Students record the class question in their science notebook.

Testable Prediction

Based on the class question, students identify a material that they will test as an insulator and predict how effective they think it might be. The teacher might introduce this step by saying, "The next thing your group will decide is which material on the materials table you think will provide the best insulation. Remember that the best insulator will block the most heat from transferring to the ice cube and will cause the least amount of melting."

The earlier inventory walk stimulated ideas about potential insulators. Now, each group decides which of the available materials might provide the best insulation. Ask students to fill at least ten lines in the science notebook to ensure the problem has been thought through. A greater quantity of ideas can help trigger a more realistic insulation solution to the problem. Students also consider what outcome determines the effectiveness of the insulation solution (less melting).

This prediction should be an anticipated outcome statement that can be tested in an experiment. Using a prediction template that reflects the relationship between insulation materials selected and anticipated outcome, students write:

If I change _____ , then I predict _____ will happen because _____.

Sample prediction statements include:

- If we wrap an ice cube in newspaper, then we predict it will melt slower than an unwrapped ice cube because....
- If we cover an ice cube in aluminum foil, then it will melt at the same rate as an uninsulated ice cube because ... (this statement predicts no relationship between variables, known as a *null hypothesis*).

Because this inquiry is modeled using a single question for the whole class, the data from all experiments can be pooled to achieve a larger data set from which to make claims. Therefore, it can help for the class to work together to craft a prediction template that is consistent for each work group. For example, each group might use this prediction: "If we wrap an ice cube in _____, then we predict it will melt (faster/slower) than an ice cube that is not insulated because _____." Each group would fill in the blank with a different potential insulator.

For the purposes of explanation, this question and prediction example is provided:

Question:

What insulating material would be most effective for the castle?

Prediction:

If we wrap an ice cube in newspaper, then we predict it will melt slower than an unwrapped ice cube because they wrap fish in newspaper at the fish market, and that keeps it cold.

Identifying Variables

For some investigations, two experiments are actually set up, and this is what is needed for this prediction. The first experiment is the *control,* which will provide a standard for comparison. This will be the "no insulation added" group. The teacher may demonstrate that for the control, an ice cube will be placed in a covered plastic tub (or zip top bag) without any additional insulation. The "insulation added" groups will be exactly the same as the "none added" one, except insulation materials will be added to the setup. To conduct a "fair test," each group can select only one insulation for the ice cube while keeping all other conditions the same as the control cube.

The selected insulating material constitutes the *independent variable.* This is the variable over which you have influence over and that indicates how the ice cube will be "treated." In the sample prediction given above, the independent variable can be found after "if" in the prediction template: newspaper. The *dependent variable* is measuring changes to the ice cube as a result of selecting newspaper as insulation. In this case, the weight of the ice cube measured in grams, or how much water has melted from it measured in milliliters, determines whether or not the insulation material is working. The dependent variable is identified after "then" in the prediction statement. A prediction points to the relationship between these two variables (independent and dependent).

The *constants* are the variables that will be held steady in order to minimize the impact of any other conditions of the experiment. These might include time, classroom temperature, and the surface of the table on which the experiment rests.

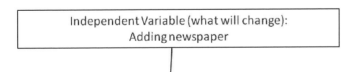

Independent Variable (what will change):
Adding newspaper

If we wrap an ice cube in newspaper, then we predict it will melt slower than an unwrapped ice cube because they wrap fish in newspaper at the fish market, and that keeps it cold.

Dependent Variable (what will be measured to see if it changes)

Figure 5.3.

Ask students to identify and record the independent variable, dependent variable, and constants in their notebooks. For the sample inquiry, students would record the following:

> **Variables:**
>
> **Independent Variable: Newspaper**
> **Dependent Variable: Amount of melt measured in milliliters (ml)**
> **Constants: Room temperature, size, and depth of container with lid**

Procedure

Roles and Responsibilities within the Group   Research shows that collaborative group work benefits critical thinking (Gokhale, 1995). Collaborative group work with designated roles within the group improves student learning even more. The following chart of roles and responsibilities may be useful in guiding students.

Team Role	Description	Student Name
Discussion Leader	Keeps the conversation focused	
Insulation Engineer	Adds the insulation to the ice cube after the group agrees on the materials and technique	
Measurement Specialist	Takes weight or size measurements as called for in the procedure	
Messenger	Communicates team concerns and findings to the teacher and class	
Data Recorder	Fills in the information on the data organizer and helps teammates transfer these data into their notebooks	

Say to students, "All good teams of scientists assign roles and responsibilities to people on the team. That way, no one gets in each other's way, and no one gets more to do than anyone else. Talk for a few moments as a group about how you might divide the responsibilities. Then write down your team's names and roles."

Writing the Procedure   Explain to students that procedures must be detailed and include the duties of each student according to his or her assigned role. The procedure highlights safety issues or other precautions, lists equipment or supplies needed, and directs the gathering of quantitative (numeric) data as well as qualitative (descriptive) data. Procedures use the imperative voice (command) for clarity and economy of words. For example, are there opportunities for students to record sensory data or draw illustrations? Try to limit each step in the procedure to one task and be sure to end by stating that the procedure is completed.

To obtain comparable results between groups testing different insulating materials, tell students, "Your ice cube and insulating materials must fit in the sealed tub on your table. How you use your insulating material is also up to you. If you use lard, will you fill your tub with lard, or just put a thin coating around the cube? If you choose cloth, will you wrap your ice cube like a present or use the cloth as a cushion?"

Students also consider the schedule for measuring the progress of the insulated ice cube. What will be the minute intervals at which the timer will be set? Teachers may need to plan other instructional activities between intervals, or groups could discuss dialogue questions at the end of this chapter (see page 76). The schedule of measurement should be common to all groups to facilitate cross comparisons of data.

A group's procedure might look like this:

1. Messenger obtains ice cube in zip top bag, chosen insulation materials, and plastic tub container with lid.
2. Measurement Specialist measures the weight of the ice cube (in its zip top bag) in grams on a scale or triple beam balance.
3. Data Recorder writes this initial weight (with units of measure) in the data organizer chart. He or she also records the initial weight of the "control" ice cube for comparison purposes.
4. Insulation Expert places ice cube in the zip top bag into plastic tub container, packs selected materials to keep it from melting, replaces container lid, and sets the timer.
5. At the next time interval, Measurement Specialist again weighs the cube (or amount of melt by pouring water from the zip top bag into a cylinder) and provides that information to Data Recorder for placement in data organizer. The rest of the group writes sensory observations or draws what is happening.
6. During the "wait time," Discussion Leader solicits group's input on dialogue questions.
7. When the control ice cube is completely melted, the inquiry is concluded and last measurements are taken.

During this time, the teacher circulates among lab groups to observe and assist with group dynamics and to listen (with as little interference as possible) to student discussions to gauge students' hypotheses and thinking processes.

The teacher may also choose to gather science notebooks for formative assessment and to give student feedback. Formative feedback is important to guide students' logical, sequential thinking. In the formative feedback process, it helps to break the task of writing a procedural sentence into these discrete units:

- **What will be done?** Write the action that will be done.
- **Who will do it?** Look at the assigned roles and assign the task to the appropriate student.
- **What will need to be recorded?** Write the kind of data that needs to be written into the notebook.

Data Organizer

A common data organizer may be designed for all groups in order for comparative data to be shared between groups. The data organizer must be able to record the initial weight of both the control and insulated cube as well as the final weights (volume of melt) at common time intervals decided on by the class in developing procedures. Follow scientific standards and use metric measurements (e.g., grams, milliliters) instead of standard measurements (e.g., ounces, cups).

The following data organizer is only one of the possibilities for data recording:

Elapsed Time	Control Ice Cube (No Insulating Material) Weight in Grams	Experimental Ice Cube (with Insulating Material) Weight in Grams
Beginning of experiment		
15 minutes into the experiment		
30 minutes into the experiment		
45 minutes into the experiment		
60 minutes into the experiment		
75 minutes into the experiment		
90 minutes into the experiment		

Working in the Science Notebook: During the Experiment

Conducting the Experiment and Recording Data and Observations

Once students are ready to conduct the experiment that they have designed, they need to minimize the amount of time the ice cube spends in exposed air. One group sets up a control: an ice cube in a zip top bag inside the lidded container, without insulation. A zip top bag allows the ice cube to be moved without coming in contact with human hands, which might transfer heat to the ice cube and mar the results. The zip top bag also allows students to drain out any liquid into a cylinder or measuring cup. This is necessary to measure the volume of melt or simply to drain off excess water before weighing the ice cube on a scale.

During the wait time between measuring intervals, the Discussion Leader brings up the following dialogue questions for the group to talk about:

1. **Explain the scientific thinking used to come up with this insulation strategy.**
2. **Why were these particular insulating materials chosen?**
3. **Why were the materials manipulated in a specific way?** (e.g., crinkled newspaper, multiple layers, only top insulated and not bottom, etc.)
4. **Would this insulation strategy also work to keep an object hot?**
5. **What would happen if the ice cube was 100 times the size of the one you are working with?**
6. **How could you make the ice cube melt faster? Slower?**
7. **How can the insulation design for this ice cube help you make a choice in advising the Prince and Princess?**
8. **What if you had two identical containers but one had a leak or no lid? Would that make a difference in your results? Why or why not?**

Students follow the procedure at the given intervals, and the Data Recorder records the data, which are later transferred into the other students' notebooks as well. Students may also sketch the arrangement of insulation within the container or any other visual cues that will jog their memories after the experiment.

Working in the Science Notebook: After the Experiment

Claims and Evidence

Each group examines its data and looks for patterns and trends. Discovering patterns in the data will help them create a *claim,* an assertion or statement made by students based on what they observed. They use *evidence*—concrete observations and data—to support their claim.

Booth, Colomb, and Williams (2003) provide a specific example of what this means. In order to claim that it rained last night, you would need more evidence than an observation that streets were wet when you awoke. Based on this evidence, the claim is not solid and could be refuted or contested by further evidence. Perhaps someone watered their lawn last night, wetting the streets, or a fire hydrant was reported leaking and flooded the street, or street cleaners were seen working in that area last night. However, if other evidence were available, perhaps the claim would have merit. For example, if evidence included someone observing rain falling, or data from a rain gauge, then that would provide validity and sound reasoning for the claim.

Using Math to Calculate the Size of the Result

One way to make certain that evidence will support a claim is to use the evidence to calculate the magnitude of the result. For this inquiry, students could use calculators to find the percentage of change in the melting of each ice cube in the various insulators (as is discussed below) or the fraction of ice cube remaining after a set time period. Using percentages to show change—as opposed to a simple subtraction—provides a standard for comparison and discounts various initial sizes of ice cubes. For example, if a student group predicted, "If an ice cube is wrapped in aluminum foil, then it will melt as fast as the ice cube left uncovered on the counter," the claims and evidence might read, "Because the ice cube protected by aluminum foil melted 100% in 30 minutes, which was the same time it took for the control ice cube to melt completely, the aluminum foil didn't change melting time. Therefore, I claim aluminum foil is an ineffective insulator." In this example, the evidence has supported the prediction.

To make a claim related to the sample prediction, "If we wrap an ice cube in newspaper, then we predict it will melt slower than an unwrapped ice cube," students must look at which ice cube had a greater degree of melt. However, merely comparing the final weights of the control and the newspaper-wrapped ice cube is not enough. This is because the ice cubes were not necessarily identical in size prior to the experiment. Deciding on the validity of this prediction requires some calculations. First, the percentage of weight change for each ice cube is calculated. Percentage change also helps us accurately compare data, as not all ice cubes have an identical weight. Students can use the following formula to calculate the change in weight in their science notebooks:

> **Calculating the Percentage of Weight Lost by an Ice Cube in 30 Minutes:**
>
> **"B" represents the weight of the cube at the beginning of the experiment**
> **"A" represents the weight of the cube at the 30-minute interval**
>
> **Formula: $(B-A)/B \times 100$ = percentage of weight lost**

For younger students, percentages may be difficult to understand or implement. An alternative is to convert the data into fractions. For example, if the ice cube weighed

100 grams at the beginning of the experiment and weighed 75 grams at the end of the experiment, then 100 g − 75 g = 25 g (the amount of weight lost). If the amount of weight lost is compared to the initial weight, 25 g / 100 g, the ice cube is ¼ smaller than it was to begin with.

Pooling Data as a Class   Each group's science inquiry helps students know if their chosen material had insulating properties, but it does not help them know if this insulator is the most effective item to use for building the royal home. And this was the problem that needed to be addressed as outlined in the story starter. To address the larger question, students must share their data to see the relative insulating qualities of various materials. By pooling their calculations of the percentage of change at a specified time. Comparing percentages or fractions yields a standard of comparison across different insulating materials used by various groups of students.

For example, if a bubble-wrapped cube lost 25% of its weight over time, and the newspaper-covered cube lost 12%, then the newspaper-covered cube had a smaller loss, and a group could claim that newspaper is a better insulator. Conversely, if another group's cube covered in cloth lost 2% of its weight over the elapsed time period, and the newspaper-covered cube lost 12%, then the class might conclude that the newspaper is not the best insulator. Multiple trials of any experiment always help substantiate claims.

If students are simply comparing their group's result to the control, then they might express their claim using sentence patterns adapted from Klentschy (2008):

I claim that _____ because _____.
Because _____ , I claim that _____.

Claims and Evidence:

Because an ice cube wrapped in newspaper melted more slowly than an unwrapped ice cube, I claim that newspaper is an insulator.

However, if students are comparing their individual group's results to those collected by the entire class, then they might claim, "cloth is a better insulator than newspaper because cloth was 10% more effective in preventing an ice cube from melting."

The teacher may wish to collect notebooks for formative assessment. The teacher can address any revealed gaps in understanding with mini-lessons for small groups or the whole class. Students can then return to their notebooks and try again. Sample mini-lessons could include how to calculate a percent, a review of what constitutes evidence, or a tutorial on how evidence is used to document a claim.

Conclusion

The conclusion to the inquiry will summarize how the claim (supported by evidence) supports or contradicts the original prediction. Some students may realize at this point that their prediction was not supported and may feel their experiment has failed. Saul and Reardon (1996) refer to this as "hypothesis syndrome" (p. 10).

At this point, the teacher needs to reinforce that an unsupported hypothesis is not a "failure," simply an opportunity to learn something that was not expected from the experiment. Teflon (the coating on non-stick cookware), microwave ovens, penicillin, and saccharin were all "accidentally" discovered when scientists were trying to test another hypothesis. One of the scientific habits of mind outlined by National Science Digital Library (NSDL, 2008) is that the process of hypothesis testing is valuable, even if the hypothesis is not supported by the data, if the hypothesis leads to fruitful investigations.

Not only does the conclusion address the original prediction, it also summarizes what was learned through investigation. Writing a summary statement simply condenses what was learned through the evidence gathered. A template for a concluding sentence is:

> **I conclude (new scientific knowledge) because of (evidence). My prediction was/was not supported.**

For example:

> **Conclusion:**
>
> **I conclude that newspaper is an insulator because an ice cube wrapped in newspaper melts more slowly than an unwrapped ice cube. My prediction was supported.**

Next Steps

When results are visually ranked or graphed, students can quickly assess the relative effectiveness of all of the insulators tested by the class. One option is to mark the various insulators along a continuum, which helps to show students which are the most and least effective insulators. Remind students that the smaller the percentage of loss, the greater the insulating quality.

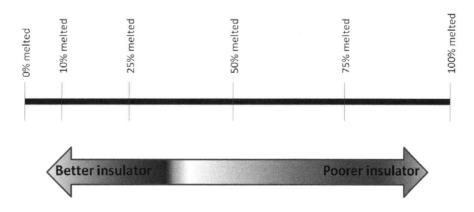

Figure 5.4.

From this, each group could give their insulation material a ranking as shown in the following example:

Percentage of Ice Cube Melt in XX Time Period	Rating of Insulating Materials
0–10% melted	5 stars (best insulating properties)
10–25% melted	4 stars
25–49% melted	3 stars
50–74% melted	2 stars
75–99% melted	1 star
100% melted– or–	
Completely melted before the control melted	0 stars (worst insulating properties)

By ranking various insulating materials in their notebooks, students understand the relative insulating value of their tested material to the other materials tested in the room and can now answer the question from the story starter.

Project and Assessment: Royal Memo

Now that students have experience with the concept of insulation, it is time to return to the original problem of the story starter: preferred building materials for the royal home.

Invite students to write a memo to the prince and the princess. Memos are different from letters. They are informational, with a professional voice. The names of the recipient and the sender are at the top of the page, along with the date and the reason for the memo. The sample memo on page 81 can serve as a guide for structuring a memo. Notice, too, that there is no signature at the bottom of the memo, though the author(s)' initials may be handwritten next to their names on the "From" line.

Royal Rubric

To evaluate the projects, consider the rubric on page 82.

Extensions

Additional Questions to Consider

1. What material could you use to keep your drink cold in your lunch box? Explain your reasoning.
2. Was this inquiry a "fair" test to determine the best insulation design? Why or why not?
3. Would pre-chilling the insulation materials make a significant difference? Why or why not?
4. Answer this question: Are materials that are the best insulators the best or worst conductors of heat?
5. What was similar about the materials that insulated the best?
6. What was similar about the materials that were not good insulators?
7. This inquiry used insulating materials to keep an ice cube cold. Would the same insulating materials also work to keep a hot object hot? Why or why not?
8. How would this experiment change if you did it outside in summer? In winter? In an air-conditioned room? In a heated room?

Memo

To: The Prince and Princess
From: Joe, Shayla, Monique, and Victoria
Subject: Building Materials for Your Royal Home
Date: October 15, 2008

_____

With a memo, you do not need to start with "Dear."

Begin the memo by stating the reason why you are
writing to the royal couple.

Use power words to define insulation and give
examples of building materials that might make good
insulators.

Write a one- or two-sentence conclusion.

No signature is needed for a memo, but you can put
your initials next to your name if you like!

Figure 5.5.

Reverse the Thinking   What would be the most effective insulation materials to keep a baby's bottle warm? Or a screw-top bottle of hot water as measured with a thermometer?

Repetition of Experiment with Multiple Variables   Can students discover ways to combine insulating materials to slow down the melting of an ice cube even further? Conversely, can they discover a way to combine conductors to further speed up the rate of melting? Students should set up an experiment with a control and record the procedure used. Refer to Chapter 8 for more information on working with two independent variables at one time.

Inexpensive Insulation for Shelters   In many urban environments, homeless citizens create shelters for themselves out of cardboard. Based on their experiences with the ice cube, would cardboard earn a 5-star insulation rating? Keeping in mind the limited or non-existent budgets of those without homes, what other insulating materials can students recommend as good insulators for these shelters?

Classification   As a class, sort all of the materials used in the inquiry activity into two categories: insulators and non-insulators. Ask students to justify their reasons based on

Name _____

Royal Rubric

	Beginning Architect (2 points)	Apprentice Architect (3 points)	Royal Architect (4 points)
Creation of Insulation Design	In order to keep the ice cube from melting, choose materials that will block the transfer of heat!	Consider the insulating properties of certain materials to minimize heat energy transfer.	Your design was scientifically sound.
Data Collection	To determine the effectiveness of insulating materials, accurately record the weight of the ice cube (volume of ice melt).	Be sure to denote relevant units of measure (grams, milliliters).	All observations recorded and labeled with all relevant units of measure.
Conclusion and Explanations	The data collected tells a story about the efficiency of the insulating materials. What is that story?	Make sure that your conclusion (claim) is confirmed by the data (evidence) you collected.	Your conclusion (claim) is supported by your data (evidence). Your choice of insulating material did a great job of blocking heat transfer!
Word Choice	The prince and princess loved science in school. They hope you will try again and include scientific vocabulary in this memo.	You use some science vocabulary. Keep going!	You use real science vocabulary to describe what happens with heat transfer and insulation.
Conventions	The prince and princess hope you will try again. Strong conventions help the writer deliver a convincing message.	You're on the right track. Consider an additional round of proofreading next time, or ask a friend for proofreading help.	Wow—your memo has outstanding grammar, spelling, and other conventions.

Figure 5.6.

their inquiry experimentation. Visit the school cafeteria to identify appliances and objects that act as insulators or conductors.

Real-World Application   Invite a building contractor to come to the class to discuss different types of insulation (e.g., blown insulation, fiberglass, extruded foam, shredded newspaper, adobe, and other locally available building materials) and the "R" factor (the industry's official insulation rating system) assigned to each.

Designing Beverage Containers for a Coffee House   Using hot—but not boiling—water, fill a water glass, a paper coffee cup (the type used at coffee chains), a ceramic coffee mug, and a polystyrene cup. (For safety purposes, the teacher may wish to pour the hot water on the students' behalf.) Ask students to gently touch each cup on the outside. Which container appears to provide the best insulation for hot beverages? Record the number of seconds it takes for students to feel the heat on their hands. Now try the experiment again using the cardboard sleeves that many coffee vendors provide. How does this impact the results? Does it take longer for the heat to be felt on their hands?

As a correlation to this book's later unit on environmental inquiry, consider the environmental impact of the reusable containers (glass and ceramic) versus the disposable containers (paper and polystyrene). Invite local coffee house owners to discuss the financial impact of various containers versus their insulating quality. Ask students to debate the overall impact of various containers.

Designing Sustainable Insulation for Building Construction   Two college students have found a completely renewable source for insulation—mushrooms! Ask students to read the story at http://www.signonsandiego.com/uniontrib/20070819/news_1h19mushroom.html. Identify the elements in the article that are *renewable* (can be duplicated naturally without chemicals) and *biodegradable* (able to break down naturally). What other creative solutions can students brainstorm for use as insulation?

Recycling Connection   During the United States Depression beginning in 1929, many Americans were so poor that they used newspaper to insulate their homes, attics, coats, and shoes. People sometimes find these old newspapers buried in their walls when they do renovations in older homes. What other items could be recycled and used for insulation instead of ending up in a landfill?

Native and Historical Insulation   Examine many types of insulation that have been used historically in the United States, including insulation that was used by native peoples. Sort them into categories: Which materials are completely biodegradable (will naturally break down over time)? Which are made out of all-natural materials? What other sorting categories can students devise? Consider the design elements of Native American homes that keep them cool in the summer and warm in the winter.

Space Technology   NASA developed a silver thermal sheeting for the exterior of its space shuttles. The same technology has been used to develop emergency blankets for those affected by natural disasters. Learn more about this space-to-earth technology at http://www.nasa.gov/vision/earth/technologies/silver_insulation.html. How does this kind of blanket keep the human body warm? Do the blankets act as conductors or insulators? Why?

How Do Wet Suits Work?   Scuba divers, snorkelers, and some surfers wear wet suits to keep them warm while practicing their sports. Most wet suits are made of neoprene, a synthetic rubber with air pockets of insulating nitrogen, but an additional insulator is water that is trapped between the body and the wet suit. You can learn more about how wet suits work at http://www.waterskiworld.com/wetsuits. Students can learn more about the properties of neoprene at http://www.wisegeek.com/what-is-neoprene-rubber.htm or http://www.dupontelastomers.com/products/neoprene/neoprene.asp.

Solar Energy   Solar panels use conductors to capture heat energy. Learn more about solar energy and compare that process to the inquiry experiment conducted earlier.

The Anasazi and Pueblo Tribes of the Southwest   All indigenous tribes used locally available materials to construct shelters and homes. The Pueblo Native Americans mixed water, sand, straw, and earth to create a ''mud'' that was then formed into bricks and baked in the sun. This mixture was called adobe and is still used for modern construction today, especially in warm, dry climates such as the American Southwest. Not only does adobe use materials that are locally available, but it is an excellent insulator against the warm desert sun. Some adobe-style homes were made in open air, and others, such as the ones found at Mesa Verde National Park in Colorado, were built against the sides of cliffs for even more protection from the elements. Visit the school library to learn more about the Pueblo tribe that made adobe, or its ancient ancestors, the Anasazi, at http://teacher.scholastic.com/researchtools/researchstarters/native_am/, or learn more about contemporary adobe construction at http://www.adobebuilder.com.

6

Temperature and Heat: The Porridge Case

Lesson Overview

From the perspective of a detective, students investigate how three bowls of porridge, with dramatically different temperatures, could come from a single source. Using a thermometer to measure heat energy, students experiment with independent variables to provide an explanation for the varying temperatures among the bowls. This lesson may follow Chapter 5's study of insulation and heat energy and is suitable for grades 3 through 6.

National Science Education Standards

- **Heat, Light, Electricity, and Magnetism:** Heat can move from one object to another by conduction (Grades K–4).
- **Transfer of Energy:** Heat moves in predictable ways, flowing from warmer objects to cooler ones, until both reach the same temperature (Grades 5–8).

Outcomes

Emerging scientists will be able to:

- Explain that heat energy moves in predictable ways, flowing from the hotter (higher temperature) to the colder object (lower temperature).
- Read a thermometer accurately to record temperature in degrees Celsius.

Practiced scientists will be able to:

- Determine the relationship between an independent a variable and a dependent variable.
- Explain that heat energy can be transferred via conduction and radiation.
- Describe how surface area, stirring, or insulation can influence the rate of radiation.

Awakening Prior Knowledge

Perceived Temperature

In Chapter 5, students saw that heat energy can be transferred by radiation or blocked using insulating materials. When describing heat energy, ideas about what "hot" means are subjective. For example, call out the following list of items and ask students to respond as to whether they would consider the items as "hot" or "cold":

- Ice cream
- Steaming soup
- Summer day
- Winter day
- Body temperature of someone with a fever
- Water coming out of the geyser Old Faithful
- Glacier

Next, work as a class to place these items on a spectrum line in their science notebooks from perceived coldest to perceived hottest. The following example is one potential student arrangement.

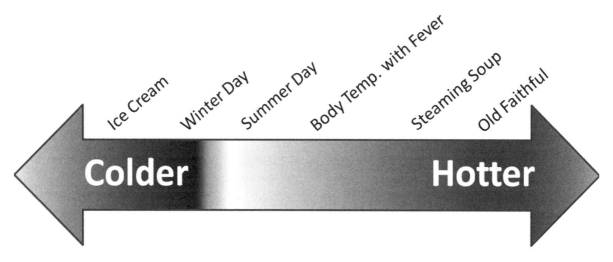

Figure 6.1.

Reading Temperature with a Thermometer

One way to arrange the listed items scientifically from coldest to hottest is to know the temperature of each item. Temperature is a measure of heat energy using a thermometer. Practice reading a thermometer is a useful skill for students and encourages active use of scientific vocabulary. Provide students with several pictures of thermometers that have been colored in red up to a certain line so that they can practice how to read numbers on a thermometer in degrees Celsius. Ultimately, students will associate a range of numbers (°C) with "hot" and another range with "cold."

Temperature is measured in degrees, and a superscript "°" is an abbreviation for degrees. The most common U.S. temperature scale is Fahrenheit (abbreviated "F"). When students living in the United States watch the weather segment of the news, the meteorologist (weather expert) reports temperatures in terms of degrees Fahrenheit. However, Centigrade (Celsius—abbreviated "C") is the temperature measurement metric scale used by scientists and by people living outside the United States. Students may convert between Fahrenheit and Celsius using the following conversion formula:

$$[°C] = ([°F] - 32) \times 5/9.$$

Additionally, there are many sites online that can automatically convert between the two temperature scales. For example, when students type "convert 212 degrees Fahrenheit to Celsius" in the Google search bar, Google will automatically convert and display the result.

Now give students the chance to measure the temperature of these objects by looking up this information online or using the list below to assign a numerical temperature to each item.

- Ice cream: (minus) −5 °C or 23 °F
- Steaming soup: 42.2 °C or 108 °F
- Summer day: 29.4 °C or 85 °F
- Winter day: (minus) −6.6 °C or 20 °F
- Body temperature normal: 37 °C or 98.6 °F
- Body temperature with a fever: above 37 °C or 98.6 °F
- Water coming out of Old Faithful (geyser): 95.5 °C or 204 °F
- Glacier: at or below (≤) 0 °C or 32 °F.

Perceived versus Scientifically-Measured Heat

Do these thermometer readings change the order of items on the coldest-to-hottest spectrum above? Discuss the differences between perceived temperature (in which students use prior knowledge or one of their five senses to estimate something's temperature) and scientific measurement of heat energy using a thermometer. This is an important distinction for this chapter's story starter, in which Goldilocks perceives the temperature of porridge by tasting.

Changes in Temperature

Another concept that will be visited in the story starter is changes in temperature. To help students begin to consider heat transfer, ask students to choose, "Which will stay hot longer?" and read the list of choices below. Have students write their responses in their science notebooks then share their answers aloud. Encourage students to expand on their answers and justify their choice by following it with the word "because."

Which Will Stay Hot Longer?

1. **A cup of hot chocolate with a lid on it or a cup of hot chocolate without a lid**? (The cup with a lid, because heat energy flows [*radiates*] from hot [inside the cup] to cold [outside the cup]. The lid helps keep the heat in [*insulation*].)
2. **A bowl of soup sitting still or a bowl of soup being stirred?** (Sitting still, because stirring brings more molecules to the surface of the soup. At the surface, the temperature difference between the cooler ambient air and the warmer soup surface means heat energy is transferred from soup to air. Eventually, the soup will become room temperature.)

```
E-MAIL

TO:        chief@forestpoliceofthekingdom.com
FROM:      officer124@forestpoliceofthekingdom.com
SUBJECT:   Break-in at Bears' Cottage
---------------------------------------------------

Dear Chief,

I followed up on the call we got yesterday from a Mrs.
Bear, who claimed that the home she shares with Mr.
Bear and their baby bear was allegedly broken into by
a young girl named Goldilocks.

Mrs. Bear claims that three crimes occurred:
  • Goldilocks allegedly ate a spoonful each of the
    parents' porridge, stating that one was too hot and
    one was too cold.  She ate all of the baby's
    porridge, claiming it was, "Just right."
  • Goldilocks allegedly sat in each of the parents'
    chairs, stating that one was too hard and one was
    too soft.  When she sat in the baby's "just right"
    chair, it collapsed.
  • Goldilocks allegedly lay down in each of the
    parents' beds, finding one too hard and one too
    soft.  However, when testing the baby's bed, she
    declared it "just right" and fell asleep.  She was
    asleep in the baby's bed when the homeowners
    returned home after a morning walk.  When she
    awoke, she was so surprised to see the family,
    known as "The Three Bears," that she dashed out the
    door and has yet to be apprehended.

Please tell me how you would like me to follow up on
these crimes.

Sincerely,
Officer Tale
```

Figure 6.2.

```
E-MAIL

To:       officer124@forestpoliceofthekingdom.com
From:     chief@forestpoliceofthekingdom.com
Subject:  RE: Break-in at Bears' Cottage
-----------------------------------------------------

Dear Officer Tale,

Thank you for your report on the alleged break-in at
the Bears' cottage.  Before we bring in the suspect
Goldilocks for questioning, I would like to encourage
you to sharpen your detective skills.

I have seen your photographs proving that there is a
broken baby-sized chair, and I have heard the
testimony of the Bear family that they actually saw
her in the bed.

But the idea that three different temperatures of
porridge could come out of a single porridge pot
sounds quite ridiculous.

Please take Detective Hansel and Detective Gretel with
you back to the Bear cottage and get to the bottom of
this matter.  And remember—they love sweets.  Keep
them away from candy houses, OK?

The Chief
```

Figure 6.3.

3. **An oven with the door open or closed?** (Closed, because the door serves as an insulating barrier.)
4. **A French fry under a warming light or on the counter?** (The fry under the warming light, because heat energy is being radiated from the light to the fry below.)

Now consider this scenario: "Which ice cream will melt first: ice cream sitting on the counter on a hot day or ice cream sitting on the counter on a cold day?" (Ice cream sitting out on a hot day, because heat is flowing from the warm outside air to the cold ice cream, which causes the ice cream's temperature to rise above its melting point.) Thinking about "why" this happens sets the stage for "The Porridge Case" story on page 88 and 89.

Story Starter: The Porridge Case

This story starter is written with the assumption that students are familiar with the story of "Goldilocks and the Three Bears." Read a version of the story to children if they are not familiar with the story already, or use a technique called "Tapping In" for students to retell the story to one another. In "Tapping In," the teacher invites one student to come forward and tell everything he or she knows about the Goldilocks story. When this student has shared all of his or her ideas or has had a minute or two to share, another student can tap the first student on the shoulder. The first student sits down, and the second student begins to share what he or she knows until another student taps in. This activity is useful for reconnecting students to a familiar story and for pooling prior knowledge that sets a foundation for the story starter—a pair of e-mails written based on the fairy tale.

Preparing for Inquiry

Reviewing the Story

Using the story starter, ask students to complete a T-chart about the facts in the Porridge Case. Clarify what porridge is: a hot cereal similar to oatmeal. On the left side, students record the facts about porridge expressed in the e-mail. On the right side, they record assumptions or inferences about porridge from the Goldilocks story that did not necessarily show up in the e-mail. For example, based on illustrations of the story that they have seen in the past, students may assume that the bowls are the same size, contain the same amount of oatmeal, or are made of the same material (e.g., ceramic, plastic, or wood). Differentiating between the "Facts of the Case" and assumptions (that are not based on facts) is an essential skill for all scientists. The following chart is a sample.

Facts of the Case	Assumptions
1. There were three bowls of porridge (two parents and one baby).	All bowls were the same size.
2. The porridges were different temperatures (too hot, too cold, just right).	Each bowl had a different amount of porridge in it.
3. Goldilocks tasted each bowl to determine its temperature (she did not use a thermometer).	Tasting is an accurate measure of heat energy.
4. All the porridge in the baby's bowl was eaten.	Goldilocks was hungry.

If students struggle with creating the table of facts and assumptions, the following questions can prompt students into focusing only on the relevant portions of the e-mail:

1. **Let's look at the three claims stated in the detective's e-mail. What physical evidence is available for the detective to notice at the cottage?** (Empty porridge bowl, broken chair, size of chairs, mussed-up beds.)
2. **What evidence would the detective not be able to observe?** (Temperature of the porridge at time of Goldilocks' visit, Goldilocks tasting the porridge, how the porridge was made, which chair Goldilocks sat in first.)
3. **The chief is concerned primarily with only one of the three claims. Which one is it?** (Porridge)
4. **What problems does he observe with this claim?** (He finds it hard to believe that one porridge pot could produce porridge of different temperatures in each of the bear's bowls.)
5. **What does the chief want the detective to do?** (Figure out if the porridge claim could have occurred.)
6. **What information in this e-mail is not important to the investigation?** (Chairs and beds in the bears' house, Hansel and Gretel, candy, candy houses.)

Connecting to Science

To demonstrate conduction of heat energy, ask students to touch a metal spoon, chopstick, and plastic spoon before placing these items into a cup of hot (not boiling) water. After a minute or so of sitting in the hot water, ask students to touch each of these utensils again. They may be surprised to discover that the metal spoon has become hot while the others have not.

To make clear what is happening in the cup, explain that heat is energy. The amount of heat energy in a substance such as water, metal, wood, or plastic, depends on the characteristics of the particles (molecules) that make up that substance. These characteristics include the speed of the particles' movement, the number (the size or mass) of particles, and the type of particles. Heat energy is added to the utensils when they are placed in the cup of hot water because heat flows from hot to cold. The result is that the particles that make up the utensils are moving (vibrating) with more energy and that the metal is vibrating with the most energy and therefore feels the hottest.

Temperature is the measurement of energy, not energy itself. Higher temperatures mean that the particles of a substance are moving faster. The converse is also true; if heat energy is removed, the temperature will go lower.

Unlike *thermal conduction* (a metal spoon in hot water), which requires particles to collide with each other to transfer heat, *radiation* does not require any medium to move heat. For example, your body is radiating heat into its cooler surroundings right now or being insulated from heat loss with a thermal jacket. The bowl of hot oatmeal cools as heat radiates from the bowl into the cooler surroundings. The greater the difference in temperatures between the bowl of oatmeal and the surrounding air, the greater the rate of cooling. The amount of surface area exposed or covered, the stirring speed, the bowl thickness, and the material from which the bowl is made would all influence this rate of heat radiation.

Inventory Walk

By displaying and/or discussing the materials that will be available for student experimentation, students become familiar with resources. Ultimately students will select from these supplies to design their experiment. Begin the inventory walk by telling students that they will use oatmeal to stand in for porridge.

Say, "It could be served in any of these types of bowls (show students bowls of different sizes and compositions). But instead of tasting the oatmeal to estimate temperature, thermometers will be used to measure heat energy in the oatmeal. Now let's walk through some of the materials for this experiment."

Materials

- Packets of instant oatmeal or box of quick-cooking oats
- Same-sized and different-sized (small, medium, and large) bowls
- Wooden, ceramic, plastic, and metal bowls
- Lids for bowls
- Craft sticks for stirring porridge
- Thermometers that can be placed in oatmeal
- Timer
- Heated water (add tap water to make sure water is not too hot)
- Measuring cup or cylinder

Important Safety Note   Keep heated water within a warm temperature range (40 °C–60 °C) that is measurable with a student-grade thermometer (Buczynski, 2006). Use alcohol-based thermometers instead of mercury-filled ones. Only the teacher should handle the hot water. Although tempting, the oatmeal in the experiment is not for eating, as the thermometers being placed in the oatmeal have not been sanitized.

Vocabulary: Power Words

Nagy (1988) identified three properties of effective vocabulary instruction: integration, repetition, and meaningful use. Word-sorting activities address all three of these points. Because vocabulary for heat and temperature are fairly common words, this is the perfect opportunity for students to work collaboratively to discuss what the vocabulary words mean to them personally, and then examine the relationship between the words in a word sort (Tompkins & Blanchfield, 2008). To do this, students write each vocabulary power word in large letters on separate pieces of paper. Then, in collaborative groups, students examine all the words and discuss their meaning and relationships. At this point, students determine which words have strong associations and begin to pair various words based on a particular relationship between the words. For example, they may pair *temperature* and *Celsius* because *Celsius* is the unit of measure for *temperature*. OR, they may pair *Fahrenheit* and *Celsius* because these are both *units of measure* for temperature. Students try to see how many relationships there are between pairs of vocabulary words.

To reinforce definitions that students have constructed for these vocabulary words in the sorting activity, students can practice in a fun, non-threatening way by playing, "Honk or Pass." For this game, divide the class into two groups and line each group up on opposite sides of the classroom. Give a bicycle horn to the first student in each line. Call out a vocabulary word. If the student with the horn can provide a suitable definition, then he or she "honks" in and answers. If he or she does not feel confident yet in defining the word, the horn is passed to the next student in line. If that student wants to answer, then he or she "honks" in. If not, then the horn continues to pass down the line. The last person in line reverses the horn's direction. Once someone has "honked in" and the word has been defined, then the student at the head of the line moves to the end of the line, and the game repeats with the next power word.

- **Heat energy**: when particles that make up a substance are moving (vibrating) with more energy.
- **Temperature**: the measure of heat energy.
- **Thermometer**: instrument used to measure heat energy.
- **Heat transfer**: occurs when heat radiates from hot to cold; occurs when heat is conducted from a warmer object to a cooler one.
- **Fahrenheit**: the temperature measuring scale most commonly used in the United States.
- **Centigrade (Celsius)**: the temperature measuring metric scale used commonly around the world and in science.

Working in the Science Notebook: Before the Experiment

Student-Generated Questions

Students now use the "facts" outlined on their T-chart and the inventory materials on display to create a question regarding temperature and porridge. The teacher may prompt student thinking by asking, "What are we trying to find out?" Students respond that their task is to be a detective and determine how it could be possible that three bowls of porridge poured from the same pot could be such different temperatures (as measured in degrees Celsius). Then ask, "Would questions that measure or compare help us figure that out?" For example:

Measuring Questions

- How long will it take a bowl of porridge to cool five degrees Celsius?
- How much (in degrees Celsius) does a bowl of porridge cool in five minutes?
- What happens to the temperature of porridge when cold milk is added?

Comparison Questions

- After twenty minutes, will an uncovered bowl of porridge lose more heat than a covered bowl?
- After twenty minutes, which bowl will retain more heat: a large bowl with 1 cup of oatmeal or a small bowl with 1 cup of oatmeal?
- What will be the temperature difference between a bowl of porridge in a metal bowl and porridge in a Styrofoam bowl?
- What would happen to temperature readings if bowls of equal size had different amounts of porridge?

Redirection of Yes/No Questions   Successful inquiry depends on posing investigable questions. Redirect questions that can be answered with "yes" or "no" so that students will have more meaningful explorations. Some examples of redirection are shown in the following chart.

Yes/No Question	Possible Redirected Question
Does stirring porridge make it cool faster than not stirring?	What effect does stirring have on temperature change in a bowl of porridge?
Does the size of the bowl make a difference in the temperature of porridge?	Which porridge will be hotter after twenty minutes, that in the big bowl or the small bowl?
Can porridge get cooler the longer it sits in a bowl?	How long will it take for a bowl of porridge to cool down by 10 degrees Celsius?

The student's research question is recorded in his or her science notebook. For the purposes of modeling, the following question is used:

Question:

If you have two identical bowls, each with different amounts of porridge, which bowl will retain the most heat ("be hotter") after twenty minutes: the one with less porridge or the one with more?

Testable Prediction

Students now reflect on their measurable question and make a prediction in their science notebooks. Refer to Chapter 3 for more scaffolding on writing predictions. Modeled after Klentschy (2008), an effective framework for a prediction is:

If I change _____ , then I predict _____ will happen because _____.

The following is a student sample of a prediction that would be written in the science notebook:

Prediction:

If one bowl has more porridge than the other, then I predict that the bowl with more porridge will have the higher temperature after twenty minutes. This is because there is more of it (volume).

Identifying Variables

In this guided inquiry, each lab group is going to change only *one* variable. This is the *independent* variable (the condition that is purposely changed or altered). All other conditions of the experiment will remain the same (*constant*). The response to this change that will be measured is the *dependent* variable.

For example, given the student prediction in the previous section, the independent variable is the amount of porridge in each bowl, and the dependent variable is the measure of porridge temperature in degrees Celsius over time (rate). Constants would be the size of the bowl; its composition, shape, and depth; use of a lid; and the amount of stirring. The *only* variable being changed is the porridge portion.

Likewise, if a prediction is formulated so that "bowl size" is the independent variable, then composition of bowls, shape and depth of bowls, the porridge amount, lid use, amount of stirring, and all other items that could vary remain the same across experiments. Temperature and type of oatmeal in the initial "pot of porridge" and even the particular thermometer used to measure heat gain/loss are kept constant. Because only one variable is changed, any temperature differences observed can be attributed to that one variable. For more information about determining variables, see Chapter 3.

Procedure

Students should generate their own directions, in their own words, for their inquiry. If students are working in a group, they agree on a procedure as a group, but each student writes the steps in his or her own words. This helps strengthen the development of a student's personal writing voice, which is an essential component of a good writer (Klentschy, 2008; Culham, 2003). A numbered procedural list also functions as a checklist; during the experiment, students may check off each numbered direction as it is completed. The teacher may guide and formatively assess the procedure before students conduct the actual experiment. The following is an example of a procedure a student might write to test the prediction made above.

Procedure:

1. In a big mixing bowl, make 3 packets of instant oatmeal following the directions on the package (each package makes 1 cup of oatmeal).
2. Line up 3 identical bowls.
3. Put 1/2 cup of oatmeal into the first bowl.
4. Put 1 cup of oatmeal into the second bowl.
5. Put 1-1/2 cups of oatmeal into the third bowl.
6. Stir briefly and leave bowls uncovered.
7. Put and leave a thermometer in each bowl to record the temperature.
8. Write the initial temperature reading in your science notebook's data organizer.
9. Set the timer for 5 minutes. When the timer goes off, read the temperature again and write it down.
10. Continue until you have 4 temperature readings at 5-minute intervals.

Remind students to check their procedure to make sure that they are manipulating only one variable. For example, if they are changing the amount of oatmeal, they cannot also change the size or composition of the bowl. Independent variable isolation can be a stumbling block for novice student scientists. Their natural enthusiasm and energy sometimes leads to making more variable changes than elementary experimental design allows.

Data Organizer

Now that students know what they will measure and when they will measure it, they need to create a data organizer—such as a chart, table, or graph—in which to record their results. During experimentation, students will fill in numbers on the empty organizer they have created. The following is a sample data table for the experiment discussed above.

Independent Variable: Amount of Oatmeal (in Cups)	Dependent Variable: Temperature (in Degrees Celsius)				
Time in minutes	0	5	10	15	20
1/2 cup of oatmeal					
1 cup of oatmeal					
1-1/2 cups of oatmeal					

Working in the Science Notebook: During the Experiment

Conducting the Experiment and Recording Data and Observations

Students now follow their written procedure and record two kinds of information in their science notebooks: data in their data organizer and observations that are written in sentence form below the data organizer. Students will have five minutes between each temperature reading. During this time, they may express their observations with illustrations, labeling relevant information.

For easy cleanup, give each group a zip top bag to dump their oatmeal into and pass around a dish tub to collect the oatmeal-covered bowls and supplies. For safety, collect thermometers separately.

Working in the Science Notebook: After the Experiment

Claims and Evidence

As noted on page 33, the Claims and Evidence thinking occurs after the inquiry. Students ask themselves, "What is the meaning behind these data?" To make meaning of data and observations, students reflect on data, review patterns of data, and synthesize their results into implications. The *claim* is their synthesized meaning, and the *evidence* is the data or observations that verify the claim. Students look for:

- **Data patterns** (Overall, did temperatures go up or down?)
- **Range of temperature readings** (What was the highest temperature recorded? Lowest? During which 5-minute time period did the greatest change occur? Least change?)
- **Comparisons** (Which bowl was coolest? Warmest? Had the least change? The most change?)
- **Rates** (How did temperature readings change over time? Was it fast? Slow?)

Elementary students are guided in writing claims and evidence in their science notebook when they are given a sentence pattern, such as this one, based on Klentschy (2008):

I claim that (assertion). This is because of (evidence).

Returning to the sample inquiry, a student's claim and evidence might be:

Claims and Evidence:

I claim that the more porridge you have in a bowl, the longer it will stay hot. This is because in our experiment, the bowl with more porridge had the higher temperature after twenty minutes.

Using "because" prompts students to provide supporting evidence, an important cognitive skill that is needed for students to write essays, speak persuasively, and defend a position in later curricular years.

Conclusion

In the conclusion, students return to their initial prediction and decide if it has been supported or not. In the sample inquiry, this prediction was made:

If one bowl has more porridge than the other, then I predict that the bowl with the most porridge will have the higher temperature after 20 minutes. This is because there is more volume to hold heat energy.

As the student discovered in the Claims and Evidence step, increasing the amount of porridge *did* keep the porridge hotter in the given time period.

In the sample inquiry, evidence supported the student's prediction, so he or she would write:

Conclusion:

I conclude that a larger amount of porridge will retain more heat energy than a smaller amount. Because the bowl with more porridge in it was hotter than the lesser amount after 20 minutes, my prediction was supported.

Notice how this conclusion has been built up slowly, in a way that scaffolds, over the last few steps. If the student's prediction had not been supported, he or she would write, "I conclude that a larger amount of porridge will not retain more heat energy than a smaller amount because the bowl with the most porridge in it cooled more after 20 minutes. My prediction was not supported."

Project and Assessment: Detective Tale E-Mails the Chief of Police

The Project

The project for this chapter highlights procedural knowledge: determining the relationship between independent and dependent variables. In addition, it taps into the content knowledge necessary to interpret results: the transfer of heat energy as measured by

Name _____

E-mail Rubric

Criteria	Police Academy Trainee (2 points)	Junior Detective (3 points)	Senior Detective (4 points)
Ideas: Understanding Temperature	Practice reading a thermometer. If the reading is high, does this mean something is *hot* or *cold*?	Think about what might cause the porridge to get cooler/warmer. How would changing *one* variable affect the temperature readings?	You could say with confidence that temperature changes observed were because of the single variable manipulated.
Voice	When you write your e-mail, pretend to be Detective Tale. The Chief is looking forward to hearing from you!	Sometimes you sound like a real police detective. Keep in mind that you are providing scientific findings to the Chief.	Wow—you sound just like Detective Tale! Your choice of words had the authority of a real detective.
Organization	Can you help the Chief understand how three porridge portions from the same pot could be different temperatures? Try again, using the order of ideas in the e-mail guidelines to help organize your thoughts.	The Chief can follow most of your ideas. Help him out by structuring all of your ideas according to the e-mail guidelines.	Wow! The Chief is impressed that you wrote such a well-organized and easy-to-understand e-mail

Figure 6.4.

temperature. Students explain relationships and provide analysis as they reexamine the original story starter: the exchange of e-mails between Detective Tale and the Police Chief. The Chief had asked Detective Tale to look into the possibility that bowls of porridge from the same pot could be different temperatures as Goldilocks claimed. Based on the students' inquiry, they now have an idea about whether this is possible or not. In the voice of Detective Tale, students will write back to the Chief. This writing activity focuses on three of Culham's (2003) *6+1 Traits of Writing*: ideas, organization, and voice. The following guidelines can help students write a rich e-mail response that includes all three:

> You, Detective Tale, have completed your Porridge Investigation and need to write a response e-mail to the Chief of Police. A strong e-mail starts by giving an answer to the Chief's question and follows up with evidence that supports that answer. E-mails that are concise (containing just the needed information) are a part of e-mail culture and better received than overly long ones. Consider these guidelines when writing to the Chief:
>
> 1. Write in the voice of Detective Tale.
> 2. Start by answering the Chief's "yes or no" question—could porridge from the same pot be different temperatures?
> 3. Go beyond this "yes or no" answer to explain Detective Tale's procedure and evidence collected that support his answer.
> 4. Remember that you are writing a professional e-mail to your boss, so use standard language. (The Chief is your supervisor and not your friend, so avoid abbreviations or instant messaging [IM] language!)
> 5. Sign Detective Tale's name.

Rubric

This rubric provides constructive comments and encouragement for struggling students as well as recognition of accomplished students. The rubric supports a student's mastery of the investigation process by offering ideas on how to improve their understanding of the scientific method. Learning to design a measurable question, accurately read a thermometer, and make connections between a temperature reading and the amount of heat energy present in the bowl of porridge are part of the learning outcomes. In addition, students are asked to incorporate their investigation into a wider framework, recognize assumptions, and analyze relationships.

Rather than making the rubric a checklist of whether or not each step of the scientific method was completed, a broader view is taken, looking at the process as a whole.

Refer to the rubric on page 98 as an example.

Next Steps/Extensions

Temperature Stations   Students enjoy working with thermometers and exploring the concept of temperature as a measure of heat energy. Consider creating a small exploration center with thermometers and/or Web access so students can find out, on their own, the temperatures of various objects, materials, or locales. Weather.com can help students identify the weather in their hometown or around the world.

Library Learning   Why do certain factors (lids, cup jackets, portion size, etc.) conserve heat energy?

Authentic Application   How do thermostats in houses or temperature gauges in cars work? Who in the community might be a resource to help answer this question?

Human Body   In a healthy state, our body temperature is 98.6 degrees Fahrenheit. Does that body temperature change when we are sick? When we have been exercising during recess? When we turn the classroom thermostat up or down?

Web Resource   Many sites on the Web feature games students can play that involve reading a thermometer or thermometer template. Surf a bit and practice thermometer reading skills.

7

Magnetism: Dance of the Magnets

Lesson Overview

A force, such as magnetism, is essentially a push or a pull causing a change in the position or motion of an object. "Dance of the Magnets" illustrates this attraction and repulsion between objects made of various materials. Students in grades 3 and above use observations of this magnet behavior to produce evidence-based claims of magnetic properties.

National Science Education Standards

- **Light, Heat, Electricity, and Magnetism**: Magnets attract and repel each other and certain kinds of other materials (Grades K–4).

Outcomes

Emerging scientists will be able to:

- Define properties of magnets.
- Explain that bar magnets have a north-seeking pole and a south-seeking pole.
- Clarify that magnetic forces attract only magnetic materials (those that contain iron).
- State that magnets come in many sizes, shapes, and strengths.

Practiced scientists will be able to:

- Infer magnetic properties of a material.
- Describe how a magnetic field surrounds every magnet.
- Demonstrate that while magnetized, temporary magnets act like permanent magnets.
- Explain that magnets can make an object move without directly touching the object (action at a distance).

Awakening Prior Knowledge

To begin this magnet inquiry, ask students what these items have in common: a refrigerator magnet, a videocassette, a compass, a credit card, a levitated monorail, or toy trains that connect without fasteners. Students brainstorm on a fresh page in their science notebooks. Many will be familiar with refrigerator magnets or have played with magnet-based toys in an activity center. The commonality of all of these items is the application of magnetism.

Discuss what students have observed about how magnets behave. What do magnets attract and not attract? How do two magnets interact with each other? What questions do students have about magnets?

The teacher can document this information on a whiteboard, bulletin board, or chart paper for future reference.

Story Starter: Dance of the Magnets

The next step is to build context for inquiry by reading the story "Dance of the Magnets," on pages 103 and 104.

Preparing for Inquiry

Reviewing the Story

First, review the characters of the story and the types of materials that they represent.

- **Bea, Benito, and Bella** are bar magnets. A *bar magnet* is a rectangular-shaped piece of iron, steel (contains iron), or magnetite (a mineral found in lodestone or natural magnets) that attracts only certain types of materials. Bea is a small magnet, Bella is a medium-sized magnet, and Benito is a large magnet.
- **Frieda** is a filing. *Filings* are small metal scrapings. Frieda must be made out of iron, nickel, or cobalt because of the way she sticks to Bea, a magnet.
- **Peter, Paulo, and Penelope** are paper clips. *Paper clips* are generally made from galvanized steel wire (steel is an alloy consisting mostly of iron). Paper clips come in different sizes, too, and some are even coated with plastic.
- **Mark the Marble** is a glass ball.
- **Carl the Cardboard Kid** is made of corrugated fiberboard or heavy stock paper (recycled, we hope).
- Are **Principal Ross** and **Custodian Dave** male or female? Can you tell from the story? (Hint: Look at the pronouns!)

Next, using bar magnets to represent the characters in the story starter, reenact the dance moves on a document camera or overhead projector. To do the magnet Hokey Pokey, play music (available at http://kids.niehs.nih.gov/lyrics/hokey.htm) and arrange four to six magnets in a tight circle. Turn each magnet so that all of the south poles face the center of the circle. Invite students up to the demonstration area to see if they can make the south pole of one magnet touch the south pole of another magnet. Point out that each end of the bar magnet is referred to as a *pole* and that if you suspended the magnet in the air, one end would point north and the other south. The magnetic effect is strongest at the magnet's poles. Even if you break a bar magnet in half, each piece will still have a north and south pole. Continue the magnet Hokey Pokey by turning the magnets around so that all of the north poles face toward the center of the circle. Students observe that when *like* (similar) poles face one another, they *repel* (or resist) one another.

If time allows, use both magnets and paper clips and reenact the "Bunny Hop" dance that was also referred to in the story starter. For music and lyrics, visit http://kids.niehs.nih. gov/lyrics/bunnyhop.htm. In this dance, move a magnet among scattered paper clips so that

Dance of the Magnets

Frieda the Filing and Bea the Medium Bar Magnet were best friends at Fernwood Magnet School. "Frieda and Bea, Bea and Frieda, always stuck together," said their friends.

When Frieda and Bea arrived at school on Monday morning, they saw a big banner over the door: DANCE CONTEST! FRIDAY AT 2 PM!

"Dance contest?" Frieda said to Principal Ross. "What's that?"

"Everybody gets a dance partner. The goal is to keep dancing. The longer you dance, the more money you raise for families in need. It's fun, and it helps others," said the principal.

All week long, Frieda and Bea practiced their dance moves. Kindergarteners tapped their toes in line. Bea saw Custodian Dave clicking his heels together and waltzing with his broom.

When Friday finally arrived, and Principal Ross came on the P.A., to announce the start of the dance, Frieda and Bea nearly flew down the stairs as they hurried to the gym, where the dance was already in full swing.

What a crowd! Magnets of all sizes crowded the dance floor, jumping and jiving to the beat. Carl the Cardboard Kid and Mark the Marble, however, were roaming around, unable to find anyone to dance with.

Principal Ross knew right away that something was wrong. Sure, some magnets had found a partner and were stuck together, dancing away.

"Wow, they're really attracting one another," said Principal Ross.

But some of the magnets were keeping away from their partners at all costs. "How repulsive!" thought Principal Ross. Some magnets were covered with metal pieces, and some items couldn't stick to any kind of magnet.

Bea came up with tears in her eyes.

"Principal Ross!" wept Bea. "Benito, the biggest bar magnet, invited me to dance, but every time I try to get closer, he scoots away! It's like he and I are rejecting one another!" Just then, Bea turned around, and WHOMP! She and Benito had a magnetism so strong that they stuck right together.

Principal Ross realized that the Dance Contest wasn't going as planned and signaled for the DJ to stop the music.

"Boys and girls, this dance isn't going the way I thought it would," announced Principal Ross. "Would everybody please clear the floor? Let's start with a demonstration. If you are on the bar magnet team, please come to the center and show us your stuff!"

Everybody knew that bar magnets loved to show off their routines. They took their positions and, to the tune of the "Hokey Pokey," began to move and sing:

You put your north pole in.
You put your north pole out.
You put your north pole in.
And get scattered all about.

Figure 7.1.

**You do the Magnet Motion.
And you turn yourself around.
That's how we repel!**

"Wow," Frieda said, poking Bea. "When they try to bring their north pole end to another bar magnet's north pole end, they actually move away from each other." The bar magnets started their second verse. This time, they did it differently.

**You put your south pole in,
Which means your north
pole's out.
I put my north pole in,
And, zoom! We're at-
tached.
We do the Magnet Motion.
And now we move as one.
That's how we "attract!"**

"So it really is true," Bea said. "Opposites do attract. That's why I didn't stick to Benito right away—our North Poles were facing each other!"

Principal Ross thanked the bar magnets and asked them to clear the floor. As Bella, one of the smallest bar magnets, was returning to the sidelines, she got a little bit too close to Peter the Paper Clip—and they attached! And then Peter's sister, Penelope the Paper Clip, got attached to Peter.

"Whoa—how did that happen?" said Frieda. "The paper clips aren't magnets."

"Ah," said Principal Ross. "Bella and her friends are showing another way to dance. Let's give them the floor!"

The DJ started to play the Bunny Hop.

Bella, Peter, and Penelope were moving around the dance floor, connected together like train cars, singing:

**We are something special!
We can make a chain!
Do the magnet pickup.
Clip, clip, clip!**

**Are you made of certain
metal?
Maybe you can join.
Can you join our freight
train?
Clip, clip, clip!**

The friends watched as their paper clip pal Paulo got attached to Penelope. More paper clips tried to join the train, and a few did, but some at the end of the line could not attach.

"That's weird," said Bea. "I wonder why some paper clips can attach and not others?"

The dance floor was starting to fill again as different objects started to see if there was a magnetic attraction between them. Some had it, and some didn't. And poor Mark the Marble just kept rolling around, unable to find any partner until he got stuck in a divet in the floor.

Principal Ross watched the dancing students and realized that there would need to be some guidelines for future dances so everybody knew how to find a partner.

Figure 7.2.

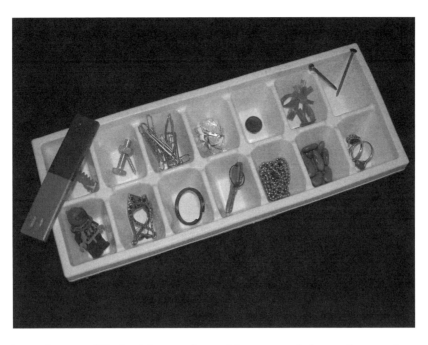

Figure 7.3. An ice cube tray filled with a variety of items can help students gain early conceptual understanding of magnetism.

students observe how either pole of a magnet can attract objects that contain iron (such as paper clips). See if a "bunny hop" procession of paper clips can be formed behind the magnet. Paper clips not only react to a magnet's "pull"; they can also become temporarily magnetized by being close to a magnet, which is why one paper clip is temporarily able to attract another paper clip, forming a "conga" line.

Finally, in separate compartments of an ice cube tray put a few coins, washers, buttons, paper clips, marbles, craft magnets, keys, key rings, push pins, nails, screws, jewelry, pieces of cardboard, aluminum foil, plastic, or other small objects to test for magnetism. Tape a piece of plastic wrap over the top of the tray to secure the items, pushing the plastic wrap down into each ice cube well. Provide a tray and a magnet for each group of students and ask them to talk about which materials are attracted to the magnet and which ones are not. What does this exploration mean in terms of possible solutions to Principal Ross' dilemma? What guidelines could Principal Ross begin to form in terms of magnet dance partners?

Connecting to Science

What Is **Really** *Happening?*   Magnets can be naturally occurring rock called lodestone, containing the mineral magnetite, or magnets can be artificially made with materials that contain iron, nickel, or cobalt. Elementary students may wonder where the attraction of this mysterious force of magnetism is coming from. The answer has to do with what is happening at the atomic level with magnets.

Magnets are made up of thousands and thousands of tiny atoms. Each atom has a center, called a *nucleus.* Around each nucleus, electrons revolve. Some go in one direction, and some go in another. Scientists tell us that if the number of electrons revolving in one direction equals the number of electrons revolving in the other, then there is no magnetism. But if there is an imbalance (more electrons are rotating in one direction than in another), scientists believe that this imbalance correlates to a material being magnetic (Koch, 2005).

To illustrate this concept, provide each student with one sheet of white paper, one piece of colored paper, and a dozen die-cut arrows. Ask students to imagine that the white sheet of paper is a magnet with millions of mini-magnets (magnetic domains) inside of it. Place all of the arrows on the sheet of paper to represent these mini-magnets. When all of the north poles of the mini-magnets (arrows) are lined up and pointing the same way, then the big magnet (white sheet of paper) will exhibit magnetic properties. This is also why when a magnet is gently cut in half, newly cut faces on the smaller pieces will become the new north or south pole.

Let the colored paper represent a non-magnetic material. In non-magnetic materials, all of these internal mini-magnets (arrows) are all jumbled up. Place all of the arrows on the colored paper in a random array. Ask students to remove all pairs of opposite-pointing arrows. When the number of mini-magnets (arrows) pointing north is equal to the number pointing south, this cancels out their magnetic effect so that the material does not have magnetic properties.

Paper clips (which are not magnets but are made of iron-containing steel) can become temporarily magnetized by exposure to a magnet. This exposure causes all of the mini-magnets in the paper clip metal to line up and point the same way. Now the paper clip will briefly exhibit magnetic properties. In the simulation, if the paper represented a paper clip that had been exposed to a magnet, would it be white or colored? (white) and how would the arrows be arranged? (all arrows pointing in the same direction)

You cannot see magnetism but you can see the effect of this invisible force through attraction or repulsion of magnetic materials. This region where magnetic forces act is called the magnetic field. Students can see the shape of a magnetic field by sprinkling powder like iron filings around a bar magnet. The filings align themselves parallel to the magnetic field lines, producing a visible image of the invisible field. The greatest concentration of filings will be at the two poles, where the field is strongest. (To see a drawing of this phenomenon, visit http://image.gsfc.nasa.gov/poetry/magnetism/magnetism.html or http://www.eia.doe.gov/kids/energyfacts/sources/electricity.html).

Safety Note   Computers, VHS or audiocassette tapes, credit cards, and even driver's licenses or student identification cards that have a brown-colored strip all use magnets to work properly. It is important not to use magnets near these items, or their function could be compromised.

Inventory Walk   The materials in the following list can be used as stimuli to build student motivation for inquiry by introducing materials that students will use to design an experiment and to lay the groundwork for understanding the abstract idea of magnetism.

Materials List

- Bar magnets
- Iron filings
- Buttons
- Cardboard squares
- Plastic cups

- Paper clips
- Coins of various denominations
- Aluminum cans
- Nails or screws
- Pushpins
- Marbles
- Students' jewelry

To begin the inventory walk, place these items in a box or sack. Gather students together on the carpet or in a central area. Pull out each item one at a time and ask a few introductory questions. Just as in language arts, where students are encouraged to connect text to their own lives, encourage students to make connections between these items and their daily lives. The following questions are examples of conversation starters that a teacher might ask about a cardboard square ("Carl" in the story):

- **What is this?** (Cardboard.)
- **How have you seen this used in the past?** (Boxes at the grocery store, box in the office that copy machine paper comes in, etc.)
- **How can you describe it? Use your senses.** (Stiff, brown, square, smooth, etc.)
- **How does the cardboard relate to magnets in the story?** (Doesn't stick to magnets.)
- **Could it be used to keep magnets away from each other?** (Depends on the thickness; powerful magnets have magnetic fields that continue to be effective through the depth of cardboard.)

Next pull a few paper clips out of the box to represent the story characters Peter, Penelope, and Paulo. Ask these questions:

- **What are these objects?** (Paper clips.)
- **What might they be used for in school?** (To hold papers together.)
- **What do you think they are made of?** (Steel, metal, wire, and some will say aluminum.)
- **Is this material magnetic? How do you know?** (Yes. They stuck to the magnet in the "Bunny Hop.")
- **How could you test whether it is magnetic or not?** (Hold a paper clip next to a magnet to see if it sticks.)
- **Were the paper clips permanently connected together in the story?** (No.)
- **Do you think you could make one paper clip stick to another, without using a magnet?** (Students may not be certain, but this is possible when a paper clip is held against the magnet for a short period of time.)

Next select Bea, a bar magnet, and Frieda, represented by iron filings, from the inventory box and ask:

- **How were Bea and Frieda able to "always stick together?"** (One must be magnetic and attract the other, or maybe they were both magnets?)
- **Can you tell by looking if there is a difference between each end of the bar magnet?** (Possibly the ends of bar magnets are different colors, but if color was not there, you could not tell the difference.)

- **Could Bea and Frieda stick together if Carl, the cardboard square, came between them?** (Students may not be sure, as the answer depends on the strength of the magnets and the thickness of the cardboard.)

Continue along these lines with each item in the box.

Creating a Visual Glossary on a Bulletin Board   At the conclusion of the inventory walk, place each item in a plastic bag and staple the bag to a bulletin board, along with a label for each item. (Place large items on a table or countertop.) This creates a visual word wall that can be referenced throughout the inquiry. At the conclusion of the inquiry, students will write those words and their definition for that word in a glossary at the end of their science notebooks. Students may draw a picture of each object in addition to or in lieu of a sentence, depending on their learning need.

Vocabulary: Power Words

Encourage students to engage in "science talk" when they are expressing what they observe. When magnets were touched to the different materials in the wells of the ice cube tray, what happened? Some students will describe a behavior where paper clips were "pulled toward" the magnet. This "pulled toward" then becomes the working definition for the vocabulary term, "attract." If science talk continues, and the question, "What is a magnet?" is raised, students may describe the shape, color, size, or strength of the magnet used with materials in the ice cube tray. The teacher can guide thinking that even though some students used round, small, gray, refrigerator magnets and some used larger, rectangular blue and red magnets, all magnets behaved in the same manner, attracting certain materials and not others.

A working definition for a magnet may begin with "an object that attracts (list what is attracted) but not (list what was not attracted)." From these observations, words associated with magnetism (attract) are being applied to specific examples. Students begin to build and use scientific language from everyday language.

- **Attract:** To pull toward.
- **Magnet:** Magnets are made of nickel, iron, or cobalt that has been exposed to a magnetic field. This exposure changes the atomic structure of these metals so that the metal has the property to attract or repel certain materials.
- **Magnetism:** A fundamental force of nature, which can cause certain materials to be attracted or repulsed.
- **Magnetic pole:** The end of a magnet where the force is the strongest. If a magnet is suspended in the air, one end will want to point north. This is called the north-seeking pole. The opposite end is called the south pole.
- **Magnetic force:** The pull or push in an area surrounding a magnet (called the magnetic field).
- **Repel:** To push away from each other.

Working in the Science Notebook: Before the Experiment

Student-Generated Questions

To craft great inquiry questions, students need ongoing assistance.

Redirecting Yes/No Questions   Use the traffic light technique from Chapter 3 so students can "vote" on whether or not a posed question is a red light (closed) question or a green light (measurable) question (Levitov, 2005). Here are some practice questions to help students recognize the difference between a yes or no question and a question that is investigable.

- Are all magnets made of metal? (Red)
- How far away can a magnet be from a paper clip and still attract it? (Green)
- Will a magnet still work if it has been frozen? (Red)
- Do magnets stick to soda cans? (Red)
- Do all magnets have opposite poles? (Red)
- Which of these materials will block a magnetic field? (Green)
- How does hammering a magnet affect its strength? (Green)

After practicing with identifying an investigable question, students can continue to develop question skills by reworking red light questions into green light questions in their science notebooks. This revision is most easily accomplished by beginning the question with "how, which, or what" (Klentschy, 2008). See the following for examples.

Comparison Questions

- Which magnet has a larger magnetic field, the small one or the larger one?
- How is the magnetic field of a U-shaped magnet different from a bar-shaped one?

Questions That Explore Scientific Concepts

- How does water, temperature, or light (students choose one) affect a magnet's ability to attract?
- What happens to a magnet's strength if a magnet is painted?

Questions That Can Be Answered with Quantification or Measurement

- How many paper clips will my magnet pick up?
- How many paper clips can a magnet hold?
- How long will an object hold its temporary magnetism?
- How far do magnetic forces reach?

Some of these questions can be answered with a single word. For example, an answer to the question, "How many paper clips will my magnet pick up?" may be, "Six," but the investigation may lead to more inquiry questions, such as "How strong is a magnetic field?" or "How do paper clips become temporary magnets?" If students struggle to construct a question, prompt them to consider the role magnetism played in the two dance moves that were enacted in the story or how various characters' magnetic properties would react in a variety of situations.

For the sample inquiry, differences between Bella, a small magnet, and Benito, a large magnet, are examined. The sample inquiry is meant merely as an example. This means that the teacher should not lead the class in replicating this model. Rather, teachers and students can—and should—develop their own inquiries.

Question:

What are the differences between a large magnet and a small one?

Students start a new page in their science notebooks for the question they are developing, putting the date and page number in the top outside corner and the name of the investigation (e.g., "Magnets") on the top line.

Testable Prediction

This is the stage of inquiry where time needs to be given to "thinking about the question" and how it might become a prediction. There are many approaches to the example question. Students may consider the role "size" plays in magnet behavior. Maybe there is no relationship between the size of a magnet and a magnet's properties. If so, then size is not a factor in determining differences. If students predict that there will be no difference between the behaviors of the two objects, this is known as a *null hypothesis*. Perhaps based on his or her experience with objects in the ice cube tray, a student thinks the size of magnet will dictate how many small items the magnet can pick up at once. This would be a reasonable method to measure the strength property of a large magnet to the strength of a small magnet. Maybe, after exploring with magnets in the ice cube tray, a student thinks a larger magnet will be able to pick up objects from a greater distance. As students consider the various possibilities, a prediction begins to emerge.

To scaffold crafting a prediction, consider the following sentence template:

If I *change* [this factor], then I *predict* [this result] will happen *because* _____ [use prior knowledge].

The first part of the prediction statement, "If I change _____ ," can help students envision the basics of the procedure. This is the "action" part of the prediction statement. If a prediction is about the pattern of the magnet fields around the magnets, then the procedural action steps would be very different than if a prediction was focused on the ability of magnets to transfer magnetism. For a prediction about magnetic patterning, perhaps iron filings would be sprinkled around each size of magnet. For a prediction about the transfer of magnetism, procedural steps might be directed toward bringing paper clips close to magnets and then touching other paper clips.

The second part of the prediction statement, "then I predict _____ will happen," forces students to take a stand. Instead of merely predicting that one magnet will be more powerful than another, students deepen the prediction by quantifying it and adding something that can be measured. For example, a scientist might predict that a large magnet can hold 50% more paper clips than a small one. Some elementary learners may use simpler mathematical comparisons, such as predicting that the larger magnet will hold five more paper clips than the smaller magnet. They might also predict that a large magnet can attract a paper clip from a distance of ten centimeters while a small magnet cannot.

Whatever direction the prediction takes, it reflects the tenor of the question in the previous step. In the sample question above, the student is questioning whether or not there will be a distinct difference between the behaviors of a large magnet and those of a small one or whether there will be no difference.

The third part of the prediction statement, using the word "because," requires students to tap into their prior knowledge and use their science power words as they explain their thinking. For modeling purposes, here is a sample prediction based on the sample question given earlier:

Question:

What are differences between a large magnet and a small one?

Prediction:

If I change sizes of magnets, then I predict the larger magnet will hold twice as many paper clips as the smaller magnet because it has a stronger magnetic field.

Identifying Variables

Most variables in an experiment can be identified in the prediction statement. The clause "if I change _____" names the *independent variable,* and the clause "then I predict _____ will happen" signifies the *dependent variable.*

Independent Variable   The *independent variable* is what will be varied during the experiment. In most elementary experiments, there is a single independent variable, as it simplifies experimental design. (Chapter 8's sample seed inquiry demonstrates how to set up a valid experiment with two independent variables.) Depending on what students want to find out about magnets' behavior, the independent variable will vary from group to group but could manipulate:

- Temperatures of magnets
- Shapes of magnets (horseshoe compared to bar)
- Categories of objects to be tested
- Thicknesses of barriers

The independent variable in the sample inquiry is the size of the bar magnet.

Dependent Variable   The *dependent variable* is the variable that will be observed and measured as it responds to changes in the independent variable. The dependent variable will be measured in units that are appropriate (e.g., size, weight, or quantity). Depending on the independent variable being tested, student may be measuring:

- Number of sheets of paper acting as a barrier of magnetic field
- Number of paper clips attracted
- Distance in centimeters of attraction field
- Weight in grams of BBs (small metal beads) attached to magnet

The dependent variable in the sample inquiry is the number of paper clips that a bar magnet can hold through the force of attraction. (The number of paper clips held is *dependent* on the size of the bar magnet.)

Constants   *Constants* are the things that will stay the same during the experiment. In the example, the constants include the size of the paper clips, whether they are coated in plastic or not, the temperature of the ambient air, the type of surface for the experiment, and even gravity. There are usually multiple constants in an experiment.

If students continue to struggle with variables, replacing the prediction sentence template with the following sentence may assist in understanding:

When I change _____ **(A), I will measure the response of**
_____ **(B). I will keep these things** _____**(C) the same.**

In this sentence pattern, (A) identifies the independent variable, (B) signifies the dependent variable, and (C) represents the constants.

For the sample inquiry, a student would write the following in his or her science notebook:

Variables:

Independent Variable: Size of bar magnet
Dependent Variable: Number of paper clips
Constants: Temperature, size and type of paper clips, testing surface

Procedure

In writing a procedure or list of steps to be followed when carrying out the experiment, students visualize in advance what they will be doing, a kind of "pre-thinking" that supports cognitive growth. Procedural writing forces students to envision an experiment first as a whole, then as a series of small sequential steps.

To plan a procedure, students think about what they want to observe as a result of their actions. For example, perhaps a student group plans to plunge a magnet into a bowl of paper clips to test how many paper clips will be attracted to the magnet. They expect this action to tell them the magnet's strength. But students must also think about the technique they use. Putting a pole end of a bar magnet into the bowl is different from exposing its flat surface to the pile of paper clips. The pole end has a stronger magnetic field but a smaller surface area, while the long section of the magnet has a larger surface area but a weaker magnetic field. To yield consistent results, the procedure must specify how the magnet is held as it is placed in the bowl. If not, the procedure would accidentally test two things simultaneously: both the strength of the magnetic field and the size of the field. Students will benefit from teacher support on visualizing the procedure as they write it in order to ensure that the experiment is actually testing what the students want to know. In the sample inquiry, what students want to know is the strength of the magnetic field.

Teachers can review student-generated procedures and provide feedback, but students should feel that the procedure is "theirs." This is a difficult concept for most teachers who like patterns to follow to make labs easier to manage. However, student ownership reinforces a student's motivation to engage in the work.

Most procedures are recorded as lists, which are faster to write and easier to read than paragraphs. (For a sample procedure in paragraph form, see Chapter 9.) The procedure should be brief, succinct, and clear so that the experiment can be repeated if needed. For the model lesson, students might write the following procedure in their science notebooks:

Procedure:

1. **Get a bunch of paper clips that are all the same size.**
2. **Untwist one end of a paper clip to form a "hook."**
3. **Hold up a large bar magnet and let the paper clip "hook" be attached to one pole of the magnet.**
4. **Very gently hang a paper clip onto the hook.**
5. **Repeat Step 4 until the "hook" paper clip comes loose from the magnet.**
6. **Record how many paper clips are on the hook.**
7. **Take the paper clips off the hook.**
8. **Write down the number of paper clips.**
9. **Repeat Steps 1–8 two more times.**
10. **Do the whole experiment again with a small bar magnet.**

Accuracy is important in science. Notice how the procedure includes, "Repeat Steps 1–8 two more times." Each repeat of an experiment is known as a *trial.* Doing a total of three *trials* of the experiment for each magnet will yield a more accurate data set. Accurate data make it easier to know if the prediction was supported or not.

Data Organizer

Now that students know what they are measuring and the procedure they will use, they can design a graphic organizer for recording those data in their science notebook. There is no single data organizer that works in every experiment. Students should have some freedom to construct a graphic organizer (with teacher guidance) that is meaningful to them. Data organizers include tables, graphs, charts (including a T-chart), or a list of sentences or text-based notes. Data charts should always include a place to record measurement of the dependent variable as well as the unit of measurement (e.g., number of days, centimeters, milliliters, grams, pieces, number of people, or seconds).

For the sample inquiry, students are recording the number of paper clips for each size of bar magnet in each of three trials. That information could be recorded in a variety of ways. Here are four examples:

	Larger Magnet Number of Paper Clips Held	Smaller Magnet Number of Paper Clips Held
First Trial	24	18
Second Trial	27	16
Third Trial	30	20

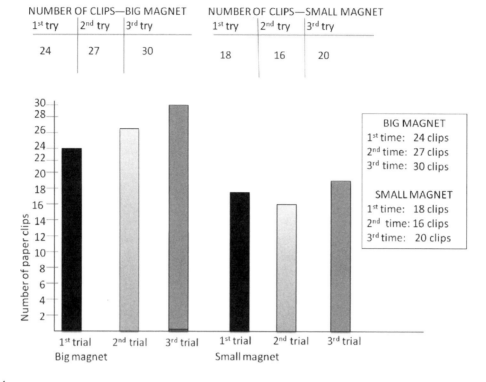

NUMBER OF CLIPS—BIG MAGNET			NUMBER OF CLIPS—SMALL MAGNET		
1st try	2nd try	3rd try	1st try	2nd try	3rd try
24	27	30	18	16	20

BIG MAGNET
1st time: 24 clips
2nd time: 27 clips
3rd time: 30 clips

SMALL MAGNET
1st time: 18 clips
2nd time: 16 clips
3rd time: 20 clips

Figure 7.4.

The student draws an empty data organizer into his or her science notebook.

Working in the Science Notebook: During the Experiment

Conducting the Experiment and Recording Data and Observations

Students are now ready to conduct the experiment. This is, for many students, the most exciting time. Based on materials referenced in student-written procedures, which the teacher has reviewed in advance, the teacher has organized a materials table that contains the resources needed for each experiment. For the sample inquiry, the student would obtain one large magnet, one small magnet, and a handful of same-sized paper clips.

Students' natural curiosity will tempt them to touch a magnet to everything they see in the classroom. Therefore, stress that students should conduct their experiment as outlined in their procedure before jumping into another experiment. At times students will improvise steps in the procedure to improve directions or find that another way of doing things would be better than what they originally thought. If this occurs, encourage students to make notes of these deviations or additions to the procedure in their science notebooks. Ultimately, someone else should be able to do the test exactly the way that they did.

Also encourage students to sketch their observations, which may communicate information that a student's words cannot. These additional observations may lead to new inquiries.

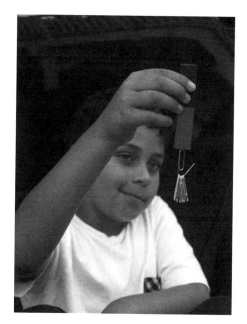

Figure 7.5.

Students may also use photographs to document their progress, as in the photo shown here, which would help future scientists understand how their hook worked.

Working in the Science Notebook: After the Experiment

Claims and Evidence

With the experiment completed, students make sure their procedural steps reflect what was actually done and then begin to examine data, observations, and illustrations. Ask students to consider data from many angles. For example, what was the range of the number of paper clips held by a small magnet (from fewest to most)? What was the numerical average (mean) number of paper clips held from all three trials of the small magnet? To calculate the mean, add up the data and divide by the number of trials. Students with special needs might use a calculator to assist computation. Using our sample data, students would write the following:

Calculation of average number of paper clips held by the large magnet:

$[24 + 27 + 30] / 3 = 27$ (if you get a number here with a remainder, round it down because you can't have part of a paper clip!)

The average number of paper clips held by the large magnet is 27.

Calculation of the average number of clips held by the small magnet:

$18+16+20 / 3 = 18$

The average number of clips held by the small magnet is 18.

The calculations provide valuable information and identify patterns that students need to make evidence-based claims. The *claim* is the statement of what was discovered, and the *evidence* is the data, observation, and/or illustration that support the claim statement. Again, students look at their calculations and figure out what the data mean. They use science power words to explain their data. If the larger magnet held an average of 27 paper clips and the smaller magnet held 18, does this mean the magnetic force of the larger magnet's pole is stronger? If so, how much stronger? Is that a claim that can be made about the differences between large and small magnets? (Yes) How does the student know? (From the data)

In the sample inquiry, the following claims might be made:

Claims and Evidence:

I claim that large magnets have stronger magnetic forces than small magnets. I determined this because a large magnet held more paper clips on average than a small magnet.

Writing claims sometimes means making inferences (see also Chapter 6). For example, students cannot see the magnetic force but *infer* its properties via indirect measures, such as counting the number of paper clips to determine the strength of the magnetic field. From counting the paper clips, the claim is made that large magnets have stronger magnetic forces than small ones. Is this claim true of all magnets? No. Depending on a magnet's composition, a small magnet could have a stronger magnetic field than a larger one. However, this claim is supported based on the evidence gathered for these two particular magnets. There are no absolutes in science!

Conclusion

Generating a claim and drawing a conclusion helps to guide students through difficult thinking steps in science inquiry. To draw a conclusion from the data, students look back at their original prediction to determine whether that prediction was supported or not supported. Reporting that a prediction is "wrong" or "inaccurate" is not recommended because these terms carry a negative connotation or imply imprecise results.

The prediction in the sample inquiry was that a large magnet could hold twice as many paper clips as a smaller magnet. Students calculated that a larger magnet, on average, held 27 paper clips, while a smaller magnet held 18 paper clips. Are nine more paper clips enough to claim twice as many? No, evidence would need to show that the larger magnet could hold 36 paper clips (18×2) for this claim to be supported. Therefore, the prediction is not supported.

Students may need reassurance that an unsupported prediction is not a blunder. Predictions are based on prior knowledge or background research, and real-world scientists often have predictions that don't pan out as planned. Scientists learn as much from unsupported predictions as they do from supported ones. For example, scientists testing a new drug may predict that it will reduce cancer by 50%. If it actually reduces cancer by 70%, then the prediction is unsupported, but the research is still valuable!

Students also reflect on potential experimental error and the scientific understanding they have gained as a result of working through the scientific method.

A possible conclusion for the example scenario might be:

Conclusion:

I conclude that larger magnets have stronger magnetic fields than smaller ones because the larger magnet could hold more paper clips on a hook than a smaller magnet. My prediction was not supported because the large magnet did not hold twice as many paper clips. I learned that even though the larger magnet had a stronger magnetic field, it wasn't necessarily twice as strong.

Next Steps/Reflections

Finally, students briefly reflect on where they might wish their inquiry to go next. Most students want to rush this step by randomly touching a magnet to various objects in the classroom to see if that object has magnetic properties. Sometimes, teachers need to slow down students' hurried activities so that they can reflect on what is happening. To nurture a slower, more thoughtful, and more sustained activity, ask students to jot down "I wonder'' questions in their science notebooks as ideas spring up during spontaneous experimentation. The following are ''I wonder'' examples:

I wonder:

- **How does my small bar magnet's ability to hold paper clips compare with my neighbor's?**
- **What role gravity played in the magnet holding such a large number of paper clips?**
- **If a magnet can pick up paper clips through a barrier, how thick could the barrier be?**
- **If I rubbed paper clips against a magnet, would the paper clip have magnetic ability?**
- **How many paper clips could be attracted to a magnet in a chain formation?**
- **How do scientists measure the strength of magnets?**

How Does the Teacher Support Next Steps?   The teacher can support these ongoing questions by leaving materials out and available as an information center for the next several days. Teachers can encourage both informal inquiry and magnet play. If existing funding or grants are available, consider making small materials kits that can be sent home for further inquiry. This brings family members into the excitement of science inquiry. The child may also take his or her science notebook home to record observations.

What If Questions Can't Be Answered with Hands-On Experimentation?   Note the final question from the above ''I wonder'' list: ''How do scientists measure the strength of magnets?'' This is a question that cannot be answered simply by students experimenting with materials. Although they may be able to design their own procedure for measuring strength (e.g., by counting the number of paper clips held by a magnet), they will not be able to divine the experts' methods. For these kinds of questions, have the students work collaboratively in small groups with the school library media specialist to pursue these interests using expert resources.

Project and Assessment: Podcast a Voice Mail from Principal Ross

During the summative project, students connect their science understanding recorded in their notebooks with the original problem in the story. In this case, the problem was that Principal Ross thought that there should be some guidelines for future dances so everybody knew how to find a partner. (Students know that principals like to call them ''guidelines'' and students call them ''rules,'' right?)

Say to students, ''Pretend that you are Principal Ross of Fernwood Magnet School. You are going to be absent on the day of the next dance contest, and you are calling Assistant Principal Lee to give him the guidelines for the dance. When you try to call, you get his voice mail instead. You need to leave him a message that will inform him of at least three magnetic guidelines that can be used for future dances. When you record your voice mail, you will need to sound like a principal and speak with authority and confidence.''

To be successful in this assignment, students must apply their knowledge of magnetism to a metaphor (dance contest) and communicate evidence-based magnetic properties to a non-scientific audience.

Making a podcast to simulate voicemail is simple! A podcast is a digital audio recording that can be posted or distributed online. You can use free software or even make a toll-free phone call using a free Gcast.com account that is converted to a podcast (Fontichiaro, 2008). For podcasting instructions, software, and tips, visit http://podcastingatschool.seedwiki.com.

Principals, of course, are polite and thorough on the phone. Consider these elements of a top administrator's voice mail:

- **Start with a greeting** such as "Hello," "Hi," or "Good afternoon." Say who you are.
- **Tell Assistant Principal Lee at least three guidelines**. For each guideline, state who is dancing with whom and the magnetic fact that makes that the rule. For example, a bar magnet and nail should be paired for the dance, but not a bar magnet and cardboard square, because nails are made of magnetic materials and cardboard is not. Feel free to indulge in the metaphor. For example, magnets with stronger magnetic forces should always lead in the dance moves.
- **End with a thank you and a** closing such as "Goodbye."

Students work alone to role-play Principal Ross. Writing out a script in advance facilitates the recording process, and using scientific vocabulary gives it the necessary authority and authenticity. Before recording, students can self-assess their scripts by labeling their work with dots: green (confident that it has fulfilled the requirements), yellow (not sure), or red (lack of understanding of the assignment or confidence that it has fulfilled the requirements). Teachers can see at a glance the self-efficacy of their students and how students make judgments about their own work and mini-conference as necessary to help students develop more accurate self-assessing strategies. After evaluating the podcast with the following rubric, a comparison can be made to determine how accurate the student's self-assessment was.

If your students post a podcast online, we hope you will send the URL to the authors of this book at activelearning@gmail.com.

Rubric

The rubric on page 119 can guide students into creating an outstanding product and allows teachers a quick method of accurate summative assessment.

Next Steps/Extensions

Some students will have formed new questions that interest them and will wish to pursue those as a next step. For others, here are some extensions to consider:

Library Learning   Is there an invention like a "magnetometer" that might measure the strength of a magnet? What are some applications of magnets in the real world?

New Investigation   How does temperature (either heating or cooling) affect the function of a magnet? What about breaking a magnet in half? Or hammering it? Do any of these physical changes impact the function of a magnet?

Language Arts Connection   Use a simile to describe a magnet by completing this sentence: "A magnet is like a _____ because _____."

Name _____

Magnet Podcast Rubric

	Need Caller ID (2 points)	Principal in Training (3 points)	Principal Ross (4 points)
Describing properties of magnets and magnetic behaviors	Use the results of your experiment to describe how magnets and other objects are behaving with each other at the magnet dance. Then use this information to form dance guidelines.	In designing the dance rules, clarify that magnetic forces attract only magnetic materials. Use power words to explain the interactions.	Yea! Your use of scientific vocabulary was awesome in describing the interactions between magnets and various materials.
Organization	Consider ordering your guidelines as first, second, third. Be sure to explain each dance rule before moving to the next. The ideas for the rules should come from your investigation.	Be sure to begin your voice mail with a greeting and end with a goodbye. Also, consider using your experimental claims and evidence to develop guidelines for the dance.	Your voice mail was courteous and your three guidelines are appropriate for the next magnet dance and have solid support from evidence in your experiment.
Voice	Can you trick us into believing that you are a real principal? Make sure you are clear and certain about what you want to say before you begin.	In order to sound like Principal Ross in the voice mail, use the vocabulary, tone, and style of a principal.	Wow—you really sound like Principal Ross. The style of your voice mail has authority and confidence.

Comments:

Figure 7.6.

From *Story Starters and Science Notebooking: Developing Student Thinking Through Literacy and Inquiry* by Sandy Buczynski and Kristin Fontichiaro. Santa Barbara, CA: Teacher Ideas Press. Copyright © 2009.

Practical Application   A compass's arrow is a magnet that points to Earth's magnetic north. Design an orienteering activity for students to explore during recess.

Technology Connection   Use KidPix software to help students understand the difference between magnetic and non-magnetic substances. Divide a KidPix document in half. Label the first half "magnetic" and the second half "non-magnetic." Students can use the stamps' libraries to identify objects for each category. For a free, open-source alternative to KidPix, consider TuxPaint (http://www.tuxpaint.org).

Playing with Magnetic Properties   Can you create new dance moves for magnets at Fernwood Magnet School? View the authors' twirling magnets video, *Can You Do the Magnet Twirl?* at http://www.teachertube.com/view_video.php?viewkey=8cec2d9700c75f7a417d.

Can you explain why this happens? Could it be the next magnet dance hit?

8

Seeds: Sprouting into the Future

Lesson Overview

Students categorize different types of seeds and determine how various environments will affect the germination of seeds. Students in grades 3 and up design an experiment to observe and document the relationship between environment and seed germination. A monologue is presented to answer the question posed by the story starter: What makes a seed get started as it begins to turn into a plant? The seedlings grown in this investigation can be used again in Chapter 9's study of the relationship between environment and plant growth.

National Science Education Standards

- **Life Cycles of Organisms:** Plants and animals have life cycles that include being born, developing into adults, reproducing, and eventually dying. The details of this life cycle are different for different organisms (Grades K–4).

Outcomes

Emerging scientists will be able to:

- Explain that all seeds perform the same function in plant growth whether the seed is edible or not.
- Describe a seed's role in the life cycle of a plant.
- Explain that water is necessary to initiate seed germination.

Practiced scientists will be able to:

- Explain the growth patterns of seeds.
- Describe the relationship between environmental factors and seed germination.

Awakening Prior Knowledge

Seeds Display

Make a collection of fifteen different types of seeds, including seeds from garden flowers, vegetables, wildflowers, weeds, seeds from preparing food, birdseeds, and snack seeds (peanuts, popcorn, or sunflowers). Invite students to glue these seeds on a poster board, store them in egg cartons, or staple them in zip top bags to a bulletin board to reflect the many sizes, shapes, and colors of seeds. As students make seed observations, ask, "Where do the seeds come from?" (Most come from inside fruits or vegetables.) Remember from Chapter 4 that one reason fruits sweeten with ripening is to entice animals to eat the fruit, thereby transporting the seeds in their digestive system to a new location.

Edible and Non-Edible Seeds   Next, students will examine whether or not all seeds are edible. Remind students that plants are made up of six basic parts (roots, stems, leaves, flowers, fruits, and seeds) and we can eat all parts, depending on the type of plant. See the following chart for examples.

Root	Stem	Leaf	Flower	Fruit	Seed
carrot	celery	lettuce	broccoli	eggplant	coconut
radish	asparagus	spinach	cauliflower	orange	sunflower

Say to students, "Have you ever met a seed you didn't like? Think about what you ate for dinner last night. Did it include seeds? Let's see if we can list the seeds that we (humans) eat (*edible*) and seeds we typically do not eat (*non-edible*)." Students brainstorm a list in their individual science notebooks. This list may include the following examples:

Seeds We Eat	Seeds We Don't Eat
Sunflower seeds	Acorns
Peas	Most flower seeds
Green beans	Apple seeds
Lima beans	Seeds from citrus fruit such as oranges, grapefruits, or lemons
Coconuts	
Lentils	Avocado
Soybeans	Peach
Chickpeas (Garbanzo beans)	Plum
Oats	Papaya
Barley	Cantaloupe
Rice	Watermelon
Rye	Cherry
Buckwheat	
Quinoa	
Many kinds of nuts	
Pumpkin seeds	
Seeds from a pepper (but only if we want our food to be really hot!)	
Seeds inside a tomato	
Corn	
Cucumber	
Eggplant (we eat the seeds inside)	
Peanut	
Wheat	
Strawberry (we eat the seeds that grow outside the fruit)	

Pool student responses on a class chart or use a wiki to gather all student data in a central location. Also collect packages of garden seeds for showing students the expiration date. How long have the seeds been stored? (Answer may surprise students.) Does that affect their ability to grow into a new plant? (That depends on the type of seed.) What would you need to do with these dry seeds to make them sprout (germinate)? (Add water.)

Seeds Have Their Own Food   To help students transition from thinking about seeds as something we (and other animals) eat to thinking about seeds as a food source for the embryonic plant, ask students, "Did you know that inside each seed is nutrition for animals but also food for a plant to use as it starts growing? Food is contained in the *cotyledon* of each seed where starch turns naturally into sugar. This is food that an embryo plant uses as it germinates. Because plants are *producers (autotrophs)*, eventually, the plant will make its own food from sunlight in a process known as *photosynthesis*. But until its leaves reach sunlight, a plant relies on the food it carries inside its seed. Once the leaves take over producing food, the cotyledon withers away. When you are eating a seed that you like, your body is enjoying that starch. Like all animals, we humans cannot make our own food, so we rely on getting it from other plants and animals. Animals are *consumers (heterotrophs).*"

Story Starter: Sprouting into the Future

See page 124

Preparing for Inquiry

Reviewing the Story

This story functions in four ways. It:

1. Establishes interest by connecting to a genre of literature.
2. Promotes questioning and stimulates curiosity.
3. Provides introductory content information.
4. Presents a context for an investigation.

A discussion of the literary elements, content, and questions of the story helps prepare students for the inquiry to come.

Literary Elements   The following questions can guide a classroom discussion and help students gain understanding of the story starter.

1. **Who are the characters they meet?** (Alumi and Nyl)
2. **How did the problem arise?** (People stopped sharing food and knowledge; now they have no food and don't know how to make it.)
3. **How do the characters figure out that the beans might be edible?** (They see that they are for growing and make an inference.)
4. **What needs to happen for the society to have food again?** (The children must figure out how to grow and harvest the seeds.)
5. **What questions still linger?** (How will Manuel and Javier get home? Will the seeds grow?)

Sprouting Into the Future

Manuel and Javier were playing in the backyard.

"Let's build a plane, big enough for both of us to play in!" said Javier.

"Sounds good to me," said Manuel.

The two boys gathered up scrap wood, the box Javier's mom kept her holiday ornaments in, two rickety chairs from the alley dumpster, and a tarp from Manuel's dad's boat. Pretty soon, they had a plane just big enough for both of them to sit in. They played Flying In A Plane until it was nearly dusk.

"Mom says I have to be home before the street lamps come on," said Javier. "And it's almost that time." He swung his leg over the edge of the plane and started to climb out.

Just then, a rumble shook the earth. Javier fell back into his chair as the plane began to move.

"Is this an earthquake?" yelled Manuel.

"I don't think so," Javier said. "If this were an earthquake, things would be shaking. But we're …. we're … we're going up!"

Sure enough, their play plane was now hovering a few inches above the ground, and with another rumble, it shot up until they were so far away from Javier's house that they could only see a speck.

"Whoa, something's really happening to us!" yelled Manuel. "What is it?" Their plane went up and up and up. They went up so far that when they looked down, all they could see were clouds.

"We've got to do something!" shouted Javier. "But we forgot to build controls into the plane, so how will we ever get back down!"

Just then, as if the plane had magically heard Javier's words, the plane began to descend. Down, down, down it went. It felt like the plane was going straight down, but when it landed, they weren't in the backyard anymore. They were surrounded by tubes and big shiny silos. Huge windmills circled overhead.

"Whoa, I've never been someplace that looked

so futuristic," said Javier.

Two girls in sparkling silver jumpsuits came toward the boys. "Welcome to the future," they said. "We are glad you are here. We have been calling for someone to help us. Here you are, just as we envisioned."

The boys were surprised. They had been called here? By these girls in weird clothes?

"But ours isn't even a real plane!" sputtered Manuel. "It's just a bunch of junk that we put together with nails and tape! How did it get here?"

"You came here floating on our wishes," said the older girl. "But we have forgotten our manners. I am Alumi, and this is my younger sister Nyl. Thank you for helping us. Centuries ago, during a time of great difficulty, our ancestors moved here to avoid the pollutions of the city. For many years, our people lived in harmony and shared their resources so that we had what we needed."

"Then everyone started getting jealous and fighting," continued Nyl. "We forgot how to share and how to take care of each other and our village. People started hoarding food."

"Not just food," said Alumi. "They stopped sharing their growing secrets. Now, no one is left who remembers how to grow plants for food. All that remains is this small jar passed down through the years. It's labeled 'Beans for Growing,' and no one has ever opened it. We don't know how to grow them."

"Neither do we," said Manuel. "We buy all of our vegetables at the grocery store: already picked, in cans or frozen bags."

"Please help us," begged Nyl. "Time is running out. Our parents are very sick because they have not had enough food to eat. You must help us grow these beans to keep them alive."

"We can try," said Javier. "But we'll have to do this inquiry together, because none of us has had experience growing seeds."

Beans for Growing

Figure 8.1.

Time Travel   "Sprouting into the Future" is a time-travel story. Students can connect to prior literary knowledge with questions such as these:

1. **Do students know any other time-travel stories?** (Common answers might include Jon Sciezska and Lane Smith's *Time Warp Trio* series or Mary Pope Osborne's *Magic Tree House* series.)
2. **What do those stories have in common?** (People travel to other places and times, they need to find a way to get home, and they usually have a problem to solve before they can go home.)
3. **Could science explain this experience of time travel?** (Not yet! Science searches for logical explanations of observations and rejects supernatural explanations.)
4. **Could the seeds have been sitting in the jar for years and still be able to grow into a new plant?** (Yes, science has documented the longevity of many varieties of seeds, even some that have been in space travel.)

Text-to-Self Connection   Children in different parts of the United States have different levels of familiarity with seeds and growing plants. Children in some areas may never have seen a seed and may only have seen food products that are seeds in cans or as frozen goods in the grocery store. What do the students in the classroom already know about how seeds turn into plants?

Connecting to Science

Seeds are the means by which most flowering plants reproduce. Produced in the ovary of a flower, seeds are fertilized when pollen nuclei reach them. Flowers may contain any number of seeds and come in a variety of sizes. For example, the seeds of the golden poppy, California's state flower, may produce thousands of tiny black seeds from just one flower, while the lima bean produces just two or three large seeds per pod.

Are Seeds Alive?   At first glance, a seed may not appear to be living, because it remains unchanged or dormant for long periods of time. However, seeds are actually self-contained for growing a new plant. The seed includes not only the embryonic plant but also food necessary to sustain this embryo until it can reach the sun, form leaves, and begin photosynthesis. *Monocotyledon* ("one seed leaf") plants such as grasses and corn have a single seed leaf. *Dicotyledon* ("two seed leaf") plants such as beans, peanuts, and peas have a seed that, when opened, reveals two seed halves.

Seeds have amazing longevity and simply need the right conditions to germinate. All seeds must be fertilized by pollen to have the capacity for germination. If the pollen nuclei never reach the seed, then the seed will not become fertilized and therefore will never form a new plant. Initially seeds germinate when they absorb water, rupturing the seed coat. Seed coats can be thin and transparent, as in peas, or thick and opaque, as in coconuts. Water starts a chain of chemical changes, which results in the development of the plant embryo.

Seed Germination   A seed is typically planted below ground so germination actually takes place in the dark. When the seed coat breaks open, the root (*radicle*) is the first structure to emerge. Next the embryonic leaves (*cotyledon*) and stem (*hypocotyl*) will emerge and break the soil surface to become the stem and leaves. In *monocots*, the cotyledon remains below ground, while in *dicots*, the cotyledons surface above ground on the stem. Once true leaves are in place, the plant can capture the sun's energy with *chlorophyll* (a green pigment) and convert light (*solar*) energy, carbon dioxide, and water into *glucose* (chemical energy) through a process called *photosynthesis*.

There are five basic requirements for seed germination: proper temperature, water, air, time, and room to grow. Some seeds, such as Alaska sugar peas, have been cultivated to grow in cold temperatures. Other seeds, such as tomatoes, need the warmer temperatures of summer to germinate.

Why Seeds Don't Germinate   Many factors can contribute to poor seed germination. For example:

- If the flower was not pollinated, then the seed could not have been fertilized and therefore the seed will not germinate.
- If the seed is over-watered, then the seed will suffocate due to lack of oxygen.
- If the seed is planted too deep in the soil, then all of the temporary food (*endosperm*) is depleted before the first true leaves (*plumule*) can reach the light and begin photosynthesis.
- If the seed is not provided with enough water initially to soften the seed coat, the germination process is not initiated.

Seedling Response to Stimuli   The developing seedling will respond to light and gravity. Developing shoots grow against gravity ("up"), while developing roots grow toward gravity ("down"), a process known as *gravitropism*. This will happen even in the dark. Developing shoots grow toward the light, a process known as *phototropism*.

Inventory Walk   Begin by helping students build a definition of *materials*. Ask students to think about what they would need to bake a cake. They may list cake mix, egg, oil, a bowl, a spoon, cake pans, an oven, a timer, a cooling rack, and even a toothpick to test if the cake is done! These are the *materials* needed to bake a cake. If you wanted to germinate a seed, what materials might you need? Have students generate a list of materials, then suggest additional materials until the class's list resembles the following:

Materials List

- Dried bean seeds
- 1-cup containers
- Zip top bags
- Paper towels
- Thermometers
- Soil
- Lamp
- Spray bottle with water
- Paper or plastic cups
- Permanent markers

Tell students that these materials will be available for their experiment.

Vocabulary: Power Words

The study of seeds introduces some challenging scientific vocabulary to define some words that are quite common in children's vocabulary.

Common Word	Scientific Word	Definition
Sprouting	Germination	To begin to sprout or grow.
Baby plant	Seedling	Young plant growing from a seed.
Seed food	Cotyledon (cah-tuh-LEE-dun)	Provides energy and nutrients for developing seedling.
First leaves	Plumule (PLOOM-yule)	Structure that begins producing food through *photosynthesis*.
How plants make food	Photosynthesis (foto-sin-the-sis)	Using sunlight energy and chlorophyll to combine carbon dioxide and water into sugars.
One seed part	Monocotyledon (mah-no-cah-tuh-LEE-dun) Abbreviated: monocot	"One seed leaf," meaning that the seed cannot be split in half into two parts, e.g. grass, corn, lily, palm, or orchid. The prefix "mono" means "one," as in monologue or monorail.
Two seed parts	Dicotyledon (DI-cah-tuh-LEE-dun) Abbreviated: dicot	"Two seed leaves," meaning that you could split the seed in half, as in a bean, pea, or peanut. The prefix "di" means "two" as in dialogue.
Producer	Autotroph	Organisms that can synthesize sugar (glucose) and make their own food.

After introducing vocabulary to students, duplicate the table and cut it apart, giving each child in the room one square from the chart. (You may need to make multiple copies of the chart.) Then invite students to walk around the room and find the other students whose cards are either identical to theirs or contain a synonym or definition for their word.

Students can then write a definition in their own words in their science notebook glossary.

Working in the Science Notebook: Before the Experiment

Student-Generated Questions

Help students return to the problem of the story to initiate questioning. What is the problem that needs resolution? Are these bean seeds still capable of producing new plants even though they have been in storage for a long time? Ultimately, the characters in the story want the seeds to produce plants that will make more seeds that could be eaten by their parents and others in future generations. The story characters do not know how to get the beans to start growing, so an obvious question might be, "What would you need to do with the seeds to make them sprout (germinate)?"

To scaffold this question, create a jar of beans labeled "beans for growing," similar to the one in the story. Reach in and grab a handful of bean seeds to show students. Ask:

- **Are beans for growing different from beans for eating?** (No.)
- **Where do you think these beans came from?** (In this case, the pods of bean plants.)
- **Are these seeds "alive?"** (Yes, though students may think otherwise. The seeds exist in a *dormant* (resting or, literally, "sleeping") state until conditions are right for germination.)
- **If the seeds are "alive," then why aren't they growing into bean plants?** (They need water, proper temperature, air, time, and room to grow.)
- **What would you need to do to make beans sprout?** (Add water, put at suitable temperature, spread them out, make sure there is air, and wait. Some students may indicate that soil is necessary for sprouting, but soil is not essential.)

Observation Questions   After examining the seeds in the "beans for growing" jar, students record observations that will lead to generating measurable questions. How do the seeds look, feel, or smell? How old is the seed? Can you tell by looking at it? Has the seed been fertilized? What does the inside of a seed look like? Does the seed easily split into two halves or remain whole? Drawing a seed's insides may help a student develop a plan for what the seed may require for germination.

Measuring and Counting/Compare and Contrast Questions   Students collect straightforward data with measuring and counting questions that start with "how?" (how many, how long, how often) because these questions are often answered with a single number. Eventually, these types of counting questions can lead to comparison questions. The comparison questions may still be answered with a single word but require some evaluation of the data.

Measuring and Counting Questions	Compare and Contrast Questions
How long will it take for a bean seed to sprout?	Which comes out of the seed first, the root or the shoot?
How many seeds out of ten will actually sprout?	Will larger seeds take longer to germinate than smaller seeds?
How much water does it take to loosen a seed coat?	Will more beans sprout in a warm place than in a cold place?
	What is the difference between how many soaked seeds will germinate and how many unsoaked seeds will germinate?

Questions to Redirect

Remember to redirect "yes/no" questions by starting the question with "what, which, or how."

"Yes or No" Question	Redirected Question
Are all seeds planted going to sprout into seedlings?	How many of the seeds planted do you think are going to sprout?
Can seeds sprout without water?	What effect does adding water to a seed have?
Do seeds need light to sprout?	Which grows faster, a seed grown in the dark or in the light?

"Can You Find a Way to ..." or "I Wonder ..." Questions

Students also develop more sophisticated "can you find a way to" questions. In developing these questions, students consider solutions that might address the problem. These problem-posing questions are "I wonder" questions and lead to formulating predictions.

"I Wonder" Questions

- I wonder ... how does removing a seed's coat help speed up germination?

- I wonder ... to what extent does soil help a seed germinate?

- I wonder ... what would happen if really old, outdated seeds were planted?

- I wonder ... would growing a seed in water only make a bigger plant than starting the seed in soil only?

- I wonder ... what would happen if seeds were placed under a grow light?

- I wonder ... how would putting a seed in a cup of water on the first day help it sprout?

For purposes of illustration in this chapter, these questions are asked:

Questions:

Which will sprout more seedlings, a set of seeds soaked in water or a set not soaked in water? How does light influence the germination of these seeds?

Testable Prediction

Cothron, et al. (1996) suggests two questions that can be used to help structure a brainstorming process as the prediction statement is developed. The first question centers on what will be changed in the experiment. Students may brainstorm everything that could be changed that might have an effect on seed germination, as shown below.

What Could I Change (Set of Materials, Actions, or Environment) to Affect Seed Germination?						
Seed	Water	Soil	Light	Container	Fertilizer	Temperature
age	amount	amount	intensity	size	amount	range
variety (type)	frequency	type	source	composition	frequency	duration
coat	source	additives	color	drainage	method of application	source

Adapted from Cothron, et al. (1996).

The next question centers on **how the response of the seed to this change will be measured or described**. Students brainstorm possible answers, such as the following:

- First signs of plant growth, measured in days.
- Number of seeds out of the whole set of seeds that germinate, measured as a percent.
- Count the number of seeds that germinate, measured as a whole number.
- Amount of seeds germinating fastest, measured as rate (per unit time).
- Fastest seedling growth, embryonic plant length measured in centimeters.

After students have had a chance to brainstorm these two questions, they can use this template (Klentschy, 2008) to write their prediction:

If I change _____ , then I predict _____ will happen because _____ .

From a question such as, "I wonder what would happen if the seed coat was removed before germination?" a prediction such as, "If I remove a seed coat before germinating a seed, then I predict that the seeds without a seed coat will germinate faster than seeds with seed coats still on. "Faster" is the measurement, and students can measure "faster" by counting the number of days it takes for a sprout to appear. The students could have predicted "slower" instead; the direction of measurement depends on their rationale or background information for expecting this result.

The "because" clause supplies a student's rationale for their prediction, such as, "*because* already having the seed coat removed is one less thing for the seed to have to do before germinating" or, "*because* shedding the seed coat will allow the seed to absorb more water."

Taking a Stand   It is important that the prediction "take a stand." "If I water one seed but not the other, then I predict the seeds will germinate differently" is not a stance because "differently" is not a specific, measurable outcome. However, predicting that the seed will germinate "faster" or "slower" is forecasting what direction the difference will take, which helps guide the experimental design and data collection. More practiced scientists will quantify the stance and predict 10% faster, twice as fast, or three times as fast. On the other hand, no difference in germination rates for seeds with and without water could also be predicted. Stating that no differences in germination rates are anticipated due to watering would be making a "*null hypothesis*." A null hypothesis predicts that there will be no relationship between the variables. In this example, the student predicts that watering has no difference on germination: "I predict that watering a seed will not make it germinate any faster than a seed that is not watered because cactus plants grow in the desert without water."

Predicting with Illustrations   Young children, English-language learners, or pre-emergent readers may make a drawing or illustration of their prediction. For example, the prediction, "I predict the root (not the leaves) will form first from the seed as measured by observation, because then the root can take up water" could be illustrated with a root coming down from a seed without a shoot emerging. If students are illustrating, they should then clarify their thinking by talking through their prediction with their teacher and labeling where appropriate.

Prediction for Sample Inquiry   For the sample inquiry in this chapter, two questions are posed in order to better help the story's characters decide how to best proceed with growing bean plants from their "seeds for growing" jar. Notice how adding another question impacts the complexity of the prediction.

Questions:
Which will sprout more seedlings, a set of seeds soaked in water or a set not soaked in water? How does light influence the germination of these seeds?

Prediction:
If I pre-soak one group of seeds in water but not another group and place half of each group in the light and half in the dark, then I predict more seeds will sprout in the water-soaked set in the dark because seeds are usually planted underground where it is dark and watered.

Identifying Variables

Understanding *variables* is key to good experimental design. Experiments are, at their core, exploring relationships: What will happen if I change something? Scientists know that they cannot change too many variables at once; if they do, they cannot be certain how or what to attribute any changes observed.

This sample experiment models how two independent variables can be manipulated simultaneously. For illustration purposes, water is one independent variable. One group of bean seeds can be pre-soaked in water, and another group of seeds will not. The second independent variable is light or the absence of light. These two independent variables will be sorted systematically so that results can be attributed to particular combinations of the independent variables. The pre-soaked seeds will be divided into two subsets. Half of the soaked seeds will be placed on moist paper towels and placed in a lighted spot and half will be placed on moist paper towels in a darkened area. Likewise, the non-soaked seeds will also be subdivided, but kept dry. Half of the non-soaked seeds will be placed on dry paper towels in the light and half of the non-soaked seeds placed on dry towels in the dark. The use of paper towels stands in for the planting medium (moist or dry), and putting these towels in clear zip top bags allows students to observe the progress of seeds' sprouting.

For this sample inquiry, the dependent variable is the number of seeds that *might* sprout. The change must be qualified with "might"—and not "will"—because not all independent variables elicit a response. In this case, the number of sprouted seeds will be counted in each combined condition of the independent variables.

Finally in this sample inquiry, there are some things that will be held constant: air temperature, length of time for soaking the seeds, length of time for the experiment, size and type of container, and use of a paper towel for a growing medium.

Students should record a list of each variable in their science notebooks. This is a brief list, not an extended paragraph. The following is a sample:

Variables:
Independent Variables: Water: (pre-soak seeds or not).
Light: (exposure to light or not).
Dependent Variable: Number of germinated (sprouted) seeds.
Constants: Air temperature, length of time for the experiment, size and type of container, and use of a paper towel for a growing medium.

Procedure

The procedure must consider each combination of independent variables (water/no water and light/no light), the response of the seeds to these combinations (germination), and how that response will be measured (counting). Finally, the procedure considers how many times the experiment will be repeated (*trials*) and what has to be kept constant the entire time.

The Independent Variable's Role in the Procedure   Because this sample experiment will demonstrate how two independent variables can be applied in purposeful ways, students can construct a flowchart to illustrate what will be done. This will facilitate writing the procedure.

Some students may select different independent variables to combine in a single investigation, such as seed coats removed/not removed, placed in either a hot or cold environment, or perhaps different varieties of seeds compared in different soils (e.g., slightly acidic or basic). As long as the independent variables are combined systematically, then meaningful results can be ascribed to the configuration of variables. Having two independent variables in a single experiment opens up many avenues of data analysis and presents opportunities to tier experimental design for advanced students..

The Dependent Variable's Role in the Procedure   The procedure must include testing more than one seed in each category. For example, if one bean was pre-soaked and not another, and different results occur, we cannot say with certainty that the changes are due to soaking. Many possibilities are not accounted for. For example, possibly one seed was not fertilized by pollen (and therefore will never germinate) or possibly one seed is too old to germinate. It is helpful to have a sample size of seeds that is large enough so that these anomalies do not give false results. The large sample size is also good for calculating average behaviors of the seed germination process.

List versus Paragraph Style for Procedure   Students usually prefer to list their procedure as numbered line items. However, if students are working on developing mastery of

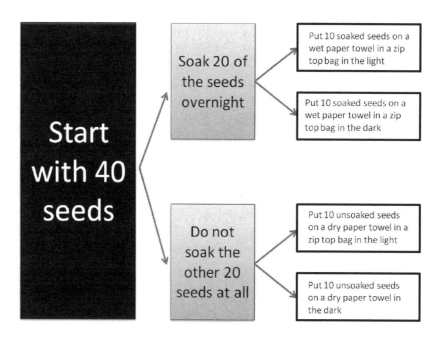

Figure 8.2.

an organized paragraph, then the instructor might recommend a paragraph format. If writing in a paragraph, consider the following structure:

- The first sentence is the *topic sentence.* It tells the reader the purpose of the experiment.
- The next sentences give the procedural steps for the experiment. For clarity, begin these sentences with transition words like, "First," "Second," "Next," and "Finally." A list of helpful "signal" words for power writing is available at http://cte.jhu.edu/techacademy/web/2000/campbellk/PowerWritDef.html.
- In the last sentence of the paragraph, make it clear that the experiment has concluded.

Visualizing the directions first as a chronological list functions as an outline for writing the procedure in paragraph format. An example of the list format is given below.

Procedure:

1. Get two identical containers.
2. Count out two piles of the same kind of bean seeds. Each pile should have 20 beans.
3. Put 20 seeds in each container.
4. Set one container aside. Don't do anything with it.
5. Fill the other container with 1 cup of tap water.
6. Place this second container of seeds next to the first set and leave overnight.
7. The next day, soak two paper towels with water and get two dry paper towels.
8. Put one wet paper towel into each of two zip top bags. Label one bag "Soaked/Light" and the other bag "Soaked/Dark."
9. Put 10 soaked seeds into a zip top bag labeled "Soaked/Light" and put the other 10 seeds from this container into the zip top bag labeled "Soaked/Dark." Seal the bags.
10. Put one dry paper towel into each of the other two zip top bags. Label one bag "Not Soaked/Light" and the other bag "Not Soaked/Dark."
11. Put 10 unsoaked seeds into the zip top bag labeled "Not-Soaked/Light" and put the other 10 seeds from this container into the zip top bag labeled "Not-Soaked/Dark." Seal the bags.
12. Store the two bags labeled "Light" on the counter. Store the two bags labeled "Dark" in a cupboard.
13. Every day, when you get to school, look at the seeds.
14. Open each bag and count how many have sprouted.
15. Write it in your notebook.
16. If the paper towel is drying out in the two soaked bags, spray water from a misting bottle into each bag so the towels stay moist.

Data Organizer

Information (measurements and observations) collected in an investigation is termed *data.* This is a plural term. One way to organize data collected is to design a table, graph, or chart. Rather than restricting students to a single teacher-selected graphic organizer, ask students to design a chart or table that will help them think about the relationship between independent and dependent variables. The teacher can move around the room to monitor and give feedback to make sure that the data organizers are logical and will work with the project. Alternatively, if time is limited, the teacher can collect the notebooks, review the data organizers, and provide constructive comments in the notebooks' margins.

Baseline Data   Try to develop the habit of recording *baseline data* on a graphic organizer. Baseline data are a scientific way of saying "what the data looked like when the experiment began." These data are often referred to at the conclusion of the experiment, as many scientists look at the original data and then at the final data to draw mathematically based conclusions.

Sample Data Organizers   For the sample investigation, a variety of data organizers are possible. The following are a few possibilities.

Day	Number of Sprouts in the Soaked/ Light Bag	Number of Sprouts in the Soaked/ Dark Bag	Number of Sprouts in Not-soaked/ Light Bag	Number of Sprouts in the Not-soaked/ Dark Bag
Monday (first day—baseline data)	0	0	0	0
Tuesday				
Wednesday				
Thursday				
Friday (last day—final data)				

An alternative might be a bar graph with the day of the week on the horizontal (left-to-right) "X" axis and the number of sprouts on the vertical (up-and-down) "Y" axis. Each day, students would consider graphing four bars: two for the soaked seeds (light and dark environments) that had sprouted and two for the not-soaked seeds (light and dark environments) that had sprouted. Colored pencils easily color-code the data; students should include a key to make clear what is being measured. For example, see the following graph:

After students select a data organizer, they draw it by hand in their science notebooks, using a ruler or straight edge. By keeping all data in the science notebook, the students are building a daily cumulative record of their thinking, which becomes very useful at the end of the experiment, when conclusions must be drawn.

Working in the Science Notebook: During the Experiment

Conducting the Experiment and Recording Data and Observations

With the procedure and data organizer in place, students have a clear vision for how to move forward.

Time to Record Data   The experimental design of this sample inquiry means that data will be collected for a few minutes each day. The teacher can help to make sure that this time is available. Each day, data are recorded until the experiment reaches its pre-

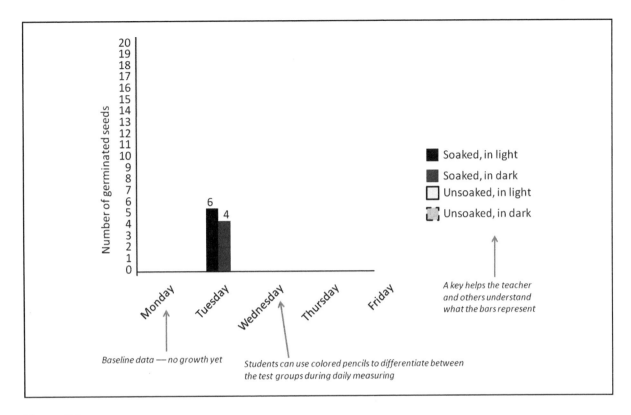

Figure 8.3.

determined conclusion. Given the busy curricula schedules in elementary school, the teacher may work jointly with the students to help them decide on a conclusion date for the experiment. Make sure that all constants are held steady and the seeds remain in their designated bags under specified experimental conditions.

Sketching Observations   Recording of information goes beyond recording numbers, however. Encourage students to use hand lenses or magnifying glasses for a close-up view of seed growth. These visual observations help make their learning concrete as they view what part of the plant emerges from the seed first or how much each of these parts of the plant grows each day.

Many students are visual learners, and sketching the progress of the seeds can help students think through and construct meaning about what they are observing. Encourage students to draw not only the silhouette shape of what they are seeing but to provide as much realistic detail as possible. See Chapter 2 for suggestions on how to draw scientifically. Labeling these drawings provides an authentic opportunity to use science vocabulary.

Young children, who may lack the fine motor skills to draw seeds in their small actual size, should be encouraged to fill their paper with an oversized seed drawing so that there is plenty of space to draw details.

Observing for Validation of Prior Knowledge   When making predictions using the templates, students use "because" to explain their prediction. This explanation reveals their prior knowledge. Students can use observation time to watch to see if their prior knowledge is accurate. Using written notes or drawings helps students track the seeds' daily experience and begin to think about whether or not their prior knowledge was accurate.

Working in the Science Notebook: After the Experiment

Claims and Evidence

Students now look at the data—instead of relying on prior knowledge or their "hunch"—to find patterns. The patterns will lead them to form a "claim" about what is happening, and the data patterns provide the supporting evidence. Especially with beginning scientists, conferencing with the teacher is important to be sure that they are using data—and not prior knowledge—to construct the claim.

In the sample experiment, there were ten beans in each test group. This makes it relatively easy to compare data from the soaked/light, soaked/dark, not-soaked/light, and not-soaked/dark columns of the data organizer. However, converting these numbers into percents can provide another kind of useful data. Use this formula below to convert the data into percentages.

Calculating the percent germination for each set of seeds allows class data to be compared even if the original data sets' size were different.

To make a claim, the data can be examined from multiple angles. At first a student may look at the overall variable of soaked and not-soaked seeds. Each time, the evidence is presented followed by an assertion. For the sample case, the following might be what a student would write in his or her science notebook:

> **Claims and Evidence:**
> **Because only soaked seeds sprouted in both the light and in the dark and none (0%) of non-soaked seeds sprouted in either the light or dark environments, I claim that water plays a role in seed germination and light does not.**

Conclusion

During the conclusion stage, a student reexamines the original prediction in light of what was discovered during inquiry. The sample inquiry prediction suggested that more sprouts would grow from pre-soaked beans than from not-soaked beans. Given the sample

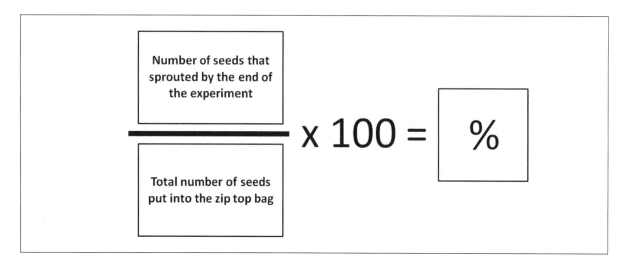

Figure 8.4.

data, that prediction was supported. Students also learned that light did not play a role in germination as soaked seeds spouted in both light and dark environments. This suggests both a conclusion and an inference. The inference is that because seeds are capable of germinating in the dark, they are not using sunlight to make their food at this time so their food source must come from the seed itself. And the conclusion is that seeds need water to germinate. The fact that no unsoaked seeds placed in dark or light environments germinated also provides evidence that supports this conclusion.

A review of the data does not support the original prediction, as an equal number of seeds sprouted in the dark as in the light environment.

Conclusions also ask students to summarize findings and think about experimental error.

Conclusion:
I conclude that light plays no role in seed germination because equal numbers of soaked seeds sprouted in the light and dark. My prediction was not supported. I also learned that water is necessary for seeds to germinate because only those seeds exposed to water sprouted. Experimental error may have included letting the paper towel dry out for those soaked seeds in the dark.

Scientists can often answer more than one question by studying a single set of data. For example, the question, "What sprouts first, the shoot or root?" could be answered by examining daily drawing of seed growth from a science notebook. Which sprouts first: beans that are pre-soaked and their seed coats loosened or those seeds that are pre-soaked and their seed coats do not loosen? Which has a higher germination rate, pre-soaked seeds that are kept wet or pre-soaked allowed to dry out or seeds that are not pre-soaked but placed on wet paper towels?

Next Steps

When students develop new questions along the way, they may be motivated to explore those new queries. For example, here are some "next step" queries that might have come out of this chapter's sample inquiry and might require a continuation of data collection or collecting a brand new data set:

Next Steps:
- **If we ran this experiment for more days, would any of the not-soaked seeds ever sprout? What would be the final germination rate for soaked seeds in the light? In the dark?**
- **Why don't all seeds grow into plants?**
- **How old can a seed be and still germinate?**
- **What would happen if the seeds were left to soak for three days? Could a seed drown?**
- **We didn't use soil in our project. How would our experiment have been different if we had used soil instead of a zip top bag and paper towels?**
- **Would a damp cloth towel work the same way as a damp paper towel? Or does the towel need to break down over time to support the germination process?**

Some of these questions can be answered by initiating a new round of hands-on science inquiry. Other questions may require expert knowledge, such as books or online resources. The school library media specialist can be a key player in "expert knowledge" research, identifying useful materials, database references, and Web sites, working either with the whole class or with small groups.

Project and Assessment: A Seed Monologue

The story starter, "Spouting into the Future" asks students to provide some guidance for growing a jar of seeds that have been sitting around for a long time. Students are to provide information on the best environment for getting seeds to germinate to Alumi and Nyl. One way to convey this information back to the story characters is through a seed monologue or short speech. In this case, the seed will "speak" back to Alumi and Nyl. This provides students an opportunity to be creative with the scientific information they have learned about seed germination.

Creating a Monologue

TV shows and live stage plays sometimes have a moment where one character talks for a paragraph or two without interruption. This is known as a monologue. To create a monologue, students take on the character of a seed and ponder: What does it feel like to soak overnight? Feel the seed coat split? Send out the first root, then the first leaf or leaves? Students should use the sequence of seed germination as the basis of their monologue and embellish it with observations. The setting for the monologue could also be futuristic, but all information concerning seed germination has to be based on evidence collected from their investigation. To bring closure to the story starter, the seed will "speak" to Alumi and Nyl about the germination experience and offer advice on how they can get their seeds to germinate. Here are some questions to stimulate student thinking and help compose the monologue:

- A seed sitting in a jar for a long time is dormant. How does it feel to "wake up?"
- Was soaking in water overnight beneficial?
- Are you a monocot or dicot? What is the difference?
- Are you a producer or consumer? What is the difference?
- What is the hardest or easiest thing for you, as a germinating seed, to do?
- What helped you the most in shedding your seed coat?
- What are you looking forward to the most after germination?
- Are you in a hurry? How fast are you growing?
- The seeds in the bag next to you are not sprouting at all. What do you say to them?
- Do you feel the need for water every day or was one jolt at the beginning enough?
- What changes do you make from day to day?
- Which did you grow first, your root or shoot? Why?
- What advice would you, the germinated seed, give to our time travelers for growing your fellow seeds?
- What advice do you give to Alumi and Nyl so that they can successfully germinate seeds to provide a sustainable food source for their friends and family?

Presentation

In *6+1 Traits of Writing: The Complete Guide,* Culham (2003) lists six writing traits and a "plus one": presentation. This project gives students a chance to orally present their thinking to the class. After completing the writing workshop process, students share their monologues with the group. Here are some suggestions for stellar oral presentations:

1. Write or type your monologue on every other line. If you are using a computer, use an extra-large font so you can read quickly.
2. Practice your monologue in front of the mirror, in the car on the way to school, with a friend, or in the shower. The more you practice, the more confident you will become.
3. Try practicing twice as slow as you normally speak. That will help you to not speed through it when you are nervous.
4. Try to "read ahead." Look down to read the beginning of the sentence, then look up from your paper to speak the entire sentence.
5. Take a deep breath before you start. Exhale your anxiety!
6. Have fun.

Psst ... I Spy a Prefix

Remember earlier in the chapter, when we learned that a monocotyledon has only one seed leaf? The prefix "mono" means one, so a monologue is a speech by one person. A dialogue has the prefix "di," meaning two, so a dialogue is a conversation between two people, just as a dicotyledon is a seed with two seed leaves.

Technology Connection: Podcast It!

Consider podcasting or videocasting the seed monologues instead of presenting them in person. See Chapter 7 for more information about creating a podcast.

Rubric

See page 140 for a sample rubric.

Extensions

Questions to Consider

1. Which of the following factors must be present to begin seed germination?

   a. paper towel
   b. *water*
   c. soil
   d. many seeds together

2. What is the source of nutrition for the embryonic plant?

   a. sunlight
   b. water
   c. *seed cotyledon*
   d. air

Seeds Monologue Rubric

	Acting Apprentice (2 points)	Supporting Actor or Actress (3 points)	Master Thespian (4 points)
The Science of Seeds	Let's look together at the results of your experiment and some books about seed germination so you can try again.	Think about the conditions in which your seeds germinated in the experiment. How can you, as a seed, use these results to inform Alum and Nyl?	Your monologue tells how necessary water is to the germination process. Bravo!
Idea Development	Go back and answer some of the idea development questions provided. This should help expand the monologue. Let's try again.	This monologue is from the point of view of a seed that is in the process of germinating. What started that process? What happened next?	The seed germination process was clear and easy to follow through your monologue.
Presentation	It's OK to feel nervous. Find a practice buddy who can help you for the next time.	Try saying your monologue with feeling instead of in a monotone.	Your monologue was presented with confidence. Thanks for practicing before performing.

Figure 8.5.

3. Which of the following describes an independent variable?

    a. *action or material that will be altered in the experiment*
    b. measured response to variables changed in the experiment
    c. conditions that will be kept constant
    d. observations made during the experiment

4. A *producer* is best described as any organism that

    a. must obtain nutrients from another source
    b. *can make its own food*
    c. is also a consumer
    d. is an animal

5. Which of the following vocabulary words has the same prefix as *monologue*?

    a. dicotyledon
    b. *monocotyledon*
    c. dialogue
    d. motivation

6. What is the function of an experiment's data organizer in your science notebook?

    a. *a place to record the results of an experiment*
    b. a method of identifying types of variables
    c. a way to arrange the steps of the procedure
    d. a glossary (location of vocabulary)

7. How do "Sprouting into the Future" characters figure out that the beans might be edible?

    a. They draw a conclusion after cooking them.
    b. They experiment by adding water.
    c. They make an observation by tasting them.
    d. *They make an inference by reading the label on the jar.*

8. Which of the following is a "red light" (yes/no) question that needs to be made measurable?

    a. How many seeds would actually germinate if really old, outdated seeds were planted?
    b. *Can you tell by looking at a seed whether or not it will germinate?*
    c. Which sprouts first, the root or shoot?
    d. What is required to begin seed germination?

9. What are baseline data?

    a. *a record of the beginning conditions in an experiment*
    b. a record of the final results of an experiment
    c. the claim made based on the evidence gathered
    d. the basis for a prediction

10. The step-by-step instructions for an investigation are called the:

    a. prediction
    b. *procedure*
    c. evidence
    d. conclusion

Estimation   Read Margaret McNamara's book *How Many Seeds in a Pumpkin?* (2007), in which a first-grade teacher brings three pumpkins of different sizes to school. Students try to estimate how many seeds are in each. Charlie is surprised to learn that the tiniest pumpkin his teacher brought to school has the most seeds. The readers learn about estimation and the fact that the deeper and more plentiful the ribs are on a pumpkin, the more seeds it has. Try replicating this book's experiment in your classroom.

Life Cycle of Plants   Explore the life cycle of plants with Gail Gibbons' *From Seed to Plant* (1993), Allan Fowler's *From Seed to Plant* (2001), or Helene A. Jordan's *How a Seed Grows* (1992).

Drama   Read Eric Carle's *The Tiny Seed* (1987). Using the ensemble pantomime technique, in which all children play the same role at the same time, ask all of the students in the class to portray the tiny seed. Alternatively, split the class in half: have half play the tiny seed and half play the other seeds (Fontichiaro, 2007).

Alternatively, have students act out what is happening as another student reads his monologue aloud.

Another drama technique for very young students is to act out Ruth Krauss' *The Carrot Seed* (2004), which chronicles a boy's care of a seed until it grows into a carrot.

Math   Estimate how many seeds are in a green bell pepper. Then cut the pepper into quarters. Count the number of seeds in that quarter, and multiply by four for a more accurate count. Do green, yellow, and red bell peppers have similar numbers of seeds?

Compare growing edible seeds and non-edible seeds. Are there differences in germination rates of seed? Rates of plant growth (height/time)? Try growing a really large seed (avocado) in a cup of water.

Cross Sections and Long Sections   To learn more, scientists sometimes cut things to look at what is inside (See Chapter 4). When they cut something in half the short way, it is called a cross section. If you cut a cross section of a cucumber, you will end up with a round slice, like you might find at a salad bar. Open a cucumber at the cross section and draw what you see in your science notebook. Now cut it lengthwise (so each half is a long oval). Draw what you see. What did you learn about how cucumbers make seeds from this activity?

Online Plant Explorations   Put on your detective hats and go online to the University of Illinois Extension's *Great Plant Escape* to learn more about how plants grow and what they need for survival. Visit http://www.urbanext.uiuc.edu/gpe/case1/index.html.

More Ideas for Teaching about Plants   Try http://teachers.net/lessons/posts/1480.html for more lesson plans about plants. Additional resources are available at http://askabiologist.asu.edu/expstuff/experiments/pocketseeds/Pocket_Packet_1.pdf, including photos of the inside of a seed and a seed embryo.

9

Plants: Six Magic Beans

Lesson Overview

Students consider the relationship between a plant's location and its growth pattern as well as whether or not plants begin their life cycles as producers, able to make their own food. After reading a variation of "Jack and the Beanstalk," students explore what conditions are best for plant growth—not just short-term, but for long-term sustainability. The seedlings started in Chapter 8's investigation can be used here by students in grades 3 and up to consider various environmental influences on further growth.

National Science Education Standards

- **Regulation and Behavior:** All organisms must be able to obtain and use resources, grow, reproduce, and maintain stable internal conditions while living in a constantly changing external environment (Grades 5–8).

Outcomes

Emerging scientists will be able to:

- Measure the rate of plant growth.
- Explain that plants begin growing by using food stored in the seed.

Practiced scientists will be able to:

- Document the relationship between plant growth and environmental conditions.
- Describe that once seed food has been used up, the plant either makes its own food or perishes.

Awakening Prior Knowledge

What Happens When You Run Out?

To begin a discussion on sustainability, ask students these questions:

- **What happens to a car when it runs out of gasoline?** (The car stops moving.)
- **What would happen to restaurant business if the restaurant ran out of food?** (Customers would stop coming until more food was ordered.)
- **Could a plant run out of food?** (No, because a plant can make its own food using sunlight.)

What Do Students Already Know about Plants?

Ask students to talk about what they know about plants growing. What might they have observed at home, at school, or in the community regarding plant life? What do they see as successful environments for plants to grow? What do they see people doing to keep plants growing?

Next, turn students' attention to a *seedling*, a plant just starting out. If plants make their food from sunlight, how can a seedling make its own food if it starts out as a seed underground in the soil and has no contact with light? Just like a lot of living organisms need help getting food at the start of their lives—from mother's milk or from an egg's stored nutrients when hatching—seedlings also get some assistance from food stored in seeds. Emerging seedlings have a built-in, life-sustaining mechanism that helps the seedling survive until the stem surfaces from underground and green leaves are formed to absorb sunlight and make food. This mechanism, however, has a limit. If a seedling's true leaves do not reach sunlight before the seed's built-in food supply runs out, the plant will die. What might cause a delay in a seedling's true leaves reaching sunlight? It could be that the seed was planted too deep in the soil or was planted, strewn, or blown by the wind into a place where plants won't grow, such as under a log, a shade cloth, or in a dark place.

Note these possible causes of delay on a piece of chart paper, on a bulletin board, or on a part of the whiteboard that will not be erased until the conclusion of the experiment.

Story Starter: Six Magic Beans

Please see the reproducible on pages 145 and 146.

Preparing for Inquiry

Reviewing the Story

Fairy tales, by their very nature, ask us to suspend belief. Events are happening that could not possibly be real, such as talking animals, wizards, and magic seeds. Begin by discussing these elements of the story starter with students. Then ask, "What magic could a bean seed possess? Is it magic? Or is it nature?" It may appear magical that an entire plant can emerge from a single seed given very little input from Mother Nature in the form of rain. However, seeds that have been fertilized by pollen contain a plant embryo and enough stored food to give a seedling the energy it needs to germinate and push up from the dark soil into the light above ground. The following questions and ideas can spark a classroom discussion:

- **Ask students to speculate on the significance of the rainfall in the story**. (Seeds need only water to begin the process of germination.)
- **In "Six Magic Beans," how was Bluebell, the cow, seen as a *sustainable* (continuing) resource by Jack's mother?** (The cow could provide milk over and over again.)
- **How were the six magic beans also seen as a sustainable resource?** (Bean seeds grow into bean plants, which, in turn, produce more beans to eat or seeds to plant.)
- **Would it be cheaper to raise a cow or raise bean plants?** (In many climates, it is cheaper to grow plants, because bean plants make their own food; cows must be fed.)
- **The beans in the story were simply thrown out the window. If you throw a seed on the ground, will it grow into a plant?** (No, not without water. Students may also incorrectly answer that the seed cannot germinate unless it is buried in dirt.)

Six Magic Beans

Once upon a time, there lived a boy named Jack, who lived with his mother. Life was hard for them, and they often went to bed hungry.

One spring day Jack's mother told him that the situation had become desperate. "You will have to take our cow Bluebell to market and sell her. Be sure you get a good price, because we will need the money to buy food for the next few months," she said.

"I'll make sure I trade you for the best deal I can get," he whispered in Bluebell's ear as he reluctantly tied a rope around her neck.

Jack and Bluebell walked slowly along the worn dirt road. As the road bent sharply to the left, a man in a long black cloak suddenly appeared in the middle of the road. "My boy!" he said. "Why are you traveling down this road with a cow?"

"Mother says we have to sell Bluebell," said Jack. "We need the money for food."

"Money?" said the mysterious man. "I can trade you something far more valuable than money." The man held out six beans. "These are magic beans that are better than money. These beans will change your life. Would you consider trading these six magic beans for Bluebell?"

Jack believed in the magic beans and quickly agreed to the trade.

Jack hurried home, eager to share his good news with his mother.

"Jack! Back so soon? You have the money already?"

"No. I've got something better—magic beans!"

"What! There's no such thing as magic. I thought you were smarter than to trade our precious Bluebell for a handful of ordinary beans! Now we have nothing!"

She threw his beans out the window and sent Jack to bed without any supper. (Which, to tell the truth, wasn't that unusual, because they rarely had enough food for dinner anyway.)

To add to Jack's melancholy, it rained all night long.

The next morning, Jack ran to the window and looked out into the yard. He couldn't believe his eyes. There, where his mother had thrown the beans so angrily the day before, he saw some sprouts —a few in the dark corners of the yard, a few in the sun, even a few that had been dusted over with dirt. Could the beans be magic after all?

For the next few days, Jack and his mother watched the beans. They hadn't all landed in the same place. Some were in the sun, some in the shade, and some in the darkest corners of the yard. Some landed in dirt, and some didn't. None were the same.

Before you think you've heard this story before, think again. This isn't the story of a magic beanstalk or a golden harp or giant

> ## These beans will change your life.

Figure 9.1.

From *Story Starters and Science Notebooking: Developing Student Thinking Through Literacy and Inquiry* by Sandy Buczynski and Kristin Fontichiaro. Santa Barbara, CA: Teacher Ideas Press. Copyright © 2009.

that says, "Fee, Fi, Fo, Fum!" This is a different tale.

Over time, Jack noticed that some beans were growing faster than others. Some were so pale that they were nearly white, and some were bright green. Some still never sprouted.

Jack's mother regretted having given up the cow, which gave them milk each day, which had been so important to their daily diet. She realized that the bean plants could be sustainable, too—if she could get all of the beans to grow, they could eat beans all summer and be healthy and happy. She watched the pale plants that had grown in the dark grow the fastest … and then, suddenly and without warning, the pale plants withered and died.

"Why would the tallest plants die so quickly?" she asked Jack.

"I don't know, Mom, but you always say we should ask an expert. What if we wrote to Holly Hock and Cal LaLilly, who write the World of Gardening column in the newspaper? Maybe they could help us know how to keep the other plants alive."

"Luckily, we still have some paper and a pencil," said his mother. "I'll get started."

Dear Ms. Hock and Mr. LaLilly:

We tossed six beans into the yard, and they're all growing differently. The ones that grow in the dark seem to grow really fast and spindly. The ones deep in the soil haven't come up at all. What conditions are necessary for plants to grow well?

Thank you in advance,

Jack's Mother

Figure 9.2.

- **The most important detail from the story starter is that rain fell overnight. How would you know if the seeds received any of the rainfall?** (The seeds could only have germinated if they had received water, so germination is evidence of rainfall. Reference Chapter 8 to remind students that water is essential for germination of seeds.)

- **Each of the seeds landed in a unique place for germination. What were some of the environments that seeds ended up in?** (Sun, shade, dark, dirt, no dirt, landed deep in soil.)

- **If you were a scientist, what might be an environment you could test to know if it is possible for a seedling to grow under that condition?** (Water only, in a closet, in a shuttle orbiting earth, etc.)

Connecting to Science

The story starter indicated that a seedling shot up fast but then perished. What would cause that? That is probably a question that children cannot answer without knowing more about the science behind seed growth.

Figure 9.3. A plant growing in the dark has a pale color and a tall, spindly stalk.

Very long, skinny, weak stems and small leaves that are a pale yellowish color are characteristic of plants grown in the dark. The seedling's yellow color is termed *chlorosis* (kluh-ROH-sis) and is due to a lack of chlorophyll, the green pigment that captures light energy for *photosynthesis*. The rapid increase in stem height enhances the probability that the seedling will reach light and be able to begin the process of food production through photosynthesis.

This phenomenon is known as *etiolation* (ee-tee-oh-LAY-shun) and is caused by an increased concentration of *auxin* (AWK-sin). Auxin is a plant hormone found in the shoot's tip that, in the absence of light, increases the stem's rate of growth. In nature, this mechanism gives seedlings an advantage in the forest where larger plants may be blocking sunlight. However, etiolation over a long period of time can be a disadvantage because the plant is growing fast and consuming its seed food resources without creating any new food from sunlight. When the seed's food reserves are used up, a plant grown in the dark will die. If the etiolated plant is exposed to light, then photosynthesis takes over the food supply. As a result, the plant revives and turns green (evidence that photosynthesis has occurred)

Figure 9.4. A plant growing in the light has a healthy green color and no spindly growth.

The photos on page 147 demonstrate the difference between a plant experiencing *etiolation* after growing in the dark (see figure 9.3) and one grown in daylight (see figure 9.4.)

Inventory Walk   One way to provide an opportunity for students to begin framing productive questions is to give them direct contact with a variety of seedling growth patterns as listed below. For the inventory walk, pantomime Jack's mother throwing the six magic beans out of the window. Then show students some sample seedlings that have resulted after the rains at Jack's house. Can the students describe a possible environment that might produce a seedling that looks like the examples shown?

Materials List

- **6 dry bean seeds**
- **6 bean seedlings for demonstration.** Show students a variety of possible beanstalk scenarios: bean seeds that did not grow at all and bean seedlings that are tall, short, bushy, spindly, green, yellow, water-logged, dried out, healthy, or in poor health. Different varieties of bean seedlings could also be displayed, such as lima or green beans, or bush or climbing varieties of bean plants. Ask students to wonder what could have caused this diversity of seedling results. (Environment and/or genetics.)
- **Germinated seeds.** If this inquiry follows the germination inquiry in Chapter 8, it is fine to use those seeds. If not, seeds will need to be germinated from scratch, and enough will be needed for each student group to place several seeds into multiple environments for experimentation. Any package of dry beans from the grocery store (such as pea, lima, or pinto beans) can be used, or packets of garden seeds can be germinated.
- **Plastic or paper cups with a hole punched in the bottom**
- **Gravel**
- **Bag of soil**
- **Measuring cup**

Vocabulary: Power Words

Powerful words create an impression in our minds. Plant study generates some fairly significant scientific vocabulary. One approach to this vocabulary is to help students form a mental image to remember how the word is pronounced. For example, "ee-tee-oh-LAY-shun" may conjure up a conversation that goes something like this: E-T (as in phone home), Olé (bullfight cheer), shun (slang for lotion). Or perhaps use small words that students might be more familiar with to string together forming the pronunciation of the scientific word. For example: foe–toe–sin–the–sis could be remembered as foe (as in fee, fye), toe (on your foot), Sin (try to avoid), the (the), sis (short for sister) and producer as pro (sports pro)–do (can do)–sir (yes sir). Once students are comfortable with a scientific vocabulary word's pronunciation, they are comfortable using the word as part of their science talk. Vocabulary words useful in this inquiry investigation are as follows:

- **Etiolation**: Rapid elongation of a plant's stem due to absence of light.
- **Photosynthesis**: Process by which plants convert carbon dioxide and water into glucose (a kind of simple sugar) using solar energy and chlorophyll pigment.
- **Producer**: An organism capable of making its own food (plants, blue-green algae, and some bacteria).
- **Seedling**: New plant growth emerging from seed.

Working in the Science Notebook: Before the Experiment

Student-Generated Questions

To generate a question for investigation, students need to know, "What are we trying to find out?" Ultimately, students want to learn what conditions are necessary to grow plants well so that they can write back, as Holly Hock or Cal LaLilly, to Jack's mother with advice. From the inventory walk, students see that six magic beans could have grown into very different seedlings according to the environment in which they landed or the type of seed it was to begin with. It is also possible that the seedlings did not grow at all. The assumption from the story is that the variations in seedling growth are ascribed either to the various environmental conditions in which the seed landed or to the variety of seed. Since it rained overnight, students know that water was provided for the seeds. The story starter offers many avenues for questions.

"A Plant Growing Well"   The first consideration from the story that students may address is what constitutes a "plant growing well." They need to be able to define the characteristics they would look for to determine if a plant were healthy. To generate this definition, ask students to list in their notebooks characteristics that they expect to see in a healthy plant. Responses might include: a nice green color, getting taller daily, bushy, a certain number of leaves, or production of flowers or fruit.

Once traits of a healthy plant have been listed, ask students to think about how they would measure each trait and to add that measurement to the list in their notebooks. For "getting taller," height can be measured in centimeters. For "bushier," width can be measured in centimeters. To determine "number of leaves" requires counting. "Nice green color" could be determined by comparing the leaves to a color chart created with colored pencils or paint chips, with each color having a corresponding numerical rating. Taking these types of measurements over time will show change in the plant's growth, documenting the path of a "plant growing well."

Measuring Questions   Measuring questions build students' confidence in learning to use measuring tools such as a weighing scale, cylinder, ruler, or color charts. These types of questions necessitate students being careful about taking accurate measurements and also generate numbers that serve as solid evidence for later claims. Measuring questions might include:

- **How many centimeters does a bean seedling grow per day in a(n) ____environmental condition?** (Future growth projections can be made from the resulting data.)
- **How long will seed food sustain a plant's growth when the plant is grown in a dark environment?** (This may yield a surprising answer because some plants can survive weeks of being grown the dark.)
- **How many days will it take a seed planted 5 centimeters deep in soil to emerge to the surface of the soil?**

Comparison Questions   Comparison questions set up two separate experiments, each of which is identical except for the change of a single variable, the independent variable. From the story starter, students suppose that the independent variable is an environmental condition or genetic trait that impacts the seedling's growth.

As students design questions, teacher feedback is an important component of the think-through process. Comparison questions with possible teacher feedback might look like this:

- **How much taller will a seedling grown in the dark get compared to a seedling grown in the light?** (Feedback to student: Does this height mean that the seedling is growing well? Why?)

- **If one seed is planted 5 centimeters deep in the soil and another is planted 10 centimeters deep, which seedling will get the tallest in 10 days?** (Feedback to student: What if one of the seeds is planted so deep it never surfaces? Should you consider multiple seeds at gradual depths?)

- **Which bean seed will grow into the "healthiest" plant, a larger seed or a smaller seed?** (Feedback to student: How will "health" be measured? What is the environmental condition for this growth? What conditions would be held constant for the two different-sized seeds?)

"What Happens" Questions   We often see young students experimenting with "what happens" questions: What happens if I pinch that flower bud? What happens if I stomp my foot in a puddle? What happens if I let the air out of a balloon? These types of questions also begin to form a basis for predicting an outcome. "What happens if this is done? Then I predict that _____(prediction) will happen." Examples include:

- **What happens if I cut a seed in half before planting it?**
- **What happens if fertilizer is applied to a seed before planting it?**
- **What happens if I pinch off the tip of a seedling grown in a dark/light environment?**
- **What happens if I start growing a seedling in the dark but move it to the light?**
- **What happens if I cut off the remaining seed of a plant after the stem has emerged from the soil?**

Redirecting Yes/No Questions   Teachers can help students convert simple questions into questions that are investigable by using what, which, and how.

Original Student Question (Answerable with "Yes" or "No")	Revised Student Question
Are seedlings going to grow tall?	What causes a seed to grow tall?
Can seedlings live in the dark?	What happens to seedlings grown in the dark?
Do seedlings need to be fed to live for a long time?	Which seedlings will live longer: those "fed" fertilizer or those not "fed?"

For the purpose of example in this chapter, this question is posed:

Question:

How long will seed food sustain a seedling's growth in a dark environment?

The answer to this question will provide an opportunity to learn what conditions are necessary to grow plants well. That knowledge, in turn, will be reported back to Jack's mother as advice at the conclusion of the inquiry. But first, students think about and consider the answer to their question by forming a prediction.

Testable Prediction

As discussed in Chapter 3, a prediction crafted in an *if/then* pattern followed by the word *because* helps make students' prior knowledge explicit to the teacher and helps students learn that their predictions should be backed up with a rationale (Klentschy, 2008). As long as the prediction is grounded in a rationale, teachers should help students to pursue them and not step in to "correct" the situation. Real scientists learn a great deal when their initial prediction does not pan out, and so will students. The scientific method includes returning to the prediction at the end of the process, giving students a chance to revisit the prediction and reevaluate assumptions based on the information learned during the investigation.

Students may generate predictions similar to the following:

- *If* I never put a seedling in the light, *then I predict* it will die after two weeks *because* plants need light to make their own food.
- *If* I grow a seedling in a dark environment, *then I predict* seed food will sustain the seedling forever *because* plants have their own food. (Feedback to student: Nice job of using the question's original wording to formulate the prediction. Think about how you will measure "forever." Do most plants live this long? How would you know?) (Teacher monitors, but does not correct, the student's misconception that the seed food lasts forever.)

Students who struggle with written expression might differentiate by sketching instead of writing. For example, they could draw what they anticipate the plant might look like at the end of a ten-day period.

For the sample inquiry, the following is a prediction that grows out of the question from the previous step:

Question:

How long will seed food sustain a seedling's growth in a dark environment?

Prediction:

If **I grow bean seedlings in a dark closet,** *then* **I** *predict* **seedlings will get taller for 10 days and then die** *because* **the seed only has limited food.**

Identifying Variables

In the sample inquiry, the environmental factor that will be different for each set of seedlings is exposure to light. Any differences in the rate of plant growth can then be credited to this one changed aspect of growing, the *independent variable*. The way you measure the independent variable's impact is by examining and measuring the *dependent variable*.

The dependent variable in the sample inquiry is the growth rate of a plant. To calculate a "rate," measurement is taken over time. If a plant's height is used as the indicator of plant growth, then the plant's height would be measured in centimeters. By taking this measurement every day, we can calculate the growth rate (increase in height per day) of the seedling.

After the experiment, students can use these data to make inferences about how the built-in seed food impacts the life cycle of the plant. Depending on the structure of a student's inquiry, comparisons can be made between the longevity and growth rates of plants grown in the dark with those grown in the light, or other varying degrees of darkness.

In order to say with certainty that growth rate (the dependent variable) is a result of the absence of light (the independent variable), then everything else about the experiment must be kept the same; these are the *constants*.

For this sample inquiry, students might make the following notes in their science notebooks:

Variables:

Independent Variable: Absence of light in the growing environment.
Dependent Variable: Growth rate of plant, height measured in centimeters/day.
Constants: Type of seed, type of soil, amount of soil, amount of water, temperature of environment, and type of planting container.

Procedure

In designing a procedure enough detail needs to be given so that when the procedure is replicated, similar outcomes will result. To illustrate how much detail is necessary in a procedure, students can practice "giving directions" for tying shoes, making a peanut butter sandwich, blowing a bubblegum bubble, or getting to the playground from the classroom. In writing these types of sample procedures, students can gain understanding on the amount of detail required by a procedure.

For example, if a student is writing a procedure for walking from the playground to the classroom, it probably isn't necessary to say, "Stand up," or, "Put one foot in front of the other," but information like, "Walk forty paces, then turn left," is critical.

In the illustration of a sample procedure, several plants are placed in each environment to stress that larger *sample sizes* (the number of items placed under each type of experimental condition) minimize error. With a larger sample, students can observe patterns and average data they record, which are more accurate than testing a single plant in each environment.

The following is a sample procedure in a numbered list. Notice how the procedure has a trial period that lasts longer than the prediction's ten-day time period. This is to allow for the possibility that the prediction's results may occur over a period longer than ten days.

Procedure:

1. **Get six bean seedlings that are in identical containers.**
2. **Number each seedling and measure its height. Record this in your notebook.**
3. **Put three of the seedlings in a dark cupboard.**
4. **Put the other three on the windowsill where it is light.**
5. **Use a thermometer to make sure the temperature in both places is the same.**
6. **Measure the amount of water so that you give the same amount to all plants when needed.**
7. **Measure each plant every day using a ruler with centimeters.**
8. **Record the plant height in your science notebook every day.**
9. **Also record and draw observations of what the plant looks like.**
10. **Continue measuring the plants for 30 days.**

The next example is the same procedure in paragraph form:

Procedure:

First, get six bean seedlings in identical containers. Number each container from 1 to 6. Second, measure the height of each seedling and record this data. Next, place three of these bean seedlings in a dark cupboard and place three bean seedlings on a windowsill. Finally, measure the amount of water so you give each plant exactly the same amount of water, as needed. Use a thermometer to measure the temperature, because you need the temperature to be the same in the cupboard as on the windowsill. Every day, measure the height of the plants in centimeters with a ruler. Write down the height of each plant in your science notebook. Also draw or write what the plant looks like each day. Continue measuring the plants for 30 days.

Data Organizer

From the sample procedure above, students can determine the type of information needed on the organizer, such as the number of plants (six), changed variable (light and dark), the units of measurement (centimeters), the frequency with which data will be collected (every day), and total length of the experiment (30 days). The data organizer must, then, be large enough to accommodate 30 days' worth of data gathered from six plants each day.

Because each work group is designing an inquiry around a unique question, different types of data organizers may be necessary. There are often many ways to collect data even for a single inquiry. Students can design data organizers that are accurate and support their preferred thinking modality. Their data organizers are drawn by hand using a ruler or straight edge into the science notebook. The following is a sample data organizer for the sample inquiry:

	Plant 1 (dark)	Plant 2 (dark)	Plant 3 (dark)	Plant 4 (light)	Plant 5 (light)	Plant 6 (light)
Day 0 (Monday)	2 cm	4 cm	5 cm	3 cm	5 cm	2 cm
Day 1 (Tuesday)						
Day 2 (Wednesday)						
Day 3 (Thursday)						
Day 4 (Friday)						
Day 7 (Monday)						
Day 8 (Tuesday)						

Figure 9.5.

Conducting the Experiment and Recording Data and Observations

The teacher has had the opportunity to talk with each group informally as they planned their procedure and data organizer, so he or she is aware of the status and material needs of each group. He or she has assembled the necessary materials and is confident about what each group is about to do. Everyone is prepared.

The teacher should stress the importance of accuracy in measuring plant height. Use the same ruler each day and for each plant. Begin measurement from the base of the plant (the spot where the plant stem meets the dirt) and record measurements in the correct place on the data organizer.

Also encourage students to make annotated illustrations in their science notebooks, attempting realistic drawings as opposed to symbols (see Chapter 2). Observations of details become more evident when students illustrate data. Annotated illustrations add another layer for making meaning of the experiment in the Claims and Evidence section. This is especially true if students are considering not only the longevity of a plant but also that plant's quality of life (coloration, number of leaves formed, overall health of the plant, etc.).

As this sample experiment is designed for data to be recorded over a month, teachers allow approximately ten minutes each day to get out the science notebooks, water the plants (if needed), measure the plants, make observations, and record data.

After the Experiment

Students must have regular practice with the question, "What does this data mean?" (Klentschy, 2005). The following steps scaffold the experience for elementary learners as they work toward a lifelong mastery of data interpretation.

Claims and Evidence

Scientists look at evidence or data, which has been either measured or observed, and ask the question: "What are these results telling me?" This becomes the *claim*. The supporting reasons are the *evidence*. Klentschy (2008) recommends drawing a T-chart or two-column table in the notebook at this stage to help to organize student thinking. Not all students will need a T-chart; some may be able to visualize this concept in their minds and simply write a sentence in their science notebooks.

Claim	Evidence
I claim that seeds provide food for seedlings.	This is because plants grown in the dark survive at the beginning of their life cycle without light to make food.
I claim that plants grown in the dark are not making their own food.	This is because plants in the light were dark green, an indication of photosynthesis (food making) and plants in the dark were yellow.
I claim that plants grown in the dark are not making their own food.	This is because all three plants grown in the dark died before 30 days had passed.

Conclusion

Writing a conclusion empowers students to compare scientific results to prior knowledge, rethink misconceptions, and make a definitive statement. In this way, the conclusion can be viewed as a summary statement of what the student learned. The checklist on page 36 can assist in scaffolding this step.

The original prediction of the sample inquiry was, "*If* bean seedlings are grown in a dark closet, *then* seedlings will get taller for 10 days and then die *because* the seed only has limited food." Sample results revealed the plants only lived half as long as the students predicted they would. This means that the original prediction was not supported by their work. The student can therefore conclude:

> **Conclusion:**
>
> **I conclude that plants grow faster in the dark, because their average growth rate was twice that as those grown in the light. However, I predicted that the seedlings would live for 10 days, and they only lived for five. Therefore, my original prediction was not supported. I learned that plants will grow quickly in the dark but that they cannot keep growing without light. Possible experimental error came when we put the seedlings in the under-the-sink cabinet and the custodian left the doors open, letting in light. That could have affected our results.**

Students may feel that they have "failed" if their prediction was not supported. An unsupported prediction is not a sign of a failed experiment or of poor student thinking. It is through trial and error that new scientific understanding is sometimes found. Practicing scientists regularly discover that their predictions are not supported.

Sometimes an answer is found through *inferences*. Inferring is like "reading between the lines." To make an inference, observations are combined with past experiences to draw a conclusion (Ansberry & Morgan, 2005). Observations are based on using one or more of our five senses (sight, hear, taste, smell, touch) to explain experimental results. For example, through observation it is noted that a seedling grown in the dark is pale yellow and has no green leaves. This observation implies an absence of chlorophyll, a pigment that would make the plant appear green. Chlorophyll is essential for the food-making process of photosynthesis. The observation-based inference is that plants grown in the dark are not making their own food.

After students have shared a summary of their experiments and conclusions with the class, the teacher can remind students of the scientific names behind the phenomena they observed, such as etiolation and photosynthesis. A definition, pronunciation guide, and drawing may be recorded in the glossary section of the science notebook.

Project and Assessment: Newspaper Advice Column on Gardening

Now students are ready to return to the problem identified in the story starter and provide some gardening advice to Jack's mother in the voice of a newspaper advice columnist. Ask the school library media specialist for assistance in gathering a series of sample advice columns from newspapers, magazines, or the Web. As a class, look over the sample advice columns. What do students notice as common features? They may observe that the letter writer is often assigned a pseudonym or "pen name" that describes their conundrum, that the letter asks for help solving a problem, and that the columnist writes a letter back, starting with a greeting and following with practical steps for a solution.

In the case of the story starter, there are two potential columnists, Holly Hock and Cal LaLilly, so that children can write in a character's voice of either gender.

Based on the real-world advice column samples, brainstorm as a class what will be included in the letter. The final list of requirements would be written in the science notebooks for student reference during the writing process. The following is an example:

> **Directions for Advice Column Created by Our Class:**
>
> - **Start by copying Jack's mother's letter into the column.**
> - **Instead of signing it, "Jack's mother," give a pen name instead.**
> - **In the voice of Holly or Cal, start writing back. Use "Dear (pen name)" on the first line.**
> - **Remember to sound like a grown-up gardener!**
> - **Give suggestions and strategies to use for growing plants well.**
> - **Provide gardening strategies to avoid based on what you learned from plants that did not grow very well.**
> - **End with a closing like, "Good luck!"**
> - **Sign your character's name (Holly Hock or Cal LaLilly).**

One fun way to publish this advice column is with a desktop publishing software such as Microsoft Publisher or Pages for a Mac. Framing their work in an "authentic" format can excite kids into doing better quality work. What other articles could be put in the newspaper based on what was learned in this or other chapters?

Rubric

When students receive the rubric ahead of time, they can work toward the teacher's expectations. This minimizes confusion or misread signals. As in other chapters, the rubric brings in two traits from Culham's *6+1 Traits of Writing* (2003): voice and conventions. Often when we read great writing, we "hear" the author's words. That is referred to as *voice*. In this column, students use the voice of a gardening expert, not their own voice. This means that they may adopt the style and vocabulary of an adult expert. The second Culham trait in this activity is *conventions*. These are the mechanics of writing: spelling, punctuation, and grammar. Conventions are the workhorses that give writing a sense of professionalism and polish.

A sample rubric is available on page 157.

Next Steps

Often, after a plant experiment is concluded, students are given the plants to take home and plant in a garden. Consider leaving these plants in the classroom instead so students can use them for further experimentation. What if plants grown in the dark are then transferred to the light? How long will it take before these plants turn green? Or produce bean pods? This allows unanswered or new questions to be explored by students as they arise naturally.

Gardening Column Rubric

	The Gardening Advisor is out! (2 points)	Plant Growth Consultant (3 points)	The Next "Dear Abby" for Gardeners (4 points)
Voice	Who is giving this advice? Make it clear that you are writing to Jack's mother in the voice of a gardening expert.	Sometimes, you sound just like Cal or Holly! Sometimes, I am not certain that you are writing as a gardening expert.	It is immediately clear that you are writing in response to Jack's mother as an advice columnist.
Conventions	Stop the presses! Ask a proofreader to check your work before you publish it in the newspaper.	You're getting there. Another round of proofreading and peer editing, and you will be ready to publish in the paper!	This looks just like a real gardening column! You use great grammar, spelling, and punctuation.
Tips for growing plants well	You hint at what Jack's mother could do to grow plants well. Now provide specific strategies.	Keep using the results of your inquiry to provide reasons why your suggestions should be followed.	You offer Jack's mother many ideas for growing plants and include the reasons that advice should be followed.
Gardening practices to avoid	Words of advice are nice, but why should this advice be followed?	Thanks for the pointers. Tell us more about the scientific reasons for why seedlings did not grow well.	You offer tips on what gardening practices to avoid and the reasons why.

Figure 9.6.

Extensions

Math   Students can determine the average daily growth of a plant by adding up the number of centimeters of each day's growth and dividing by the number of days.

Advanced students can calculate the percent difference of growth for plants grown in various conditions.

Varieties of Beans   How might the story starter be different if it was changed to "Jack and the Radish Plant?" Or "Jack and the Corn Stalk?" Do different seedlings grow the same amount under the same circumstances? Which would grow most quickly? Which have the heartiest stems for Jack to climb? Is there a difference in how dried bean seeds and fresh beans grow?

Local Farming   Different plants are grown in different areas of the country. What kinds of vegetable varieties are grown in your area of the country? How do organic and mainstream farmers work differently to grow healthy vegetables?

Fertilizer   How does fertilizer impact seedling growth? If plants can make their own food, why is "plant food" necessary?

Fractured Fairy Tales   What other fairy tales can students think of that they could rewrite into science inquiries?

Sustainability and Nutrition   If Jack and his mother had kept Bluebell, they would have had a continual source of dairy products. With plants, they can have an ongoing source of vegetables. In the school library, learn more about the nutritional benefits of dairy products and beans and decide which might have more nutritional value for them in the long term.

10

Surveys: Taste Testers to the Rescue!

Lesson Overview

Surveys are powerful tools to measure the likes and dislikes of particular populations, providing valuable input for decision-making. This lesson applies survey methodology to inquiry investigations. As students in grades 3 and up design and execute a survey, peer reactions to various foods are documented, analyzed, and used to inform the school cafeteria. Surveys can also be a first step in developing a science fair project or to give a real-world application for using skills gained in math class, such as graphing and percent calculations. This lesson can be scaffolded for use with all levels of elementary students.

National Science Education Standards

- **Understandings about Scientific Inquiry:** Scientists use different kinds of investigations depending on the questions they are trying to answer. Types of investigations include describing objects, events, and organisms; classifying them; and doing a fair test (experimenting) (Grades K–4).
- **Understandings about Scientific Inquiry:** Different kinds of questions suggest different kinds of scientific investigations. Some investigations involve observing and describing objects, organisms, or events; some involve collecting specimens; some involve experiments; some involve seeking more information; some involve discovery of new objects and phenomena; and some involve making models (Grades 5–8).

Outcomes

Emerging scientists will be able to:

- Explain that surveys are tools for collecting data to determine the preferences or behaviors of a population.
- Develop a strategic approach for organizing data according to categories.

Practiced scientists will be able to:

- Discuss the mean, median, and mode of a data set.
- Read, interpret, and make comparisons and predictions from data represented in charts, line plots, picture graphs, or bar graphs.
- Confidently communicate survey results.

Awakening Prior Knowledge

Ask if students can provide examples of surveys taken in authentic contexts. Their responses might include political polls; consumer testing; general product marketing; parent attitude and need surveys by school districts; and episodes of *Family Feud* on television, which uses survey results as their answer categories.

Young students may have less familiarity with surveys. Invite them to interview family or staff members to gather information or to search in newspapers for samples of graphed survey data. *USA Today*, for example, often publishes survey information in colorful pie charts and graphs. The school library media specialist may have additional examples of survey data that can be explored by students. Another way to introduce surveys is by establishing a free classroom survey with SurveyMonkey (http://www.surveymonkey.com) or Zoomerang (http://www.zoomerang.com).

From these examples, have students list some styles of surveying in their science notebooks. The list might include:

- a written document asking questions of the *respondent* (person who takes part in a survey) that can be sent in the mail;
- questions asked over the telephone (telemarketers calling at dinner time);
- an e-mail-based survey (a feature built into Microsoft Outlook facilitates this);
- an online survey; or
- a face-to-face survey (such as those seen at a shopping mall).

Now that students have a general sense of what a survey is, they read the story starter to inspire them to design and conduct a survey.

Story Starter: Taste Testers to the Rescue

Please see the story on page 161.

Preparing for Inquiry

Reviewing the Story

As an inquiry methodology, surveys can be powerful and useful tools for collecting data on human characteristics, attitudes, thoughts, and behaviors. The goal of a survey is to accurately predict, from a sampling of a population, the attributes or preferences of the larger population. However, the story starter shows an ineffective way to gather data about people's likes and dislikes.

Review the story with students. The following questions can help students develop their understanding of surveys and the purpose for the taste test that they will design for this inquiry.

- **Why did the cafeteria manager, Ms. Gourmand, want to survey the students?**
  (To find out which foods might be popular with those who eat in the cafeteria so she can adjust the menu.)
- **What was the ineffective survey strategy, and why didn't it work?** (Asking people in line was a strategy that did not work because it slowed down the process of getting through the lunch line.)
- **What might be another strategy that could be used to gather this information?** (Ask people when they are not in line.)

TASTE TESTERS TO THE RESCUE!

Malia and Leilani were waiting in line in the cafeteria.

"What's taking so long?" said Malia.

"The line is twice as long as it normally is," said Leilani.

When they got to the front of the line, Ms. Gourmand, the cafeteria manager asked, "Do you prefer your mozzarella cheese in slices or as string cheese?"

"Huh?" said Leilani.

"Crunchy or smooth peanut butter?" asked Ms. Gourmand.

"Umm, I don't get it," said Malia.

"Macintosh or Granny Smith apples?" asked Ms. Gourmand.

"I'm really sorry," said Leilani, "but I don't know what you're talking about."

"I'm taking a survey," said Ms. Gourmand. "I'm asking each person in line just two or three questions about the kinds of food they like best. By the time the whole school goes through my line, I'll know a whole lot about how to redesign our cafeteria menu for next year."

"Oh," groaned Malia. "So that's why the line is so long."

"Yes, but it's for a good cause," said Ms. Gourmand. "Now, do you prefer baby carrots or carrot sticks?"

"Ms. Gourmand, we'll be here all day if you ask us these questions," said Leilani.

"And there are a gazillion kids behind us in line," said Malia.

"How else can I get the information I need?" asked Ms. Gourmand. "This is the only time of day when I see everyone."

"Maybe we can help," said Leilani.

"Yeah," said Malia. "Mrs. Tyler is teaching us all about survey design in science. Let's ask her how we can help."

"Thanks," said Ms. Gourmand. "Now, can I interest you girls in a sample from our new frozen yogurt machine?"

She handed them each a tiny cup of yogurt.

"Yum! Tart!" said Malia.

"Blech! Tart!" said Leilani.

"See, girls? That's why we do surveys! To find out what people like!"

Figure 10.1.

From *Story Starters and Science Notebooking: Developing Student Thinking Through Literacy and Inquiry* ?by Sandy Buczynski and Kristin Fontichiaro. Santa Barbara, CA: Teacher Ideas Press. Copyright © 2009.

- **Does Ms. Gourmand need to ask every single student in line?** (No, a few students could be pulled from the line and polled. Their preferences would represent the greater student body. However, the larger the number of students interviewed [known as the *sample size*], the more likely the results will reflect the greater student body.)
- **In the story, who is the population Ms. Gourmand must consider? (This can be called the "general population.")** (Everyone who eats in the cafeteria.)
- **Are there subsets of (or smaller groups within) this larger population whose preferences could be compared?** (Yes: children, adults, male, female, third graders, fourth graders, vegetarians, carnivores.)

The story also provides an example of a taste test. In a taste test, a food or beverage sample is offered to someone who, in exchange, offers their opinion about the product.

- **How is the taste test administered?** (Two people taste a small amount of the same product.)
- **How do the two tasters react?** (One loves the tart flavor; one does not.)
- **What does this tell us?** (Different people have different taste preferences.)
- **How would you know which of the girl's reaction is most similar to what other girls their age would prefer?** (We do not know enough merely from polling two girls. The best strategy is to extend the taste test to a larger group. The size of the group used for a survey is known as the *survey sample* representing a subset of the general population.)
- **Are there other ways to give a taste test?** (Yes. A blind survey hides the brand name, which reduces response bias, in which people automatically select the brand name they already know. In a comparative survey, brand names are revealed, and the respondent is asked for his or her preference.)
- **Based on other inquiries you have done, what kinds of data organizers might help you with a taste test?** (Tally marks, bar graphs, or charts.)

Spend time reviewing these questions and aligning the story with the vocabulary to help develop a stronger schema that will empower students in the inquiry process.

Connecting to Science

Considerations for Survey Design   A *survey* is a method for collecting information about people's preferences, attitudes, and thoughts via responses to questions, samples, or other stimuli. *Sample size* refers to the number of people you will interview or test in the survey. The larger the sample size, the better the results, because the pool of respondents will more accurately represent the general population from which the sample is drawn. For example, if you want to know the hottest band among fifth-grade girls, the more fifth-grade girls you ask, the more accurate your result will be. If you only ask one girl, you will hear only her opinion, which might not reflect the majority of girls' perspectives. On the other hand, you don't want to have to survey every fifth-grade girl in New York City, either!

There are also limitations of using survey as a methodology for inquiry. First, surveys rely on "self-reporting" data. This means that the soundness of the survey results depends on whether or not the respondents (the people giving answers to the survey) are being truthful in reporting their preferences and tastes. Usually the data collected from surveys are presented in such a way that no one can identify specific individuals who completed the survey. This anonymity helps participants provide honest responses.

Second, although surveys can accurately represent the opinions of a selected population, this does not necessarily mean that these opinions are "correct." The survey results merely reflect the preferences of the population that was consulted. The last limitation of surveys is that while data collected can establish whether or not a relationship between two variables exists, the data are not sufficient to be able to say that one variable causes the other.

Examining Survey Data   There are several ways to examine survey data. Because the survey sample is a subset of a larger population, the tester can look across all the data collected or only look at particular population subgroups. Marketers will divide a larger population into smaller segments, using demographic criteria such as age, gender, socioeconomic status, or even preferred activities or brands. For example, marketers of a new microwave food might want to focus their efforts only on working parents (perhaps advertising in parenting magazines or on the subway), whereas marketers of a new cartoon movie might want to target only children from ages 5 through 9 (perhaps by putting a figurine representing one of the movie's characters into a McDonald's Happy Meal). Marketers then develop specific strategies to try to sell a product, campaign for a vote, or change someone's mind on an issue.

Inventory Walk   Students will provide inventory (two kinds of similar food or drink products) from home for this inquiry, so no formal inventory walk is required. Students can brainstorm possible taste test items in their science notebooks and share their ideas with a partner, small group, or the class.

A taste test works best when the two items are quite similar. Students can *microscale* the samples (make them quite small, about one bite's worth of food or one sip's worth of beverage) to save time and money. Each portion should be placed on an individual napkin or cupcake liner or in its own small cup. Here are some inventory options to get students' creative thinking flowing:

<u>Food Varieties</u>

- **Fat versus fat-free/light/reduced fat** (e.g., milk, cheese, yogurt, cookies, crackers, chips)
- **Natural versus processed** (apple juice, honey)
- **Organic versus non-organic** (vegetables from organic and regular sections of a store)
- **With sugar and without sugar or with artificial sweetener** (e.g., a no-sugar variety of jam and a variety of jam with sugar made by the same company)

<u>Branding</u>

- **Two similar products made by competing brands** (e.g., Oreo versus Hydrox cookies or the 1980s Coke versus Pepsi taste test)
- **Brand name versus "no name"/generic** (e.g., Ritz versus store-brand crackers)

<u>Preference of Products (Flavors)</u>

- **Can you tell the difference between these products?** (e.g., Coke Classic versus Caffeine-Free Coke Classic; fruit-flavored water with caffeine versus fruit-flavored water without caffeine; fresh-squeezed orange juice versus juice from concentrate)
- **The same food served in different ways** (e.g., chilled versus room temperature; baked versus made in the microwave; broiled versus fried)

Vocabulary: Power Words   There are a number of reasons why vocabulary knowledge is important in survey research. First, a strong relationship exists between vocabulary knowledge and reading comprehension. Nagy and Herman (1987) point out that children with larger vocabularies have a better understanding of text. Vocabulary knowledge impacts how well students are able to make connections between what they already know and what they are finding out through research. Second, vocabulary knowledge has high value because it reinforces important utility terms in a way that serves as building blocks to other learning. For example, the word "data" is a high-utility term used not only in survey research but also in fair test investigations. Finally, building vocabulary knowledge is necessary to be a part of the science academic discourse. A member of the science inquiry community must be able to communicate effectively both orally and in print using appropriate vocabulary (Spencer & Guillaume, 2009).

To help students connect survey-related vocabulary terms and construct meaningful connections between them, students will assemble word chains (Stephens & Brown, 2000). This will encourage students to explore concepts in relation to each other and to think about how the vocabulary words they are studying are related. Using sample templates for word chains, students place vocabulary words in a linear or circular order and provide a specific explanation of how the two words are related. For example, vocabulary terms might be ordered in a line, such as the one shown below. Students then create and explain a rationale for the relationships between two items in a series. Other constructed sequences may offer different explanations of connections.

Linear Chain

Sample Student Writing

A **sample** size is the portion of population selected for a **survey**. **Respondents** are people in the **sample**. A **rating scale** is what **respondents** use to make their opinions known. The results of the **rating scale** are **data**. One way to display **data** is in a **bar graph**.

Figure 10.2.

Alternatively, the words can be arranged in a circle. Using the example above, the boxes could be arranged in a circle so that *bar graph* connects to *survey,* closing the loop.

These vocabulary terms are useful for describing surveys:

- **Bar graph:** A chart with bars whose lengths match collected data.
- **Data:** A collection of facts from which a conclusion may be drawn.
- **Demographics:** Special traits of a population (e.g., gender, grade level).
- **Respondents:** People giving answers to the survey.

- **Rating Scale:** A range of answers indicating the strength of respondent's agreement.
- **Sample Size:** Number of people interviewed or tested in the survey.
- **Survey:** A questionnaire or interview designed to gather data about a population.

Safety Precautions

This chapter's survey approach involves food. To keep the process sanitary and safe, these tips are helpful:

- Use napkins or cupcake liners for each serving to avoid putting food directly on a desk.
- Ask students to wash their hands before serving and to use serving utensils such as a spatula or spoon to minimize direct contact with food.
- Be sensitive to student allergy issues, particularly concerns about peanuts or dairy products.
- As a precaution, ask parents to send feedback about foods that may not be permissible for their children to eat, such as candy or caffeine. A sample permission slip is below.

Permission Form for Student Participants in Taste Tests
*Please return this form to school by [date] *

Dear Parent or Guardian,

Your child is conducting a product survey for our science class. In addition he/she will be participating in other students' surveys. As a participant, your student will be asked his/her opinion about various foods and drinks and also to provide two similar food items that can be used in running their own taste tests with the class.

All food and drink products in the survey test should be purchased from a store (not homemade).

Please list below any known food allergies your child may have, as well as any foods/ drinks that you do not want your student to taste.

I ☐ give / ☐ do not give permission for my child, _____ , to participate in the taste tests on _____ [date].

Food Allergies _____

Foods to Avoid _____

Parent Signature _____ Date _____

Working in the Science Notebook: Before the Experiment

Student-Generated Questions

Closed Questions   It is usually better to ask a closed question in a survey than an open-ended question. This is a departure from the kinds of questions generated during inquiry, as shown earlier in this book.

Take, for example, a taste test in which the surveyors want to know if tasters prefer Product A or Product B. Ask an open-ended question like, "Do you like the taste of 'A'?"

This could be answered with, "Yes," "I love it," "Sort of," "Not so much," "It's terrific!" "No, it is disgusting," "Sometimes," or "I don't know." The wide variety of answers generates a confusing data set. However, if the question is closed, such as, "Which tastes better to you, 'A' or 'B'?" then the respondent only selects one of the two options: "A" or "B." This makes the incoming data much easier to quantify and analyze. Questions with a limited set of responses also place fewer demands on respondents, who simply choose from the available responses.

Examples of Close-Ended Survey Questions   To help children brainstorm the kind of question they might like to create for their inquiry, consider this list as a class:

- **Which jelly bean tastes the most like its color?** (The respondent may have more than two options from which to choose, but still only provides a single answer.)
- **Which do you think is the creamiest potato soup for the cafeteria to serve: A, B, or C?**
- **Which would you rather have served for lunch in the cafeteria: Snack A or Snack B?**

Leading Questions   Scientific surveys avoid leading questions. A leading question is one that influences the respondent to answer in a biased way. For example, imagine a survey with the question, "Do you agree with experts that Coke tastes better than Pepsi?" Respondents might feel pressured to choose Coke because it aligns them with the expert point of view, and they might resist picking Pepsi because it's not the expert choice. A less biased approach would be to ask, "If you could choose to buy Coke or Pepsi, which would you buy?" This question avoids the hint that there is a "correct" answer.

Rating Scales   Rating scales are another kind of close-ended question. For more advanced students, that answer menu might include a numerical rating scale. For example, "On a scale of 1 to 5, with 1 being low and 5 being high, how would you rate the appearance/taste of ____?" A scale with a prescribed set of responses such as this is known as a *Likert* (LICK-ert) scale. For example:

- **From $1–5, how much would you pay for product X?**
- **On a scale of 1–5, with 1 being low and 5 being high, how much did you enjoy eating X?**
- **How do you rate your current cafeteria service? Please answer with "Excellent," "Very Good," "Average," "Needs Improvement," or "Unacceptable."**

Survey designers also think about whether they want an even or an odd number of choices when designing their surveys. Some people, by nature, don't really have a preference or don't care to share their preference. If a survey question has five choices, those people are likely to choose the middle choice, which often yields data that reveals little about true preferences. For that reason, some survey designers have an even number of choices, which eliminates having a safe "middle" choice.

When students generate number-based data sets, they can give insight into consumer patterns by examining the mean, mode, median, and range. To check the *mean*, students calculate the numerical average, taking a sum of all responses and dividing by the number of responses. The *mode* is the most commonly given answer. Students also learn in math class about the *median*, the number that is right in the middle of the data, but on a five-point scale, the median does not provide significant pattern or trend. The range of all collected data provides the breadth or span of responses. Post the simplified definitions on the bulletin board for easy reference.

- **median**—middle number
- **mode**—most frequent number
- **mean**—average
- **range**—difference between greatest and least number

One interesting aspect of having different types of averages is that people who do marketing for a living can choose how to analyze their data. If a student gathers data on a rating scale, calculating both the mean and the mode can generate quite different answers. Professional advertisers and marketers may choose to use the number that favors their product or service most.

Comparison Questions   Comparison survey questions are designed for the taster/customer to make their preferences known. Does A taste worse, better, or the same as B? Other questions might include:

- **Which is the more interesting commercial during the Super Bowl, the chips ad or the soda ad?**
- **Who is more accurate at telling the temperature of an object by touch, adults or children?**

Yes/No Questions   Throughout this book, the use of questions for inquiry that can be answered with a simple "yes" or "no" has been discouraged. However, when gathering survey data, these concrete answers are very useful. However, student evaluators should be careful not to lead the participant toward the brand/product that represents their own personal preference. Yes/no questions might include:

- **Can you tell the difference between Brand A popcorn and Brand B popcorn?** (Yes, the taster can tell the difference, or No, they cannot tell the difference.)
- **Would you enjoy a field trip to the cider mill**? (Yes or no.)
- **Should the school day be longer?** (Yes or no.)

Agree/Disagree/No Opinion   Sometimes, affirmative statements are made and the respondents are asked if they agree or disagree. These types of queries are similar to yes/no questions. For example:

- **The school day should be longer.** (Agree/Disagree/No Opinion)
- **Teachers should use red pens when they grade.** (Agree/Disagree/No Opinion)

In the sample inquiry for this chapter, a student has talked about potential survey items with his parents. He notices that when they buy oranges from the health food store, they cost a lot more than oranges from the produce section of their regular grocery store. He wonders if people can detect any difference in the taste of organic versus "regular" oranges and wants to conduct a taste test to find out. His sample inquiry question might be as follows:

Question:

Which of these two oranges tastes better? (The survey leader will provide one organic orange slice and one regular orange slice of similar sizes.)

This question is recorded on a fresh page in the students' science notebooks. The page is titled and dated, and a page number appears in the upper outside corner. Because they will later be participating in one another's surveys, students should not show their science notebooks to classmates until after the survey is completed.

Testable Prediction

From the question, the student makes a prediction about the results of his or her survey. The student is careful not to reveal his or her prediction or personal preference during the survey, as shown in the following example:

Question:

Which of these two oranges tastes better?

Prediction:

If I do a taste test with an organic orange and a regular orange, then the organic orange will taste better because organic produce is grown without chemicals that might make the fruit taste bad.

Here are some additional predictions:

- **If a taster gets two cups of soda, one with caffeine and one without, then children will be more likely to taste caffeine than adults because children have more sensitive taste buds.**
- **If students taste a sample of Coke and Pepsi, then most third graders will prefer Coke because it is the drink that they are most familiar with already.**
- **If a taster is asked to taste regular yogurt and non-fat yogurt, then a majority of kids will prefer the regular yogurt because non-fat yogurt is more watery.**

The prediction is recorded in the science notebook.

Identifying Variables

In a survey, there are still *independent* and *dependent variables*. The independent variables are the choices that the taster is given. The dependent variable is the taster's preference or ability to differentiate between products. For the sample survey, the following would be the variables:

Variables:

Independent Variable:
Type of orange (organic or not)

Dependent Variable:
Preference of person doing taste test

Constant Variables:
Size and temperature of orange slice, whether the rind is left on or off, type of napkin used, time of day (e.g., right after lunch), location

Procedure

Students make many decisions when designing a procedure. They choose the style of survey to administer, when and where it will take place, and the sample size.

What Kind of Survey Will It Be?   Students also make many decisions in the design of their survey. Will it be a *blind taste test*? In the case of a blind taste test, the taster does not know which product is in which cup. One of the most famous blind taste tests was the Pepsi versus Coke taste test of the 1980s, in which thousands of people tried to figure out which cup of soda tasted better. In that blind taste test, the cups were not labeled to reveal which product was which. (The respondent found out after the taste test which product he or she had selected.) In the classroom, students might label the cups as ''A'' and ''B'' so that the respondents do not know what is in each cup. The data organizer would also be labeled ''A'' and ''B'' so that if it is seen by the respondent, they will not know what is really in each cup. However, students would record a key in their science notebooks so that they can reference which item is ''A'' and which is ''B.'' The code must be used consistently to achieve an accurate data set.

In other cases, such as the frozen yogurt sampling in the story starter, the tester has already identified what the item is, and the girls are simply giving their opinion on the pre-named product.

Where, When, and Who?   In a survey, an added consideration in the procedure is deciding where and when the survey will take place and the size of the survey sample. Some surveys take place in quiet conference rooms, in the morning, with just a small group of people. Some surveys are conducted throughout the day in busy places such as shopping malls or libraries because a larger sample size is desired. Does the survey designer wish people to linger over the sample or hurry by? Location can determine the degree to which volunteers choose to participate. In the real world, respondents can volunteer, be paid a small fee, or be offered coupons or reward points for participating.

Location, time of day, and sample size should be recorded in the science notebooks along with the steps of the procedure.

Here is a sample procedure for how the taste test about oranges could be conducted. Keep in mind, however, that each child or group is pursuing a unique survey.

Procedure:

Location: School lobby
Time: Just before lunch
Sample Size: 24
A = organic orange slices
B = non-organic orange slices

1. **Set up one table along the wall.**
2. **Cover the table with a tablecloth so it stays clean.**
3. **Label 24 cupcake cups ''A.''**
4. **Label 24 cupcake cups ''B.''**
5. **Cut up six organic oranges into quarters.**
6. **Put one quarter of an orange into each ''A'' cup.**
7. **Cut up six non-organic oranges into quarters.**

8. **Put one quarter of an orange into each "B" cup.**
9. **As students pass through the lobby on their way to lunch, ask one person at a time to taste from an "A" and a "B" cup.**
10. **Offer the "A" cup first sometimes and the "B" cup first at other times.**
11. **Offer a sip of water between tasting to clear the palate.**
12. **Ask each taster which orange slice they like better.**
13. **Give the taster the option of saying that they have no preference or cannot tell any difference in the two orange slices.**
14. **Write the response in the data organizer.**
15. **Clean up when you are done.**

Notice that the procedure includes set-up and clean-up.

Data Organizer

Students have a wide range of choices for data collection instruments when conducting a survey. The following is a sampling of some options.

Another option is to design a data organizer using a spreadsheet program like Microsoft Excel or Google Spreadsheets (http://docs.google.com). Students create the blank data organizer and print it out. During the taste test, they record data on the printout, then return to the computer after concluding the experiment to input the data and use the software's built-in tools to electronically convert their data table into a bar graph, line graph, or

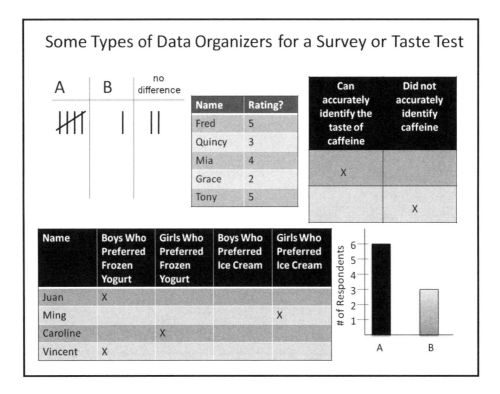

Figure 10.3.

pie graph that helps to communicate their results. The results are then printed out and taped or stapled into the science notebook in the Claims and Evidence section.

The bar graph in the lower right-hand corner of figure 10.3 illustrates data from the orange taste test example survey. In their science notebooks, students would create an empty graph grid and label each axis for clarity.

Working in the Science Notebook: During the Experiment

Conducting the Experiment and Recording Data and Observations

Conducting this experiment and recording the data are easy steps for children, as it builds on their interest in social interactions. It can be useful to divide the class in half. Have half administer their surveys while the other half act as respondents. Then, have the students change roles. Keep a dustpan and a few damp cloths on hand for unexpected spills, and have recycling and trash bins at the ready for quick clean-up.

Recording Additional Data   Students may choose to augment data by jotting down additional comments made by their respondents. This may generate useful additional data.

For example, imagine that a marketing company did a taste test comparing a prototype of a new toothpaste (Brand B) against the most popular brand (Brand A). In the process of recording people's preferences, the marketers realized that not only are people choosing Brand A, but they keep spitting out Brand B and saying how horrible it tastes. In this case, recording that additional descriptive data gives an important message to the toothpaste manufacturers that the problem is so severe that perhaps the product should not be put on the market until the offending taste is eliminated.

Working in the Science Notebook: After the Experiment

Claims and Evidence

Survey data are often quite simple for students to analyze. A simple "majority rules" may apply, or students may dig deeper to find the mean or the mode as described earlier in this chapter. Remember that mean and mode calculations can yield surprisingly different results! After analyzing their data, students can use this template to scaffold their thinking:

Because of (evidence), I claim that _____.
or
I claim that _____ because of _____.

For example,

- **Because 75% of the tasters picked B, I claim that Brand B is more popular.**
- **I claim that boys prefer cold pizza to hot pizza because 89% of boys picked the cold pizza to eat over the hot.**
- **Because the most common response to the question about liver was "1," the lowest ranking, I claim that most people dislike liver.**

In the sample inquiry with oranges, it was discovered that out of a sample size of twenty-four respondents, twenty preferred the non-organic orange slice and four preferred the organic orange slice. Putting these data in a pie chart would show that the response was overwhelming in favor of the non-organic oranges. A claims and evidence statement might read as shown in the following example:

Claims and Evidence:

Because a majority of people preferred the non-organic over the organic orange slice in a taste test, I claim that non-organic oranges taste better than organic.
or
Because 0% of those surveyed responded "no preference" in our taste test, I claim that there is a difference in taste between organic and non-organic oranges.

The claim must be based on the collected data. Therefore, a statement such as, "I claim that non-organic oranges are more popular because they cost less" is not valid because price was not included in the survey design or the resulting data. However, in the Next Steps phase, students may choose to conduct additional research to see if price might also be a factor in orange selection.

Conclusion

During the conclusion, students look at their prediction and compare it to the claims and evidence to determine what was learned. In addition, the conclusion could include observations on experimental error or ideas for future investigations. The following is a sample conclusion to the oranges taste test:

Conclusion:

In the taste test, I learned that non-organic oranges were more popular than organic oranges among elementary students. Five of the six (5/6) people I interviewed said they preferred non-organic oranges. My prediction was not supported. However, there could be experimental error. Our cafeteria only serves non-organic oranges, so maybe people were just stating a preference for what's familiar.

There is usually a practical application for the results of a survey. In marketing, statistics from surveys are used to tell us that their product is really popular or recommended by experts. For example, Trident gum was promoted for years under the tagline, "Four out of five dentists recommend Trident to their patients who chew gum."

Exit polls on Election Day are a kind of survey that is conducted as people leave the place where they vote. Reporters are not allowed to know the number of actual votes until the end of Election Day, but they do ask people how they voted as they exit. Those exit surveys were used for years to help reporters predict the winners of elections. The data do not always mirror the actual voting patterns, however. In the year 2000, for example, exit polling led a few television networks to predict that Al Gore, not George W. Bush, had won the state of Florida and would be the next U.S. President. In elections since 2000, news agencies have been more cautious about announcing their predicted winner until more actual voting tallies were available.

Next Steps

Most students are very fond of surveys, especially food surveys! Many students may wish to repeat the survey again, perhaps tweaking the experimental design or changing the product. With survey data, it is important to remember the concept of sample size and location. Perhaps this sample had an overwhelming preference for non-organic oranges, but could the survey results be different if the survey were repeated in front of a health food store? That might make an interesting future inquiry.

In their science notebooks, encourage students to reflect on the experience and record any new questions, such as the following notation:

Next Steps:

I was surprised by the results of my taste test, because people always say they buy organic because it tastes better. Everyone could taste a difference between the two types of oranges, so I guess that people realize that they have different tastes and are really choosing the one they prefer. I wonder if people pick non-organic oranges because that is the flavor they are used to. I wonder if one orange was not as ripe (sweet) as the other. I wonder if my results would be different if I surveyed only health food fans or people at a gym. I wonder if the results would be different if I did this experiment with grown-ups. I wonder if the pesticides used on oranges have a special taste and if that is why people like them. I wonder if washing the oranges beforehand makes a difference. I wonder!

Project and Assessment: Science Fair Poster

Now that the surveys are completed, the results of surveys can be used to guide future offerings in the cafeteria. For this project, students report back to Ms. Gourmand and the class about the likes and dislikes of their fellow students. An oral presentation is a good way of communicating results, but adding a visual display strengthens the message.

Students will need a science fair display board for this project. Tri-fold boards can stand by themselves on a table. Make the display board from any sturdy material such as cardboard or foam core board. Lightly scoring the sides of the board with a craft knife or scissors blade will ease folding of the sides forward to create three sections. The folds can be reinforced with tape on the backside of the board. Pre-made tri-fold boards can be purchased at craft or office supply stores. If wall space or easels are available, then flat poster board would work as well.

The boards can be a synopsis of the science notebooking experience, as shown on page 174.

The main section of a display poster is what will draw people's attention. Students can think of it as a commercial for their survey. Students use the contents of their science notebook to organize their survey information to include the following sections.

Title   Titles for each subheading on the display board can be created on the computer, cut out of construction paper, or lettered by hand. The lettering of the title should be large enough so that it can be seen clearly from a distance. Each subheading should be brief (under ten words) and reflect the survey results. Some examples are: "Coke Wins Over Pepsi," "Go Generic for Cereal," or "Kids Can Taste Caffeine—But Adults Can't!"

Figure 10.4. A student shows off the results of her taste test.

Results   Students summarize their data in a graphic form. Visual representation of results gives extra impact to the presentation. A picture is worth a thousand words. Include a photo that shows the taste test being done, if possible.

Purpose/Question   Here, the students clearly state what they hoped to find out by conducting the survey. What question did they ask each respondent?

Procedure   Drawing from what they wrote in their science notebooks, students copy the main steps of their procedures into this section.

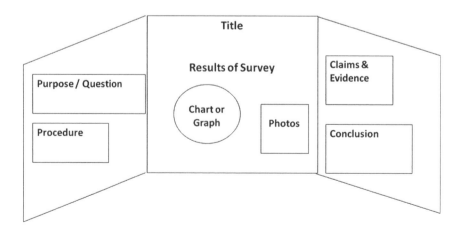

Figure 10.5.

Claims and Evidence   Students select the most compelling claim and the evidence that supports that claim and put it in this section of the display board.

Conclusion   In this section, students summarize what they have learned from their taste test survey and how they think these results impact their school. What recommendations will the student make to the school cafeteria based on the survey results? How does the student plan to apply the survey results? What did the student learn? What experimental error could have influenced the results?

Rubric for Survey Display Board

The rubric on page 175 can be used as a reference throughout the project to help students prepare for the final assessment.

Next Steps

Consumer science such as a taste test tends to "hook" kids, and they are frequently motivated to try again with another survey or to explore new aspects of a product they used for a survey, such as the oranges follow-up activities described on page 176. Students record these ideas in their science notebooks for follow-up at a convenient time.

Surveys provide feedback and validation. Surveys also provide evidence to support those seeking change or action. Well-crafted surveys can identify some of the major issues with your school environment, products, and provide evidence to support an argument or possible solution to that issue. Students can then take actions and become involved in a good cause.

Extensions

Are Statistics Misleading?   Describe a situation in which consumers could be misled by statistics. Sometimes instead of reporting on all people polled, marketers will report only on numbers from a *microtargeted* group of people (a small "niche" subgroup such as males with blue eyes or first graders whose names start with "S"). How might microtargeting make a difference in reporting results?

Combining Survey and Experimental Inquiries   Survey inquiries can be combined with experimental inquiries. For example, the student documents which brand of popcorn tastes best, then experiments to see which brand pops the most kernels or which brand produces the greatest volume of popcorn. One brand may not score the highest in all types of inquiries!

Nielsen TV Ratings   The Nielsen ratings take a sample of the television habits of selected American households. Television networks use Nielsen ratings to determine which shows should stay on the air. Has a favorite show of yours ever been canceled? Is the Nielsen system a fair one?

Are All Surveys Valid?   In preparation for the 2008 Presidential Election, the *New York Times* reported on a practice in which pollsters made correlations between what kinds of food people had in their homes and which candidate they were likely to vote for (Severson, 2008). Read the article and hold a debate in class about this idea.

Survey Rubric

	Beginning Marketer (2 points)	Progressing Marketer (3 points)	Master Marketer (4 points)
Survey Process	Think about how to organize a survey so that you can collect meaningful data.	Surveys need to clearly show the preferences/tastes of those polled. Be sure to accurately count and record each response.	Survey shows evidence of logical thought for information gathering.
Data Interpretation	Organize your data so that it can tell a story about what products your respondents preferred.	You generally understand your data.	I learned something new from your data, and so did you!
Display Board	Your exhibit should be organized, neat, and visually attractive.	Pretty good! Make sure that you have both great information and an eye-catching display.	Each poster section describes parts of the survey process. Pictures and graphs clearly illustrate overall results.
Conventions	Ask a friend to help you proofread your work.	Looking good! Most of the time, your conventions are strong.	Super spelling, grammar, and punctuation!
Presentation of recommendations based on survey results	Keep practicing your eye contact, volume, preparation, and confidence.	You can win over the audience with a practiced presentation and confidence in your results.	You used a strong voice and eye contact to persuade audience of your findings.

Figure 10.6.

11

Alternative Energy: The Budget Crisis

with Victoria A. Pascaretti

Lesson Overview

Not all science inquiry is hands-on. Scientists also use print, online, and multimedia resources to learn about science concepts from experts or fellow scientists.

In this chapter, the classroom teacher collaborates with the school library media specialist. Students in grades five and six use online research to gather information about various alternative energies under development, choose one for in-depth research, and then evaluate the practicality of that energy for adoption by their local school district. This lesson is adapted from the work of Swartz (2008) and Fontichiaro, Pascaretti, and Buczynski (2009) and is an excellent precursor to the rigorous research skills expected at the secondary level.

National Science Education Standards

- **Transfer of Energy**: Energy is a property of many substances and is associated with heat, light, electricity, mechanical motion, sound, nuclei, and the nature of a chemical. Energy is transferred in many ways (Grades 5–8).

Outcomes

Emerging scientists will be able to:

- Identify and discuss traditional energies used in the United States.
- Identify and discuss a variety of alternative energies.
- Explain the differences between traditional and alternative energies.

Practiced scientists will be able to:

- Explain the advantages and disadvantages of various types of alternative energies.
- Develop decision-making criteria and use it to determine whether a particular alternative energy is beneficial for local use.

Awakening Prior Knowledge

What Energies Do Students Observe in Daily Life?

Before embarking on this project, discuss the kinds of energy use that students observe on an ordinary day. Students work in pairs or small groups to brainstorm these ideas on a fresh page of their science notebooks, then share them as a class. The teacher records group contributions on chart paper, a blank bulletin board, or an overhead projector chart. Observed energy use might include gasoline (to power cars and buses), electricity (to power toasters and lights), natural gas (to power furnaces or clothes dryers), human power (for walking or biking), or wood or coal (to fuel a stove or power plants).

What Does "Saving Natural Resources" Mean to Students?

Continue by asking students what they think about when they hear "saving natural resources." What things do they observe people doing to save resources? Again, students brainstorm these in their notebooks and then share their ideas in a class discussion. Ideas might include recycling of plastic, glass, metal, or paper; energy-efficient light bulbs; efficient low-flow toilets that require fewer gallons of water; large windows to let in sunlight and minimize the use of light bulbs; better insulation so furnaces and air-conditioners run less; reuse of clothing and household items via hand-me-downs, second-hand stores, or charity shops; natural cleaning products; and more.

Why Do People Care about Saving Energy and Resources?

Ask students to brainstorm in their notebooks why they think people are interested in reducing energy use or saving natural resources. Students may say that they want to minimize waste, preserve natural resources, share, or save money.

These questions focus thinking for the story starter.

Story Starter: The Budget Crisis

This chapter's story starter, on page 179 and 180, takes the form of *reader's theater*. Reader's theatre is an informal dramatic form in which students read and or perform their roles holding their scripts in their hands. There is no memorization or expectation that students will deliver a polished performance.

Depending on the class's needs, students can either stay in their seats during the reading, or chairs and tables may be arranged as a makeshift set and students may move about within that space while delivering their lines. A row of desks or tables with eight chairs behind it may be placed on one side of the front of the room to accommodate the Board of Directors, and a pair of desks or table with two chairs behind it can serve as the TV studio.

Additional set pieces (such as windows or a television studio backdrop) can be drawn onto a whiteboard behind the chairs and tables. Reader's theater is meant to be an improvisational, think-as-you-go type of theater, not a rehearsed and polished performance.

Preparing for Inquiry

Reviewing the Story

As a class, discuss the issues presented in the script using the following guided questions:

- **What are the "hot button" issues that board members brought up based on rising energy costs?** (Loss of staff, loss of bus service, climate control discomfort for building occupants, and cutting of art and music programs for students.)

THE BUDGET CRISIS

Characters:
Male TV Anchor
Female TV Anchor
School Board Member #1
School Board Member #2
School Board Member #3
School Board Member #4
School Board Member #5
School Board Member #6
School Board Member #7
School Board Member #8

MALE TV ANCHOR: This is the eleven o'clock news. I am your anchor, Mark Broadsheet.

FEMALE TV ANCHOR: And I'm Felicity Caption. Our top story today: our local school district reports that it does not have enough tax money coming in to be able to pay for all of the programs that the school district wants to offer next year. Let's go live to the School Board meeting, where the debate is going on.

BOARD MEMBER #1: I hate that it has come to this, but the truth is in the numbers. With our budget numbers looking so bad, we're going to have to cut programs.

BOARD MEMBER #2: How about music? Art? P.E.? The librarian?

BOARD MEMBER #3: I would hate to see them go, but we have to balance the budget.

BOARD MEMBER #4: Gosh, my son loves art and music, and my daughter loves reading and being active in P.E. Don't we have any other choices?

BOARD MEMBER #5: Well, the price of gas has just skyrocketed this year. Fuel for our school buses has gone up 25%. If you look carefully at the budget, you'll see that's where a lot of extra money has to go that we weren't expecting.

BOARD MEMBER #6: We have to have buses, because some of our students live miles and miles away from school.

BOARD MEMBER #7: Look at how much it is costing to heat and air-condition our schools. That went way up this year as well. That's eating up more money than we budgeted for, too.

BOARD MEMBER #8: I sure would hate to lose special programs just so we could pay the heating bill, but what can we do? We've already installed energy-efficient windows.

Figure 11.1.

BOARD MEMBER #1:	Last year, we installed motion-sensor light switches so we're not paying for electricity when no one is in the room.
BOARD MEMBER #3:	Our media specialists scheduled all of the computers to turn off after school so they don't burn unnecessary energy overnight.
BOARD MEMBER #5:	In the winter, we turned down the thermostat and encouraged everyone to wear a sweater instead.
BOARD MEMBER #6:	In the warmer months, we let kids wear shorts and sandals to school instead of keeping the air-conditioning turned up so high. And we keep the blinds closed on the hot sides of the building so less heat comes in through the windows.
BOARD MEMBER #8:	We turn the buses off in front of the school so they don't idle and waste gas.
BOARD MEMBER #7:	We've already implemented the easy strategies for saving energy. Maybe we need to think bigger about how to really overhaul our energy use to save money.
BOARD MEMBER #4:	I agree. I sure would hate to lose those special staff members at our school.
BOARD MEMBER #6:	Me, too. Plus, reducing our staff only solves this year's financial problems. Next year, we'll probably still have problems paying for our energy use. If we can reduce our energy costs now, we'll save money each and every year in the future. That's a much better solution.
BOARD MEMBER #2:	All in favor of hearing ideas from interested citizens about reducing our district's energy use, say "Aye."
ALL BOARD MEMBERS:	Aye.
BOARD MEMBER #2:	All opposed?
(Silence.)	
BOARD MEMBER #3:	The motion is approved. We'll hear citizens' ideas at our next meeting.
MALE TV ANCHOR:	You heard it here first. The Board of Education has just agreed to hear reports from citizens with ideas for saving energy.
FEMALE TV ANCHOR:	If you care about saving the Earth's resources and saving the jobs of some of our schools' favorite teachers, we hope you will come up with an alternative energy plan for presentation to the School Board.
MALE TV ANCHOR:	Local 5 News will be there to report live on the results. Thank you for watching, and good night.

Figure 11.2.

From *Story Starters and Science Notebooking: Developing Student Thinking Through Literacy and Inquiry* by Sandy Buczynski and Kristin Fontichiaro. Santa Barbara, CA: Teacher Ideas Press. Copyright © 2009.

- **What measures have already been taken by the school district in attempting to curb rising fuel costs?** (Motion-detecting lights, adjusting the thermostat, shutting down computers after school, and modifying the dress code to accommodate temperature.)
- **Can you think of other measures that could have been taken by the schools in recent times to reduce energy costs?** (Canceled field trips, canceled use of facilities after school hours, incentives for carpooling/biking to school, and planting trees to shade windows receiving full sun.)
- **Define the energy objectives emerging from the school board's discussion.** (Maintain or reduce current operating expenses. Maintain school occupants' comfort levels. Reduce the impact of unpredicted energy expense hikes [rising price of fuel].)
- **What energy objectives do you think are important but were not addressed by the school board?** (The environmental impact of the use of fossil fuels on the environment, additional easy fixes such as changing to energy-efficient light bulbs, starting an energy awareness educational program to promote conservation, and altering landscaping to take advantage of nature's contribution to energy conservation.)

Connecting to Science

One way to decrease our dependence on fossil fuels and other non-renewable resources is to consider alternative fuel choices. Work with students to develop a definition of alternative energy. What does it mean for something to be *alternative*? Some students may be familiar with the expression *alternative music,* which means songs that are outside of the mainstream genres that are played on radio stations or stocked in major music stores. The Natural Resources Defense Council (n.d.) defines alternative energy as energy that is typically environmentally sound but has not gained popularity (e.g., solar and wind energies). Drawing a distinction between popularly used traditional energies and alternative ones that are not commonly used is essential for students to be able to address the overarching issues.

Traditional energies used in the United States include fossil fuels such as coal, natural gas, oil (petroleum), and electricity generated by burning fossil fuels. Burning fossil fuels adds carbon dioxide (a greenhouse gas) to the atmosphere, which contributes to global climate changes. As gasoline prices reach record highs and the world oil supply continues to diminish, new attention is being paid to alternative energy sources that hold the possibility of lower long-term costs and a reduced impact on the environment. These energies include wind and water turbines, solar energy, hydroelectric energy, geothermal energy, nuclear energy, hydrogen, alternative fuels such as ethanol produced from corn and fuel manufactured from other plants (sugarcane, rice straw, switchgrass), biodiesel fuel made from recaptured used vegetable oil, and others. As of the time of this book's publication, none of these alternative energies has established a firm foothold in the American economy. This can be attributed to a variety of factors, including start-up costs, cost to the consumer, renewability, practicality of use, and aesthetic concerns (such as appearance of the energy-capturing or energy-producing object and odor). Profitability of some alternative energy production is possible only because of government *subsidies* (federal financial aid).

Ask students if they can learn about *all* of these kinds of energy in a hands-on inquiry. It may be possible to conduct some small-scale solar, wind, or water energy experiments in a school setting, but certainly not nuclear or geothermal energy! If they cannot use hands-on experiments, then, how can they find the information they need? It requires library research:

using expert writings and resources to gain information, then processing that information to create new understanding. It also means calling on the expertise of the school library media specialist who keeps pace with the latest and best resources available.

The students will discover that real-world decision-making about science issues can be complex and that a thoughtful weighing of advantages and disadvantages, as well as thinking through the importance of those advantages and disadvantages, can lead to more meaningful decision-making about the adoption of alternative energies in their local area.

Vocabulary: Power Words

Unlike in previous inquiry chapters, the vocabulary words for alternative energy are drawn and defined primarily through the student's own research. Students identify and construct a definition for new words as they encounter them in their research, noting them in the glossary of their notebooks. Their vocabulary may include the words in this chart:

Types of Energies	Units of Measurement	Factors to Consider	Additional Words
Fossil fuel	Miles per gallon (mpg)	Aesthetics	Crude oil
	Miles per hour (mph)	Abundance	Carbon emissions
• Coal	Barrel	Renewability	Carbon credits
• Oil	Gallon	Sustainability	Recession
• Natural Gas	Watt	Consumer	Speculation
	Megawatt	Producer	Non-renewable
Electricity	Dollar	Advantages ("Pros")	Subsidies
Alternative energy	Hertz (Hz)	Disadvantages ("Cons")	Energy efficient
Biodiesel	Parts per billion (ppb)	Consumption	Energy conservation
Ethanol	Decibel (dB)	Cost/benefit	Photovoltaic solar cell
Hydroelectricity	Gauss (G)		Hydrogen fuel cell
Geothermal energy	Pascal (Pa)		
Wind energy	Particulate matter (PM_{10} & $PM_{2.5}$)		
Wave energy	Degrees Celsius ($^{\circ}$C)		
Tidal energy			
Turbine-generated energy			
Nuclear energy			
Solar energy			
Biomass energy			
• Wood			
• Animal dung			
• Plant oils			
Human energy			

Homework to Develop Prior Knowledge

Distribute the following information to students for their homework. The handout on page 186 can be cut in half and pasted into the students' science notebooks for reference. If Internet access is not available at students' houses, consider doing this step in the computer lab or school library media center instead.

It may be surprising that students are asked to print out the article and make notes on the printout instead of moving directly to note-making in the science notebooks. However, students sometimes display gaps in understanding when they initially read an article written for an adult audience. By keeping the notes with their printout, potential misconceptions can be sorted out with the instructor right away without needing to return to the computer.

Students should use pens or pencils to make notes in lieu of a highlighter. Harvey and Goudvis (2007) and Harvey (1998) point out that beginning researchers often have a difficult time differentiating between "important" and "not important" information. These students tend to highlight far more than is necessary. In contrast, students using pens or pencils process the content before they make margin notes, resulting in higher levels of comprehension. Note-making encourages students to summarize information, identify key ideas, write questions that can be answered in future research, and connect the reading with prior knowledge.

Students both enjoy and express a certain amount of wariness about this exercise. They enjoy the open-ended assignment and the ability to choose an article that is meaningful to them. However, this same open-endedness may make some students nervous, as they worry that their article will not meet the teacher's expectations. This is typical for authentic research.

Working in the Science Notebook

Sharing Homework to Develop Schema and a Working Vocabulary

On the assigned day, students bring their printouts to class, and they paste or tape the article onto a fresh page of their science notebooks. If the article spans more than a single page, consider stapling it in the standard upper left-hand corner, folding the paper in quarters so that the stapled corner is on the bottom, and taping the stapled corner into the notebook.

The teacher leads a discussion about what was discovered using a variation of the *bansho* methodology common in Japanese lesson study, during which teachers track student thinking by scribing students' contributions onto a blackboard, whiteboard, or overhead projector. The teacher acts as recorder and facilitator, but the students guide the conversation by contributing the content. The goal of this activity is for students to pool their individual learning, deepen their initial understandings, and look for possible connections between their research and that of another student.

Thinking is tracked throughout the lesson so that students have a visual reference of the flow of the discussion. Yoshina (2001) points out that this use of the "blackboard" (*bansho*)

- **documents student ideas.** Teachers make at least a brief note about each contribution made by a student. Using key words and phrases in lieu of complete sentences speeds up the process.

Name _____

THE BUDGET CRISIS: YOUR FIRST TASK

Before we can create a Board presentation about alternative energy, we need to know more about what alternative energies exist and are being tested. To do this:

1. Go to Google News at http://news.google.com, which collects news stories from around the world.

2. Type "alternative energy" into the search box.

3. Browse the results until you find an article about alternative energy that interests you and provides some useful information that you could share with the class. It can be about one specific energy idea or give an overview of a handful of types of energy. Print out the article. If the URL of the article does not show up on the printout, please write it in so you can find the article again online if needed.

4. Make notes in the margin of the article about the most important or potentially useful information. Please use a pencil or a pen that is not black ink so your notes will show up against the printout.

Please bring your notated printout to class on _____. You will paste it into your science notebook and talk about it with the rest of the class.

- -

Name _____

THE BUDGET CRISIS: YOUR FIRST TASK

Before we can create a Board presentation about alternative energy, we need to know more about what alternative energies exist and are being tested. To do this:

1. Go to Google News at http://news.google.com, which collects news stories from around the world.

2. Type "alternative energy" into the search box.

3. Browse the results until you find an article about alternative energy that interests you and provides some useful information that you could share with the class. It can be about one specific energy idea or give an overview of a handful of types of energy. Print out the article. If the URL of the article does not show up on the printout, please write it in so you can find the article again online if needed.

4. Make notes in the margin of the article about the most important or potentially useful information. Please use a pencil or a pen that is not black ink so your notes will show up against the printout.

Please bring your notated printout to class on _____. You will paste it into your science notebook and talk about it with the rest of the class.

Figure 11.3.

- **models good note-making strategies that help students organize their thoughts**. Students can direct the recorder to cluster similar ideas together, use different marker colors to help identify trends, or draw arrows to connect ideas.
- **is a visual record and summary of class discussion.** By noting each student's idea on the board, a document of the discussion process is created. The teacher can point out pieces of information and model summarizing skills by "talking aloud" during the process.

To keep the discussion organized, it can be helpful for the teacher to invite one student to share his or her thoughts, and then ask if there are any other students who also recorded information on that same topic from their article. All students who found articles about wind energy can contribute successively; this helps to keep all of the wind energy information together.

Notice that although the teacher calls on students and models organization and summarizing, the teacher is not the content provider. The conversation arises naturally from the students' independent reading. This shifts the traditional instructional paradigm, in which the teacher's edition guides conversation. In this approach, student discovery drives the conversation, and the teacher's role is to facilitate, record, and guide students into making connections.

"Kneading" the Conversation and Creating Guiding Questions

After class members have had an opportunity to contribute their information, the whiteboard is full of data and questions. In another stage borrowed from lesson study of Japan, students work collectively to make meaning of those data. In lesson study, this stage is known as *neriage,* or "kneading" the conversation to come to consensus. Just as bakers knead bread, rolling and punching it repeatedly until it is ready for baking, students work and manipulate the data until understanding is gained. The teacher may use provoking questions to guide students to that understanding but should avoid telling students what "the" summary is.

Here are some useful guiding questions that lead students to consensus:

- **What were the common hurdles or roadblocks to implementing alternative energies?** (Expense, mindset, logistics, negative aesthetics, diversion of resources, risk of accident.)
- **Many solutions were suggested for making changes from traditional energy to alternative energy. What are they?** (Incentives: tax credits, carbon offset credits, retrofits to existing infrastructure, subsidies. Consumer success stories: hybrid cars, tankless water heaters, solar panels to heat water.)
- **I noticed that three times we wrote that certain types of energies would require that a new factory be built. How would new factories impact implementation?** (Expensive for the investor, but it would create construction jobs and might save money later if that energy production costs less than existing models.)
- **What general applications of alternative energy uses have emerged from the collective reading?** (Transportation, temperature control, replacement for fossil fuel-based electricity/gasoline, residential heating.)
- **Based on what you have read, what common ideas do you see between energies?** (Not widely implemented; expense of getting started with that energy.)

Avoiding Leading Questions   During *neriage*, try to avoid statements that provide opinion, set a specific direction for the discussion, or are negative in nature, which would inhibit further input from students, such as:

- Biodiesel smells like French fries, and wind farms are sometimes unattractive. Do you see how aesthetics could be an important factor to consider?
- Wow—this stuff looks expensive. No wonder no one has implemented this source of energy on a wide scale yet.
- I see that three of you mentioned that your energy would require building a new factory. That won't work.

As teachers help students summarize the main ideas, these will guide the students' upcoming research. Swartz (2008) identified these major areas for research, which could be translated into researchable questions. For example:

- **Abundance/renewability:** How can we make, get, or grow more once we use it up?
- **Accessibility:** How easy is this energy to get?
- **Cost of production:** How expensive is it to make this kind of energy?
- **Cost to consumers:** How much will it cost to buy it?
- **Safety:** What dangers are there in using this kind of energy?

In addition to Swartz's five ideas, the following might also be generated:

- **Aesthetics:** How does this energy impact the five senses of smelling, tasting, touching, seeing, and hearing?
- **Barriers:** What barriers must be overcome in order for this energy to be used in a mainstream way?
- **Definition:** How would you define this type of energy if you had only thirty seconds to explain it to someone on an elevator?
- **Staffing:** How many people are required to build the necessary infrastructure up front and later help harvest or process the energy?

Most of this discussion takes place with the whole class. If the teacher prefers, he or she can arrange students into groups who then refer to the whiteboard for information and generate their own main categories for research, then pool the categories in a whole-group discussion. These categories will guide and scaffold students' later research, giving them some context for the information they will be examining, and should be written in the students' notebooks.

Based on the pooled knowledge, students select a form of alternative energy that they would like to research further for their presentation to the School Board. List these forms of energy on the board and give each student a randomly selected playing card. Those students with aces may select first, then those holding a king, then those who drew a queen, continuing in descending order until each child has selected a form of energy and there are no more than four students assigned to any particular energy.

Before Engaging in Research

Designing a Research Question

As in hands-on inquiry, the first step in library inquiry is to determine a measurable question for the research. When students craft the questions—rather than selecting from a teacher-made list—their intrinsic motivation is stimulated and they are more committed to the research project. Students delve deeper and persist in the project more when they have a stake in its outcome that supersedes a letter grade.

Alternative energy grips the imagination of students, and they are enthusiastic in their pursuit of information. Talk with students about how their research projects must respond to the Board of Education's guiding question: "Which alternative energies could save our school district money?" However, this question is too broad and should be broken down into a series of smaller questions.

Throughout this book, questioning strategies have suggested steering clear of "yes/no" questions (red light questions) and avoiding "why" questions as too difficult for elementary students. With research inquiry, the guidelines for question development change somewhat. Any question that can be answered with a single word as well as "yes/no" questions are still to be avoided, yet now "why" questions can often be answered. These larger questions benefit from scaffolded sub-questions that direct the research to the end goal. For example, like news reporters, students consider the "who, what, where, when, why" question sequence to address the bigger picture.

Examples of Strong Research Questions

- How would adding solar energy generators positively or negatively impact our school district?
- Who benefits from the school district's immediate implementation of solar energy?
- What would be the cost savings of using solar energy over traditional energies in the long run?
- Where would solar panels need to be constructed or located to be most effective?
- When is solar energy most efficient? During which season(s) and/or for which tasks?
- What barriers stand in the way of alternative energy implementation?
- Who has the power to say no to changes from traditional energy to alternative energy?
- What are the pros and cons of the alternative energy consideration?
- Where has this alternative energy implementation been most (or least) effective? What success or failure stories can be found?
- How long after implementation would achievable monetary/environmental savings be realized?
- What elements are required in order for wind energy to be effective?
- Who determines where wind turbine farms can be located?
- How does running a wind turbine to produce one megawatt of electricity compare to the cost of producing the same megawatt using traditional energy?
- Where is wind energy most effectively captured on a global scale?
- When does capturing wind energy have a negative impact on the environment?
- What are the advantages and disadvantages of wind energy?
- Where has biodiesel been the most effective, and why?

As an example, a student might write the following research question in his or her notebook:

Question:

How would solar energy be useful in our district?.

As in previous chapters, the sample inquiry path in this chapter is provided merely to illustrate the process. In practice, each student (or group) would develop his or her own question.

Creating a Prediction

Predicting taps into prior knowledge. By the time students tackle a project such as this, they already have experience with the role and importance of a prediction. Teachers know that predictions awaken students' prior knowledge and connect background research with what students already know. A prediction template such as, "I think that my energy will be (take a stand) because (provide a rationale)" is helpful. For example, a student might continue his or her question from the previous step with the following prediction:

Prediction:

I think that solar energy will be cost effective for our district because we have lots of sunny days where we live and the sun provides free energy.

Students write this prediction into their science notebooks. Teachers can collect the notebooks at the end of class for formative assessment.

Data Organizer

In hands-on inquiry, students generally use data organizers to collect numerical information. In library research, however, data organizers more often include written text. If students have significant library research or science inquiry experience, they can often design this data organizer on their own. If the students have limited library research experience, providing a data collection chart may scaffold the experience. Ask students to open their notebooks to a new spread (blank pages on both sides of the spine). Make a series of columns. At the top of each column, students list their areas of research (e.g., cost to consumer, cost to produce, barriers, aesthetics). A sample is available online at http://www.ascd.org/ASCD/pdf/el/Swartz%20Matrix.pdf.

It is important that the data organizer be designed to collect data that will reflect information necessary to support or falsify their prediction. For example if the prediction is cost efficiency, then the data organizer might include column headings that read: comparisons between existing energy use and proposed alternative energy use; availability; logistics of conversion of existing technologies (district gas station converted to a battery charging station); cost to operate; or sustainability. This provides students with data to consider in the cost/benefit analysis. A few columns might be left blank to record unforeseen information.

To develop skills in evaluating the relevance or use of a particular piece of information, Swartz (2008) asks students to code each piece of information. Under his system, students use an asterisk (*) to denote important information, a plus sign (+) to denote an advantage or "pro" of this energy, and a subtraction sign (−) to denote a disadvantage or "con" of that energy. Additionally, a slash (/) denotes unimportant information. Each note made by the student receives a code. Coding demonstrates that students have moved beyond gathering information; they have thought about it, evaluated or judged it, and made a decision. Informed decision making is an important life skill. Students record this key (or a key with symbols of their choosing) at the very bottom of their chart.

Variables

The variables being considered in this prediction are solar energy (the alternative energy selected for investigation) and the cost effectiveness (a measured variable) of that option. These variables are weighed to come to a decision about the usefulness of this alternative energy for the school district.

Procedure

In past chapters, the word "procedure" has been used to denote a series of sequential steps to follow in conducting an experiment. In library research, however, the steps do not flow in such a linear path. Meaningful library research follows a hyperlinked pattern. One piece of research may lead students to "jump" over to another resource. Students need instructor guidance in the "procedures" of research.

Selecting Appropriate Sources   The school library media specialist has expertise in both print and digital resources. He or she can identify reliable resources in advance so that students have the benefit of age-appropriate and accurate resources and can also help students move beyond simple Google searches and into expertly-evaluated subscription databases. Relevant books can be ordered, Web sites found, and databases checked in advance for relevant information. With a quickly-changing subject like alternative energy, the Web may have the most up-to-date information.

Many teachers ask students to use a specific number of print resources and a corresponding number of digital resources. Using a variety of resources is important for developing a three-dimensional understanding of an issue. However, consider that the format of the resource is less important than the expertise of the author. Rather, have students use the quality of a resource as the overriding evaluative criterion.

Organizing Digital Resources   Consider gathering useful digital resources by creating an account with a social bookmarking site such as Delicious (http://del.icio.us). By sharing a username and password, the teacher and school librarian can work collaboratively to input useful Web sites, which can be annotated with a brief description and appropriate keywords. The students can then visit the Delicious site and use those keywords to search for information. For an example, see http://del.icio.us/beverlyenergy. For even more collaboration, invite students to share favorite links they have discovered; simply provide each student with the password and a demonstration on how to bookmark the link. Social bookmarking can be can be an efficient way of making a list of online resources. Another option to replace student Web searching is to create a Google Custom Search. Input a list of URLs, and Google Custom Search will find results only within those URLs. Follow the instructions at http://www.google.com/coop/cse/. Both services are free. When these (or other) digital pathfinders are created, have students write the URLs of the sites they use in their science notebooks for reference purposes.

Reviewing "Reading for Research"   Students read for research much differently than they do for comprehension in a language arts anthology. Researchers skim over text, using textual elements such as section headings, captions, bold or italicized fonts, or changes in margins to help them quickly find sections in a longer work that specifically relate to their research topic. Only when researchers have found a relevant section do they begin reading for meaning. (Readers, on the other hand, begin at the start of a chapter and read each word in depth.) Remind students of the importance of using textual elements such as bolded or italicized type, guide words, the table of contents, and the index to quickly find relevant information and evaluate the usefulness of a resource. Students may record these strategies in their science notebook. At the conclusion of the research project, the teacher and students may reflect on these strategies during the "Next Steps" reflection.

Verifying Information   One area of research that is difficult for elementary researchers is verifying information with a second or third source. Remind students that this is particularly important when using "surface Web" sites (Web sites that do not require a paid subscription for use), as the author's authority may be more difficult to identify.

Documenting References   Students should create a reference list that contains all print and digital resources used. To validate any statistics used in the alternative energy argument, a reliable source must be cited. Such citation is a way of saying, "My work is based on the work of others. It's not mine, but it helped me." This is essential academic practice, so the habit of citation should begin in elementary school. Consult with the school library media specialist about a developmentally-appropriate citation format, keeping in mind that a conceptual understanding of acknowledging others' ideas is an important message for students.

During Research

Data and Information Collection

Students use their data collection sheet, skimming strategies, and digital resources to gather information. Throughout this process, it is helpful to remind students of the end goal: to convince the Board of Education that their chosen form of alternative energy is—or is not—viable. Keeping the final objective in mind helps focus the research process.

Research is not linear: it is recursive. It is possible that as students work through their research, they may find a need to revisit a research source. This is something that adult researchers do, too, as they realize they need more information—or different information—than originally envisioned. Perhaps the research process has unearthed new questions or the overall research focus has shifted. The identification of this need is a sign of a mature researcher who is investigating every pathway of their topic.

Building Collective Knowledge

Once each student has completed a data collection chart, the class pools its knowledge so that all classmates gain a more comprehensive perspective on the alternative energy issue. Because each student comes to the table with unique research, the potential for the group to rely on a single leader is diminished. A wiki, a type of Web page that allows multiple authors with an interface as simple as a word-processing document, can be created.

After Completing Research

Claims and Evidence

Students evaluate their gathered information using the coding explained earlier in this chapter. Now, students examine both the information and the coding and look for patterns. What is the research saying? That, on the whole, the alternative energy is a good match to the need? Or that it is not a good match? These questions lead students to construct a *claim*. If a claim has an evaluative measure such as ''good'' or subjective measure such as ''better than,'' then it is harder for the evidence to directly support the claim.

Continuing with the sample inquiry, a student might write:

Claims and Evidence:

I claim that solar energy is not a cost-effective choice for our school district to use now because it takes 25 years to pay off the number of solar panels needed, and our budget is not large enough for this.

Conclusion

The conclusion is a summary statement. Students put all their claims and evidences together to determine a pattern, trend, or preponderance of evidence. Conclusions can be more complex in library research than they would be in elementary hands-on inquiry.

The conclusion is an important metacognitive step, as it gives students a chance to reflect on their research process, their new content understandings, and their growing skills as researchers. The following is a sample student notebook entry that a student might write:

Conclusion:

I conclude that solar energy is not a good investment for the district right now. The energy is free, but first you have to pay for the panels, and it would take the district about 25 years to save enough energy to pay for the panels. If the district could get a grant or donation to pay the initial cost of panels, though, solar energy would be cost effective. Solar energy could be used to heat water and our classrooms. I also learned that Google News is a cool place to find brand-new information about alternative energies. I learned that coding information helped me make decisions about which information was the most relevant to my project. For this research, I learned to use databases to find accurate information quickly and Delicious to keep track of my own favorite Web sites.

Project and Assessment: PowerPoint Presentation

At this stage, the student's research and the original request by the Board of Education come together. Microsoft PowerPoint, Keynote for Mac users, or the Presentation tool in Google Docs (http://docs.google.com) are all authentic presentation tools suitable for this project. Students work with other students who researched the same alternative energy to create a group presentation.

PowerPoint Tips

Have students ever seen a bad PowerPoint, where constantly spinning smiley faces detracted from the overall quality of the presentation? Consider spending some time discussing how to make a sensational PowerPoint presentation that reinforces the author's message without distraction. The handout on page 193 can be helpful.

Knowing the Audience

Knowing how to craft a message that speaks to a particular audience is key to the success of a presentation. The audience for this presentation is the School Board, a group of adults with limited district finances, little time, and important responsibilities. A successful presentation must deliver a powerful message. Merely reading the bullet points from the presentation slides will not be enough to capture their attention. While the presence of images and bullet points onscreen can summarize the content, the oral presentation must flesh out that basic information and expand on it. Having a message that is consistently persuasive is also essential. Remind students that they are not presenting a list of facts; rather, they are trying to talk the Board into taking the same position that they identified in their conclusion.

The audience also guides the style of presentation. Ask students to reflect on the appropriateness of smiley-face graphics, screeching audio, spinning images, or other flashy animations for this audience. A professional posture and wardrobe are also considerations.

Using their PowerPoint presentations, students address the panel who played school board members and the TV news anchors in the reader's theater. Outstanding presentations may be presented before the *real* Board of Education!

Rubric

A rubric for this project is found on page 194. Notice that this project has two assessment columns. The first is a student self-evaluation. This helps strengthen students' ability to assess the quality of their own work. Teachers evaluate the work only after students have filled in the self-reflection column.

Next Steps and Extensions

Next Steps

Students reflect in their science notebooks about what they learned about alternative energy, think about the new library research skills they have acquired, consider new areas for exploration, and identify questions that remain unresolved.

Extensions

Carbon Offset Credits   What are carbon offset credits, and why are people buying them to reduce their impact on the environment? Create an advertisement encouraging people to buy carbon offset credits.

POINTERS FOR CREATING POWERPOINT PRESENTATIONS WITH
Impact!

CONTENT
- Use no more than 10 words per bullet (put speaking notes elsewhere).
- Use no more than 5 lines of text per slide.

FONTS
- Use a san serif font (such as Arial, Helvetica, Verdana, or Calibri).
- Use a font size of 28 or larger.

COLORS
- Use a light font on a dark background (or vice versa) for clear viewing.
- Colors can can make viewing more difficult for some people. Color blind males have difficulty seeing red, green, and purple.

LAYOUT
- Use no more than 5 distractors per show. Distractors include changes in font character and size, colors, sounds, animations, and transitions.
- Make the slide visually appealing by adding graphics, images, captions, or word balloons.
- Give the audience some "white space" (unused space) on the screen so their eyes have a moment to rest.
- Photographs add authenticity to the slide show. However, large photos can make PowerPoint run sluggishly. Ask your computer teacher or media specialist for help optimizing images.

Figure 11.4.

Name _____

Alternative Energy PowerPoint

Your Mission

Create a PowerPoint that could be shared with district leaders about the alternative energy that you researched. Your PowerPoint must take a stand: either recommending that the district **adopt or reject** the energy you researched.

Your title slide must contain

- your first names and
- a title that describes whether you are or are not recommending it
    - Examples: A Plan for Hydroelectric Power In Our District **or** Stop Hydrolectric Power in Our District

You may then use **up to six (it can be fewer, but no more)** slides to persuade the leaders to take the same position you did. Remember: persuading is different than telling information. You must mention each criteria from your wiki, but you may incorporate them in the way you feel works best to prove your argument.

Rubric

Criteria	Point Value	Student's Self-Score	Teacher's Score
Student completed and coded the **research sheet**	10		
Student **contributed individual research to the wiki**	10		
Student **worked effectively** in a group	5		
The **title slide** lists names and takes a stand on whether the energy is a good match for the district	5		
Students' persuasive presentation includes **each of the categories from the individual research sheet**	25		
Students demonstrate understanding of the alternative energy that they are researching	25		
The PowerPoint uses **bullet points**, not full sentences or paragraphs, to give a snapshot of what will be discussed	10		
All team members present a portion of the slideshow with **energy and poise**	10		
TOTAL SCORE:	100		

Figure 11.5.

Community Service   Create a Go Green Club to develop recycling and energy conservation initiatives in your school. Create posters, videos, or podcasts to recruit members and promote your activities in school.

Environmental Impact   Do students know how their daily habits impact the Earth? Take the Environmental Footprint Quiz at http://www.earthday.net/footprint/.

School Energy Audit   Work with the local power company to develop a plan to evaluate your school's current energy use. Students begin by documenting the energy-saving behaviors that they observe among staff and students using digital cameras or writings in their notebooks. After studying the school's interior, the next step is to walk around the outdoor campus and document landscaping that contributes to energy savings. For example, are there trees that provide shade to the building, which reduces the amount of heat entering it? Students can also look at building maintenance. What is the age of the furnace? When are filters replaced? Are replacement light bulbs energy-efficient? Are door and window seals in good condition? How does the school deal with waste? Do compost heaps exist (so less biodegradable waste is trucked off campus)? Are there recycling stations so that resources can be used again? Do students and teachers use both sides of a piece of paper before recycling it? Do students and teachers use cloth towels or napkins instead of paper ones? What strategies does the power company recommend for becoming a more efficient or "greener" school?

Before implementing those strategies, create a data organizer and gather baseline data about energy usage. As those tips are integrated, ask students to note how the new behaviors are impacting energy use. Graph the change over time.

From the data, consider the following next steps:

1. Students gather success stories and share them with the community via morning announcements, podcasts, the school Web site, or the district TV or radio station.
2. Students consider the next level of energy savings. What changes could be made if additional funding were available? Prioritize the changes.
3. Seek grant funding to implement those changes. One source for funding is the Captain Planet Foundation (http://captainplanetfdn.org/default.aspx?pid=3&tab=apply). How did these more expensive changes impact the amount of energy and money saved? Which were more effective, inexpensive changes or the expensive ones? What criteria did students use to evaluate effectiveness?

Part III

Looking Ahead to Future Inquiry

12

Story-It: Creating Your Own Story Starters for Science Inquiry

Introduction

The science topics covered in this book represent just a fraction of science themes and concepts suitable for elementary learners. Why not consider writing new story starters to accompany additional science curricula or invite students to take the lead with stories of their own? When students bring story and science together, they deepen their scientific thinking, practice developing elements of a good story, and strengthen their problem-solving skills. Working collaboratively, student groups can design story starters around a particular science concept and then exchange their stories with other groups for further inquiry explorations.

Getting Started

Wiggins and McTighe (2005) discuss the importance of *backwards design* in curriculum development; that is, thinking about what students need to know and be able to do (exit objectives) at the start of planning. This helps to ensure that lesson design leads toward a meaningful learning outcome. Similarly, when envisioning a new story starter, begin with an overarching scientific concept, such as one of those listed below. Then consider the sub-topics and ''big questions'' within that concept. For example, if the concept is *adaptation*, the big questions might be, ''How do animals adapt to their environment?'' ''What is the difference between learned adaptations and inherited adaptations?'' or ''How do plant species adapt over time (evolve) to live near pollution sites?'' The goal of the story is to provide student friendly context for science content and to guide the reader into thinking about a big question. Exploration of this question via hands-on or library research will then be richer and more multifaceted.

Select a Scientific Concept

Consider using one of these scientific concepts as a starting point:

- Adaptation
- Attraction/repulsion

- Cause and effect
- Change over time
- Classification
- Cycling and cycles
- Density
- Diffusion
- Diversity
- Equilibrium
- Force and motion
- Heat transfer
- Relationships
- Relative scale
- Solubility
- Structure and function
- Systems
- Variation

Develop Background Knowledge

The school library media center is a great place for students to start learning about these topics. Learners will need some basic background of the scientific concepts before writing the story. Students can make notes in their science notebooks. Before writing, they may also wish to experiment, hands-on, to check out plausible endings for their story. The teacher and school librarian can monitor student progress to ensure that the story is built on an accurate knowledge foundation. Continue to use the "big question" as a guidepost throughout the process.

Select a Genre

Students may enjoy writing in a variety of genres, from the ones mentioned in this book to comedies, mystery, fantasy, poetry, or rap. Writers can pull from their own experiences or from their imagination. Varying the genre helps maintain student interest and promotes original work.

Structural Features

It is important for writers to also consider language and structural features that are consistent with the genre they have selected, including:

- Opening lines to capture a reader's interest
- Use of storytelling conventions (such as "once upon a time" for fairy tales)
- First- or third-person storyteller or character "voice"
- Use of past or present verb tense
- Varying sentence length for contrast and detail
- Use of dialogue to develop action and characters

When planning a story, writers need to keep the overall story structure in mind. Writers also plan a sequence of events, complication or conflict, and how they will encourage readers to investigate a resolution. They develop characters in a specific setting or plot.

Conflict That Leads to Inquiry

For a science story starter, the *conflict* (or problem) is what leads to questions and inquiry, so this is often the best place to begin planning the story. All good stories have conflicts that need to be resolved. A story starter with a meaty conflict will excite student scientists into a substantial problem solving inquiry. What is the conflict? Is it another person, a thing, or thoughts and feelings of the character? Why does this conflict occur? Students learn in language arts that conflict can boil down to these classic forms:

- Human versus human (e.g., two characters don't get along)
- Human versus society (e.g., a character stands up to a community, its culture, or its expectations)
- Human versus self (e.g., a character's tumultuous inner thoughts or emotions)
- Human versus nature (e.g., a character battling an avalanche)

As the examples in this book show, story starters are just that—the *start* to a story. Unlike most stories, the narrative of a story starter stops before the problem is solved. However, writers of story starters need to envision some possible solutions to the problem to make sure the problem is solvable through inquiry. For example, a story about a girl who became invisible and wanted to know how to become visible again could not be solved by library research, hands-on inquiry, or even current scientific knowledge. On the other hand, a story about a skateboarder who wanted to do ultimate moves but didn't have a skate park could be explored via library research to learn about skate parks and the laws of motion, then theories could be tested by building a skate park model. That inquiry would work.

Characters

Characters make the story happen. Their thoughts and behaviors bring the problem of the story to light. Decide who will be in your story. Who are the main characters? What are they like? How do other characters in the story react to this character? How do the characters or their behaviors represent scientific concepts? Use descriptive writing and realistic dialogue to bring the characters to life. For example, writers describe behaviors, outward appearance, and even facial expressions to effectively paint a mental picture of a character.

Setting

Tell about the time, place, environment, locale, habitat, and/or season in which the story takes place. Young writers can close their eyes and imagine the location, adding sensory details of color, lighting, sounds, and smells to the setting description. Where does the story take place? How does the environment affect the characters? How does the habitat or season impact the situation? What details can you include to help readers picture your setting? Is your setting realistic or unrealistic, in the present or in the future?

Inquiry

Think ahead to the types of investigations that readers might engage in as a result of the story's conflict. What are some ways the conflict could be resolved? What happens after the conflict is resolved? How do the conflict and its resolution affect the character? What happens in the end? Are there many possibilities for resolving the conflict and ending the story or just one? What will readers learn from investigating the conflict in the story?

Using Meaningful Vocabulary

Some students may struggle to come up with a story starter right away. Providing a word wall of scientific terms related to the concept or having students select a certain number of scientific terms to use in the story can scaffold and structure the activity for more concrete thinkers.

Teachers can use the reproducible on page 205 to create a word bank. A sample based on the concept of "relative scale" is shown below.

Starting the Story

Another way to scaffold the story starter writing experience for students is to give them an introductory scenario. The following questions are examples of scenarios leading to inquiries to help jump-start thinking for writing a story to explore the concept of relative scale:

Scenario	Relative Scale Inquiry
You are hiking in the rainforest/jungle/Arctic/woods when you find a super-sized _____!	How would you arrange all the characters in the story on a relative size continuum?
What if a magician made an elephant the same weight as a mouse?	Which items/characters in the story are bigger/heavier as measured scientifically (by volume, weight, mass, density)?
What if a pencil was longer than a meter?	What objects are longer/shorter than one meter?
What if you traveled on a magic carpet to a land where you moved faster as compared to everything else? What if you were slower?	In a race, who would win if comparing worms to ants or pill bugs to caterpillars? Rate the relative speeds of these animals. (Hint: draw a line with a pen and ants will follow.)
What if you had extraordinary hearing or could not hear at all?	What is a too loud/soft sound? Survey classmates to determine relative acceptable levels.
What if everything were half its size? Double its size?	How does size of an object relate to that object's function?
You throw coins in a wishing well, but they don't sink.	Compare relative densities of objects by determining floating and sinking characteristics.

These ideas for story context leading to inquiry investigations on relative scales of weight, size, density, sound, and speed can provoke possibilities for students who struggle to create a story from scratch.

Nouns	Verbs	Adjectives	Adverbs

Figure 12.1.

Nouns	Verbs	Adjectives	Adverbs
mountain	explain	major	continuously
atom	describe	minor	equally
mouse	examine	whole	perfectly
molecule	gather	part	correctly
scale	analyze	elephantine	mysteriously
bird	guide	high	speedily
Amazon	introduce	low	clearly
magnifying lens	intend	massive	suddenly

Figure 12.2.

Polishing the Story

Students can follow a process of drafting, sharing, revising, and polishing their work. After completing the text, students can use colored pencils to illustrate their work with detailed drawings. As they try to replicate the actual appearance of objects and animals, they will develop further skills in scientific-style drawing. Illustrations can be scanned as digital images, which can be placed in a word-processing program, inside a digital story in PowerPoint, or uploaded to an online tool like VoiceThread (http://www.voicethread.com), which marries a student's oral reading of his or her story starter with the illustrations he or she created.

We hope you will share your story starters and inquiries with us at activelearning@gmail.com.

Bibliography

American Association of School Librarians. (2007). *Standards for the 21st-Century Learner.* Retrieved February 15, 2009, from http://www.ala.org/aasl/standards.

Ansberry, K.R., & Morgan, E. (2005). *Picture-perfect science lessons: using children's books to guide inquiry; grades 3–6.* Arlington, VA: NSTA Press.

Arizona State University, (2005). *Pocket Seed Experiment for the Classroom & Home.* Retrieved August 11, 2008, from http://askabiologist.asu.edu/expstuff/experiments/pocketpocke/Pocket_Packet_1.pdf.

Bass, J., Contant, T., & Carin, A. (2009). *Teaching Science as Inquiry* (11th ed.). Boston: Allyn & Bacon.

Black, P., & William, D. (1998). Inside the black box: Raising standards through classroom assessment. *Phi Delta Kappan, 80*(2), 139–148.

Booth, W., Colomb, G., & Williams, J. (2003). *The craft of research.* Chicago: University of Chicago Press.

Buczynski, S. (2006). What's hot? What's not? Goldilocks investigates temperature and heat. *Science & Children, 44*(2), 25–29.

Butzow, C. & Butzow, J. (1994). *Intermediate science through children's literature.* Englewood, CO: Teacher Ideas Press.

Cameron, J, & Pierce, D. (1994). Reinforcement, reward, and intrinsic motivation: A meta-analysis. *Review of Educational Research, 64*(3), 363–423.

Campbell, B. & Fulton, L. (2003). *Science notebooks: Writing about inquiry.* Portsmouth, NH: Heinemann.

Chin, C., Brown, D. & Bruce, B. (2002). Student-generated questions: a meaningful aspect of learning in science. *International Journal of Science Education, 24*(5), 521-549.

Cothron, J., Giese, R., & Rezba, R. (1996). *Science experiments by the hundreds.* Dubuque, IA: Kendall/Hunt.

Culham, R. (2003). *6 + 1 Traits of writing: The complete guide.* New York: Scholastic.

Darling-Hammond, L. (2008). *Powerful learning: What we know about teaching for understanding.* San Francisco: Jossey-Bass.

Dewey, J. (1916). *Democracy and education: An introduction to the philosophy of education.* MacMillan Company. Retrieved August 8, 2008, from http://books.google.com/books?id=yGxIAAAAMAAJ&dq=Dewey,+democracy+in+education&pg=PP1&ots=4bBkOXOYyi&sig=Gqni3rVSFkSpwJx6wnGI_IgUPe4&hl=en&sa=X&oi=book_result&resnum=1&ct=result#PPP9,M1.

DuFour, R. (2004). What is 'professional learning community?' *Educational Leadership, 61*(8), 6–11.

Fletcher, R. (2006). *Boy writers: Reclaiming their voice*s. Portland, MI: Stenhouse.

Fontichiaro, K. (2007). *Active learning through drama, podcasting, and puppetry.* Greenwich, CT: Libraries Unlimited.

Fontichiaro, K. (2008). *Podcasting at school.* Greenwich, CT: Libraries Unlimited.

Fontichiaro, K. (2009). What Recycle Man taught us about copyright. *Knowledge Quest, 37*(3), 83.

Fontichiaro, K., & Buczynski, S. (2009). Connecting science notebooking to the elementary library media center. *School Library Media Activities Monthly, 25*(7), 24-27.

Fontichiaro, K., Pascaretti, V., & Buczynski, S. (2009). Science notebooking in the library media center: Alternative energy. *School Library Media Activities Monthly, 25*(7), 14-16.

Gallas, Karen. (1995). *Talking Their Way into Science: Hearing Children's Questions and Theories, Responding with Curricula.* New York: Teachers College Press.

Gilbert, J. & Kotelman, M. (2005). Five good reasons to use science notebooks. *Science and children, 43*(3), 28–32.

Gokhale, A. (1995). Collaborative learning enhances critical thinking. *Journal of Technology Education, 7*(1), 22–30.

Goudie, M. (2000). *#1480: From seed to plant.* Teachers.net Lesson Plans. Retrieved August 11, 2008, from http://teachers.net/lessons/posts/1480.html.

Harden, W. & Jelly, S. (1990). *Developing science in the primary classroom.* Portsmouth, NH: Heinemann.

Harvey, S. (1998). *Nonfiction matters; reading, writing, and research in grades 3-8.* Portland, ME: Stenhouse Publishers.

Harvey, S. & Goudvis, A. (2007). *Strategies that work: Teaching comprehension for understanding and engagement.* Portland, ME: Stenhouse Publishers.

International Society for Technology in Education (ISTE). (2007). *National Educational Technology Standards (NETS-S) and Performance Indicators for Students.* Retrieved November 8, 2008, from http://www.iste.org/Content/NavigationMenu/NETS/ForStudents/2007Standards/NETS_for_Students_2007_Standards.pdf.

Klentschy, M. (2008). *Using science notebooks in elementary classrooms.* Arlington, VA: National Science Teachers Association.

Klentschy, M. (2005). Science notebook essentials. *Science and Children, 43*(3), 24–27.

Kluger, A. & deNisi, A. (1996). The effects of feedback interventions on performance: A historical review, a meta-analysis, and a preliminary feedback intervention theory. *Psychological Bulletin, 119*(2), 254–284.

Koch, J. (2005). *Science stories: Science methods for elementary and middle school teachers.* Boston, MA: Houghton Mifflin.

Levitov, D. (2005). Red light, green light: guiding questions. *School Library Media Activities Monthly, 22*(2), 25.

Martin, D. (2006). *Elementary science methods: A constructivist approach.* Belmont, CA: Thomson/Wadsworth.

Moreillon, J. (2007). *Collaborative strategies for teaching reading comprehension.* Chicago, IL: American Library Association.

Nagy, W. (1988). *Teaching vocabulary to improve reading comprehension.* Newark, DE: International Reading Association.

Nagy, W. & Herman, P. (1987). Breadth and depth of vocabulary knowledge: Implications for acquisition and instruction (pgs. 19-35). In M. McKeown & M. Curtis (Eds.), *The nature of vocabulary acquisition.* Hillsdale, NJ: Lawrence Erlbaum Associates.

National Research Council (NRC). (2001). *Classroom assessment and the National Science Education Standards..* Washington, DC: National Academy Press.

National Research Council (NRC). (1996). *National science education standards.* Washington, DC: National Academy Press. Retrieved August 13, 2008, from http://www.nap.edu/openbook.php?record_id=4962.

Natural Resources Defense Council. (n.d.) *Glossary of environmental terms.* Retrieved June 24, 2008, from http://www.nrdc.org/reference/glossary/a.asp.

National Science Digital Library (2008). *Science literacy maps: Helping teachers connect concepts, standards, and NSDL resources.* Retrieved October 19, 2008: http://strandmaps.nsdl.org/?chapter=SMS-CHP-0857.

North Cascades and Olympic Science Partnership (n.d). *Science notebooks, student work.* Retrieved August 8, 2008, from http://www.sciencenotebooks.org/student_work/.

Rosebery, A. & Warren, B. (Eds.) (2008). *Teaching science to English language learners: Building on students' strengths.* Arlington, VA: National Science Teachers Association Press.

Roth, K. (1993). *What does it mean to understand science? Changing perspectives from a teacher and her students.* East Lansing: Center for the Learning and Teaching of Elementary Subjects, Institute for Research on Teaching, Michigan State University.

Ruiz-Primo, M.A., Li, M., & Shavelson, R.J. (2001). *Looking into students' science notebooks: What do teachers do with them?* Los Angeles: National Center for Research on Evaluation and Student Testing. Retrieved August 8, 2008, from http://www.cse.ucla.edu/products/Reports/TR562.pdf/.

Saul, W. & Reardon, J. (Eds.) (1996). *Beyond the science kit: Inquiry in action.* Portsmouth, NH: Heinemann.

Severson, K. (2008). "What's for dinner? The pollster wants to know." *New York Times.* April 16. Retrieved August 13, 2008 from http://www.nytimes.com/2008/04/16/dining/16voters.html?ex=1366084800&en=cd43c69001efa0f7&ei=5124&partner=permalink&exprod=permalink.

Spencer, B. & Guillaume, A. (2009). *35 Strategies for developing content area vocabulary.* Boston, MA: Pearson Education, Inc.

Stephens, E. & Brown, J. (2000). *A handbook of content literacy strategies: 75 practical reading and writing ideas.* Norwood, MA: Christopher Gordon.

Swartz, R. J. (2008). Teaching students to think. *Educational Leadership, 65*(5): 26–31. Retrieved June 24, 2008, from http://www.ascd.org/portal/site/ascd/template.MAXIMIZE/menuitem.459dee008f99653fb85516f762108a0c/;jsessionid=IJfnLOG5j2p2GxUFgL84duVqtaqirX9XDTI8g4QzsKPsUZ63FDwf!-206654257?javax.portlet.tpst=d5b9c0fa1a493266805516f762108a0c_ws_MX&javax.portlet.prp_d5b9c0fa1a493266805516f762108a0c_viewID=article_view&javax.portlet.prp_d5b9c0fa1a493266805516f762108a0c_journalmoid=3709213f53be7110VgnVCM1000003d01a8c0RCRD&javax.portlet.prp_d5b9c0fa1a493266805516f762108a0c_articlemoid=8169213f53be7110VgnVCM1000003d01a8c0RCRD&javax.portlet.begCacheTok=token&javax.portlet.endCacheTok=token.

Tompkins, G. & Blanchfield, C. (2005). *50 Ways to develop strategic writers.* Columbus, OH: Pearson Prentice Hall.

Tompkins, G. & Blanchfield, C. (2008). *Teaching vocabulary: 50 creative strategies, grades 6–12.* Upper Saddle River, NJ: Merrill/Prentice Hall.

University of Illinois Extension. (n.d.) *The great plant escape, case 1: Search for green life.* Retrieved August 11, 2008, from http://www.urbanext.uiuc.edu/gpe/case1/index.html.

Wiggins, G. & McTighe, J. (2005). *Understanding by design* (2nd ed.). Alexandria, VA: Association for Supervision and Curriculum Development.

Yoshina, M. (2001). *Developing effective use of the blackboard through lesson study.* Retrieved June 24, 2008, from http://www.rbs.org/lesson_study/currents/effective_use_of_blackboard.php.

Children's Literature

Carle, E. (1987). *The tiny seed.* Natick, MA: Picture Book Studio.

Fowler, A. (2001). *From seed to plant.* New York: Scholastic/Children's Press.

Gibbons, G. (1993). *From seed to plant.* New York: Holiday House.

Jordan, H.J. (1992). *How a seed grows.* Loretta Krupinski, Ill. New York: HarperTrophy.

Krauss, R. (2004). *The carrot seed: 60th Anniversary Edition.* Crockett Johnson, Ill. New York: HarperTrophy.

McNamara, M. (2007). *How many seeds in a pumpkin?* Brian G. Karas, Ill. New York: Schwartz and Wade.

Index

About the Authors

Sandy Buczynski, PhD is an associate professor of science education at the University of San Diego in San Diego, California. She coordinates the Math, Science, and Technology Education graduate program and teaches courses in science pedagogy and curriculum design. Dr. Buczynski's work has been published in numerous science education journals, including *Science and Children*, *Science Scope*, and *The Science Teacher* (articles can be viewed: http://home.sandiego.edu/~sandyb/). As Co-Principal Investigator of a California math and science partnership grant, she worked closely with veteran teachers to learn how inquiry-based learning practices are impacting science education in elementary classrooms. Trained as a scientist yet with more than 30 years' experience in a classroom, she sees developing students' problem solving skills as one of the biggest challenges that teachers face today.

Kristin Fontichiaro, MLIS, is an elementary media specialist with the Birmingham Public Schools in Birmingham, Michigan, and an arts education consultant. She leads frequent workshops and professional development sessions for educators in the United States and abroad, focusing on creative teaching techniques to motivate learners into deeper explorations and more meaningful learning products. She was a member of the inaugural class of the American Library Association's Emerging Leaders program in 2007 and was named the Distinguished Alumna of the Wayne State University School of Information and Library Science in 2008. She is the author of *Podcasting at School* (Libraries Unlimited, 2008) and *Active Learning Through Drama, Podcasting, and Puppetry* (Libraries Unlimited, 2007). She is a contributor to *School Library Media Activities Monthly* and writes ?its blog on school library trends at http://blog.schoollibrarymedia.com.